W9-BUO-982

FIND IT, FIX IT, FLIP IT!

MICHAEL CORBETT is currently the real estate, home, and lifestyle host of TV's number-one news magazine *Extra*, and is host/producer of *Extra's Mansions & Millionaires*, the hour-long weekend series that takes viewers on a sneak peak of the extraordinary mansions, yachts, and hobbies of the rich and famous.

This TV star turned real estate entrepreneur has been buying, renovating, and selling homes for more than fifteen years. His company, Highland Properties, has bought, restored, and sold dozens of homes and apartment buildings. Having personally flipped over thirty homes, this home expert is regularly featured on CNN and HGTV.

In addition to his current hosting and producing projects, Corbett has made his mark in daytime television. Voted "Daytime's Most Lovable Cad" by *People* magazine for his red-hot starring roles in three different soap operas, he first starred for three years on *Ryan's Hope* for ABC, next for four years on *Search for Tomorrow* for NBC, and then for eight years, known as the sexy womanizer David Kimball, on *The Young and the Restless*, the CBS number-one daytime ratings grabber in the United States, Canada, and Europe.

Corbett has hosted and been featured on the Discovery Channel, HGTV, *Live with Regis*, *Geraldo*, *The Montel Williams Show*, and *Sally*, and has appeared in *People* magazine, *Newsweek*, and the *Los Angeles Times*, among others. Corbett also coproduced and hosted two seasons of Fox's successful *Home Restoration and Remodeling Show*, which featured many of Corbett's own renovation projects. He has also hosted the E! Network series *Soap Dish*, CBS's *Action News L.A.*, and numerous specials and cable projects.

Corbett recently concluded an enormously successful collaboration with HSN, where he premiered his Michael Corbett Collection of home improvement products sold exclusively on HSN. As HSN's Home and Lifestyle expert, he provided personally selected home products that "Create a Lifestyle That Leaves You Time for Your Life!"

Visit his Web site: www.MichaelCorbett.com

MICHAEL SANVILLE

FIND IT, FIX IT, FLIP IT!

Make Millions

in Real Estate—

One House at a Time!

Michael Corbett

A PLUME BOOK

PLUME
Published by Penguin Group
Penguin Group (USA) Inc., 375 Hudson Street, New York, New York 10014, U.S.A.
Penguin Group (Canada), 90 Eglinton Avenue East, Suite 700, Toronto, Ontario, Canada M4P 2Y3
(a division of Pearson Penguin Canada Inc.)
Penguin Books Ltd., 80 Strand, London WC2R 0RL, England
Penguin Ireland, 25 St. Stephen's Green, Dublin 2, Ireland (a division of Penguin Books Ltd.)
Penguin Group (Australia), 250 Camberwell Road, Camberwell, Victoria 3124,
Australia (a division of Pearson Australia Group Pty. Ltd.)
Penguin Books India Pvt. Ltd., 11 Community Centre, Panchsheel Park, New Delhi – 110 017, India
Penguin Group (NZ), cnr Airborne and Rosedale Roads, Albany, Auckland 1310,
New Zealand (a division of Pearson New Zealand Ltd.)
Penguin Books (South Africa) (Pty.) Ltd., 24 Sturdee Avenue, Rosebank,
Johannesburg 2196, South Africa

Penguin Books Ltd., Registered Offices: 80 Strand, London WC2R 0RL, England.

First published by Plume, a member of Penguin Group (USA) Inc.

First Printing, February 2006
12 13 14 15 16 17 18 19 20

Copyright © Michael Corbett, 2006
All rights reserved

Illustrations on pages 7, 112, 113, 179, 185, 240,
275, 316, and 317 by Mindi Meader.

℗ REGISTERED TRADEMARK—MARCA REGISTRADA

LIBRARY OF CONGRESS CATALOGING-IN-PUBLICATION DATA

Corbett, Michael, 1960–
    Find it, fix it, flip it!: make millions in real estate—one house at a time / Michael Corbett;
photography by Rand Larson.
    p. cm.
    ISBN 0-452-28669-7 (trade pbk.)
    1. Real estate investment.   2. House buying   3. House selling.   4. Real estate business.   I.
Title.

HD1382.5.C68 2006
332.63'243—dc22   2005053491

Printed in the United States of America
Set in Berkeley Old Style
Designed by Joseph Rutt

CONTENTS

ACKNOWLEDGMENTS

I want to thank everyone involved in bringing this book to life.

Trena Keating, editor in chief of Plume, had a vision for this book when it was still in outline form on my desk. Her enthusiasm and support has made the writing a pleasure. From our very first meeting over lunch, Bonnie Solow, my literary agent, has been wise, wonderful, grounded, visionary, and nurturing.

I have been so blessed to combine my two passions in life—real estate and television—into one career. Lisa Gregorisch Dempsey, the executive producer of *Extra* and *Extra's Mansions & Millionaires*, has been such a supporter and mentor for me. To her I owe enormous thanks. Warren Coulter is my business partner and friend. He constantly challenges me to be better, and for that I am grateful.

Writing a book involves an incredible amount of work, and Denise Osso has been amazing throughout the entire process. Also, I owe so much of my real estate success over the years to two remarkably talented experts, Steven Wilder, and Brian Hatch.

For their constant love and support, I thank Cheryl O'Neil, Greg Wildman, and especially my mother, a remarkable woman who is incredibly talented in her own field and has been ever-encouraging for my entire life.

And finally, I would like to dedicate this book to my late father, a voracious reader, scholar, and aficionado of the written word. I think he would have been very proud of this book.

INTRODUCTION

Are you a homeowner who wants to maximize the biggest financial investment you will make in your lifetime? Do you want to learn how to flip your way to financial freedom, to create a lucrative secondary revenue stream whether the real estate market is up or down? Do you long to own your own home but think the market has passed you by? Are you afraid you will never be able to fulfill your dream of home ownership, let alone own the home of your dreams? If you said yes to any of the above, then *Find It, Fix It, Flip It!* is your road map to making millions in real estate—one house at a time!

Find It, Fix It, Flip It! is a blueprint for your financial independence. It will teach you a long-term plan that will give you the financial security you want, deserve, and can attain. It's all here: the techniques, real estate secrets, and insider tips I have used and profited from to create my own financial success, by flipping houses starting with a $10,000 investment that I built into millions of dollars of real estate.

The concept is a simple one: Each home you find, fix, and then flip creates a profit that you immediately reinvest into a slightly better property—without having to add in any more money. Repeat this process until you are able to buy a house for cash. My goal was to never pay a mortgage again, to flip my way up the real estate ladder, building equity, flip by flip. I achieved it—and so can you.

HOW I GOT STARTED

I, too, started out as a real estate novice. After college in Boston I moved to New York City to become an actor. I was lucky enough to land a Broadway show, and was discovered one night by a casting director who offered me a contract on the NBC soap opera *Ryan's Hope*. That first season, I received my first bonus check of $10,000. I was nineteen years old.

I knew nothing about real estate, or renovations. I had never even heard the term "flipping." But I always had an interest in architecture and I had heard that real estate was a very good investment. To be perfectly honest, I think I was just trying to impress my dad, who had been very disappointed that I had not pursued a law or medical degree. I thought if I could buy a house in my hometown, maybe being an actor wouldn't look like such a bad choice after all. So with that first check from *Ryan's Hope* and a big dose of guarded optimism, I bought the house next door to my grandmother's in my hometown of Collingswood, New Jersey. Luckily, through trial and error, I fumbled my way through this first flip, managed to fix it up, put it back on the market, and, thank God for good instincts, made a profit.

At last count, years later, I have flipped more than thirty-five houses and properties and turned that $10,000 into millions in real estate. I have learned through both trial and error and the experience and guidance of some of the most knowledgeable real estate professionals in the business.

During my entire fifteen years on daytime television, from *Ryan's Hope* and *Search for Tomorrow* to an eight-year run on *The Young and the Restless*, I was flipping houses on the side. Over the past five years, I have had the great fortune to combine both my career in television and my love of real estate through hosting the number-one-rated nightly news magazine, NBC's *Extra*, and *Extra's Mansions & Millionaires*. I have also made appearances as a real estate and home expert on CNN *Nightly News*; HGTV home shows, including *Renovation Generation;* The Discovery Channel; PAX; FOX; and *Good Day Live,* as well as local news and radio programs nationwide. As a result, I have been able to work with and interview the top Realtors, designers, mortgage brokers, and professional flippers in the country. The wealth of techniques, tips, and insider secrets that have saved me thousands and helped to make me some extraordinary profits are now in this book.

Hosting Extra *and* Extra's Mansions & Millionaires *combines my two loves: real estate and televison. Here on location with my cohost Dayna Devon.*

FINANCIAL INDEPENDENCE THROUGH FLIPPING

We all know that buying and flipping homes is a proven path to financial independence. You will often hear financial experts talk about it in books and on television. In fact, I was discussing the merits of real estate investing with financial guru Suze Orman. I have so much respect for her. I love what she as to say, and how she says it. In regard to creating financial independence she said, *"There will never ever be a better investment than purchasing a home you can call your own . . . If you can do it over and over and over again, and leverage what you have, if it makes sense, you can afford to do it, and you know how . . . it is going to be something that works for you better than any other investment."*

But how do you find a house worth the investment of your time and money? Once you buy it, how do you decide what to fix? And how can you guarantee a profit no matter which direction the real estate market is headed? I will show you in this book.

MY REAL ESTATE LOVE AFFAIR

My love affair with real estate began long before I decided to write a book about how to flip houses and create financial freedom.

When I was eight, I used to ride my bicycle to the nicer part of town and take photographs of people's houses. My father had bought me some basic photography equipment, and I set up a darkroom in a closet in our basement. I made eight-by-ten enlargements and framed them. Armed with my "Michael Corbett Photographer" business cards, I went back to the homeowners and sold those photos. If they didn't want to buy them, I would say, "I would like to give you this as a gift, and if you would like to give a donation, here is a self-addressed envelope."

Even then, I wanted to show people how great their home could look—and make a profit at the same time. The photos probably weren't all that good, but people wanted to reward my eight-year-old sense of business initiative and optimism. And today I still believe that the world of business will reward these qualities. But it has to start with you! Set a goal. Keep a vision of success. Take the first steps and the rest will follow.

FLIPPING SUCCESS STORY

For as long as I have been flipping houses, I have been sharing my advice with friends and friends of friends. I am proud to say that I have started many of them on the flipping path.

I convinced a buddy of mine, Mike, who at the time was the assistant manager for country legend Dolly Parton, to buy his first flip house. It was a little fixer that had come on the market and was across the street from a house I had just bought to flip. I walked him through the process and he bought it for $110,000. He had so little money left that he used old beach towels covered with huge Diet Coke logos as curtains for his front windows! Living across the street, I was horrified! What had I done?! But Mike kept scraping funds together and eventually finished and flipped that house for a $30,000 profit. Today, Mike has flipped dozens of homes and rolled that "Diet Coke" house into a sizable real estate empire with numerous homes on both coasts.

I WAS INSPIRED TO WRITE THIS BOOK

During my time on daytime television, I always had a script in one hand and a fix-it budget in the other. I loved being able to juggle acting and real estate. When the producers of *Extra* asked me to be their real estate, home and lifestyle expert and host, I jumped at the chance. When Home Shopping Network asked me to create home improvement products for their home division, I was thrilled.

Having my own line of do-it-yourself products on the Home Shopping Network was another wonderful opportunity to combine my two passions, real estate and television.

Over the years many people have asked me to write this book. I never thought I had the time. However, a few months ago I spent the day with motivational guru Anthony Robbins and his lovely wife, Sage, in their wonderful home near Palm Springs, California. His work has always been an inspiration for me. His own success and the fact that he has been a motivating catalyst for personal change for so many is equally in-spiring to me.

We were talking about giving yourself the power to accomplish any-thing on which you set your sights. It reminded me of a line from one of his best-selling books, *Unlimited Power*: ". . . You have the power to take action and *create* the world you want to live in." As we talked, I realized that I had wanted to write this book but had been putting it off. I wanted to teach others how to help themselves empower their lives financially and learn what I had learned over all these years. Well, I recognized that day that the only thing holding me back was *me*. In fact, the only thing that holds any of us back from creating what we want, including financial freedom, is *ourselves*. I was so energized that night, I went straight home and immediately started on the proposal. I took action! And this book is the result.

YOUR ESSENTIAL FLIP GUIDE

In this book, you'll discover how to find the perfect home with the highest profit potential; where to put your renovation money to maximize return; how to smartly, quickly, and practically renovate and decorate that home, giving it all the dramatic yet affordable touches that will make potential buyers beg to buy; how to get it ready for the big sale; and how to simplify the sale and maximize your profit.

This is my Spaulding house. I found the house with the right things wrong, turned it into a perfect flip home, and more than doubled my investment. You can too.

Your step-by-step guide through the entire process includes the worksheets I use to estimate improvement costs and profits. You'll find easy-to-understand charts, tables, profit and maximum-price-to-pay calculators, and sample estimated renovation budgets. But most important, you'll learn how to figure your profit before you ever sit down at the closing table.

Using the techniques in *Find It, Fix It, Flip It!* can catapult you toward your dream home and financial independence as you buy and flip your way up the real estate ladder. They will help you build equity in your current home and teach you how to increase profit, saving thousands and avoiding costly expenses on the sale of your house. You'll learn how to avoid the pitfalls of overcapitalizing. You'll learn how to find the house with the right things wrong.

You can realize this real estate financial freedom at your own pace by following one of my Four Paths to Flipping Success. You'll learn how to determine which is right for you, your goals, and your lifestyle—and how to follow it.

Flipping your way to financial success is equally powerful in both up or down real estate markets because YOU put added value into the home—not the market. In an ever-changing real estate market, this book shows you how to profit when the market is strong and on its way up, as well as when the market is soft and on its way down.

GIVING AWAY SECRETS

I received a call from a very successful flipper here in Los Angeles. He said, "I hear you're writing a book about flipping. You're not going to give away all our secrets, are you!?" I guess I am. Many of these techniques are closely guarded by the handful of real estate pros who use them. But I believe there is plenty for everyone. We can all be successful and should share our knowledge. After all, I learned so much of what I now know from those who were willing to share it with me.

I REACHED MY FINANCIAL DREAMS . . . AND SO CAN YOU!

I climbed the financial ladder to real estate success one rung at a time. I have written this book to teach you how to do the same. *Find It, Fix It, Flip It!* is truly the guide book you need to achieve your financial success, your real estate dreams, and your ultimate dream home . . . one house at a time!

Part One

FIND IT

One

FLIPPING SUCCESS

THE ESSENTIAL GUIDE TO YOUR FINANCIAL FUTURE

Find It, Fix it, Flip It! teaches you everything I know about how to use your home as a means to create profit, generate income, and build more equity. It is how I worked my way up the financial ladder. It is the essential guide for:

1. **Aspiring Full- and Part-Time Flippers** who know that real estate investment is a proven path to financial success and want to learn to flip their way to their own financial freedom and create a lucrative secondary revenue stream.

2. **First-Time Home Buyers** who think the market has passed them by and will never be able to fulfill their dream of home ownership, let alone ever own the home of their dreams.

3. **Every Homeowner** who wants to make the most of the biggest financial investment they will make in their lifetime, their home. By learning to utilize these insider secrets, real estate techniques, and tax opportunities, every homeowner can flip their way up the real estate ladder to their dream home without investing any more capital.

In order to understand how flipping works, we will review the basic concepts:

- The home as an investment—yesterday and today
- The true cost of traditional home ownership

- The strategy of flipping
- The four paths to flipping success
- My first Los Angeles flip
- How flipping works
- Getting started
- It's NOT about "no money down"
- Some flipping inspiration

THE HOME AS AN INVESTMENT—YESTERDAY AND TODAY

Few American homeowners consider their homes to be a working asset that can actually generate wealth, but it is. The way we think about our homes is based on an agricultural model that no longer exists. In the 1800s, your homestead was part of your heritage, your identity. Settlers would buy land and pass it on to their family, never moving because the land itself provided their income from farming or raising cattle.

In the twenty-first century, with America's challenging economic times, everyday financial burdens have become greater and greater and the cost of living is much higher. Land and property are more expensive. Our homes no longer provide an income the way they did for our forefathers. But they can through flipping, by creating revenue, equity, and savings.

By building wealth through flipping houses, you can create a second income-producing revenue stream. It is nothing less than the twenty-first-century way to use your homestead to live your very own American dream. It's a concept our forefathers knew that we can now embrace: Why work for your home . . . when your home can work for you?

THE TRUE COST OF TRADITIONAL HOME OWNERSHIP
Congratulations! You Have Just Paid Off
Your Thirty-Year Mortgage—and Wasted a Lot of Money

Every expert agrees that owning a home is one of the best financial investments you can make. You know the formula: Buy a home, work hard, pay off your thirty-year mortgage. Between the anticipated appreciation of the real estate market and all the equity you have built up, when you sell, you'll make a very nice profit.

What if I told you that this old formula may not make you as much money as you think? Even though it's no secret, no one ever speaks about it. Everyone seems to conveniently forget that over the thirty-year lifetime of your mortgage you are paying a very steep price for the "privilege" of financing your home via that beloved mortgage.

How Much That Mortgage *Really* Costs You!

The cost of mortgage interest makes it nearly impossible to make money through traditional home ownership. Consider this example: If you bought your house for $550,000 and put 10 percent down, that leaves you with a $500,000 mortgage. Over the next thirty years that $550,000 house will actually cost you . . . drum roll, please . . . $1,100,000!

While you're recovering from the shock, let's look at the math. Over thirty years you pay the mortgage company nearly $650,000 in interest fees for the privilege of borrowing your original loan of $500,000, for a total of $1,100,000. What a waste of your hard-earned salary.

Take a look at the chart below. Find the value of your original mortgage or the mortgage of the house you'd like to buy. Based on a 6.9 percent interest rate over a thirty-year mortgage, see how much you are really paying for that house if you hold on to it.

TOTAL MORTGAGE INTEREST PAID OVER 30 YEARS

(Based on 6.9%, 30-year fixed loan with 10% down.)

Mortgage Amount	Total Paid Out
$100,000.00	$237,096.00
$300,000.00	$711,280.00
$500,000.00	$1,185,480.00
$750,000.00	$1,778,220.00
$1,000,000.00	$2,370,960.00

The Truth About Traditional Home Owning Made Me Flip—Literally!

No matter how much that $300,000 home increases in value over the years due to normal real estate appreciation, until its worth reaches $711,280 you are losing money! That's right, you have paid out an extra $411,000 to the bank! Even if the market continues to rise at an average of 5.5 percent a year, as it has for the past thirty years, you'd be $411,000 richer without that thirty-year mortgage. Yes, granted, you were able to take a mortgage-interest deduction each year in your taxes. But as many financial experts advise, that deduction benefit is nowhere near the expense of that lifetime of interest.

Once I understood the true cost of traditional home ownership, I made the decision that I was never going to pay that price tag. And I'm sure this frightening information will motivate you into learning how to Find It, Fix It, Flip It and never pay a mortgage again.

THE STRATEGY OF FLIPPING

It really is a simple concept: Each home that you find, fix, and flip creates a profit. After the initial investment of your first down payment and the cost of renovations, you will never need to add more cash. When you sell, you take the profit and invest it in the next flip house, each time adding in your profits so that eventually you buy a house with all cash— and never pay a mortgage again! By using the techniques in this book, you can avoid paying more than double the price of your house in interest payments, keep that money working for you at its maximum potential, and be able to reinvest all profits and equity into your next flip. This makes much more sense to me.

Flipping Creates a Second Revenue Stream

If you didn't have to pay off that mortgage, think of what you could do over the next thirty years with all that extra money. You could pay off debt, take trips, drive new cars, pay for your children's college education, and buy a vacation home.

By choosing one of the four paths to flipping success, which I describe later in this chapter, you create a second revenue stream that can pay off your mortgage and then continue to provide additional revenue as well. Your small nest egg can become a real estate fortune that will ultimately make it possible for you to buy your dream home entirely with cash while you continue to earn and save money from your career.

TRADITIONAL HOME OWNERSHIP
Has Only One Revenue Stream

WORK   PAYCHECK   HOME

FIND IT, FIX IT, FLIP IT PATH TO FINANCIAL SUCCESS
Creates Two Revenue Streams

WORK   PAYCHECK   VACATIONS   COLLEGE EDUCATION   NEW CARS   RETIREMENT

FIRST FLIP HOME   DREAM HOME

I Don't Work for My Home—My Home Works for Me

I have always thought of capital from my real estate and flip investments as untouchable and separate from my day-to-day finances. I never touched the profit from my first flip. I reinvested all of it by rolling it into other flip houses. And over twenty years my initial $10,000 investment has grown by leaps and bounds. I live mortgage-free, and now the income I make from my career supports my various other projects or can go into my savings and money funds. I don't work to pay for my house any more! My house works to pay for my future.

THE FOUR PATHS TO FLIPPING SUCCESS

Now that you understand how flipping creates a revenue- and equity-producing stream, here are four different paths you can take. Each follows the exact same game plan. The difference is in how you customize a timeline to best fit your lifestyle.

1. **Power Path—The Find It, Fix It, Flip It Fast Track** This is the continuous quick turnover approach. You find a house, fix it as quickly as you can, flip it, then roll or reinvest all of the original investment plus your flip profit into the next flip.

2. **Slow and Steady Path—Find It, Fix It, Flip It Every Two Years** This is a slower approach. You find it, fix it, and then live in it for two years. It is perfect for families or a homeowner who wants to live in the flipped home for longer. You further benefit financially because you are able to take advantage of the two-year capital gains tax break for homeowners, where you pay no tax up to $500,000 of profit per couple—and up to $250,000 if you are single if the house was your primary residence for two years. This tax advantage alone is one of the most powerful equity- and wealth-building tools in your flipping arsenal.

3. **Live-a-Little Path—Find It, Fix It, Flip It, Repeat, Then Hold!** This is my most frequently recommended path for novices. You find it, fix it, flip it, then start the process again immediately. On the second house, however, once you fix it, you *hold* it for two years before flipping. This path allows you to have the full experience of the process. You make some instant equity, invest in the next one, and catch your breath. You may just find that after your two years, you'll choose to flip the next two or three houses one after another.

4. **Flip on the Side** This path treats flips as investment projects. You never live in the flip at all. It is ideal for homeowners who have cash to invest and want the financial benefits of flipping full or part time without having to move. Even if you are employed full time you can do this. The goal is to pay off your primary-residence mortgage through your revenue stream.

MY FIRST LOS ANGELES FLIP

The first house I bought when I moved to Los Angeles was a cute little 1940s Spanish cottage in the Wilshire district. I got it for $165,000 and put 10 percent down. The house had a lot of flip potential: The yard was so overgrown you could barely see the house, it needed a new kitchen and baths, and it had a few significant but fixable structural problems, along with great potential for lifestyle upgrades. You'll learn all about how to identify houses like this that are perfect to flip in chapter four: "Find the House with the Right Things Wrong."

Inside, I knocked down a wall or two to open it up and create flow and space. I added French doors leading to the backyard, creating a wonderful indoor/outdoor feeling, put in some new appliances, and highlighted the charming cottage detailing with different shades of color. Outside, I painted the front door a high-gloss hunter green, "finished it" with a shiny brass kick plate, put up new brass house numbers and complementary outdoor fixtures. I did a great job of landscaping the yard. I put on a new roof, furnished it and "dressed it for sale" (more on that in chapter sixteen, "Dressed to Sell"). The renovations cost about $23,000. I put the house on the market for $295,000. It sold in a day.

After renovations, purchasing and closing costs, carrying costs, and taxes, I made a profit of $79,500. My investment of approximately $46,000 (down payment plus cash outlay for expenses) had now grown to $124,500.

Sale Price FFP (Final Flipped Price)	$295,000
Purchase Closing Costs	+3,500
Estimated Fix-It Costs	+22,000
Carrying Costs	+4,000
Sale Closing Costs and Commissions	+21,000
– Purchase Price	–295,000
PROFIT	**$79,500**

I was then able to buy the next house at $300,000, putting 20 percent down and keeping approximately $64,500 for renovations and expenses.

By flipping, I was able to step up the real estate ladder in four ways without investing any more money:

1. Buy a better, more expensive house

2. Move up to a better neighborhood

3. Make a bigger down payment

4. Have more money for renovations

You Set the Pace—and the Lifestyle

You don't have to incur the costs of a larger lifestyle to move up the financial ladder. It's not about bigger and better. It's about building toward financial freedom in your dream home—whether it's a grand house or a smaller, cozy home. You can start small to get into the market, then take that profit and upgrade into bigger and bigger homes until you buy your ultimate dream mansion for cash. But no one says you have to invest in larger properties to take advantage of the benefits of flipping. You can stay at the lifestyle level where you started, and flip houses in that same price range until you can pay cash for your home.

Along with buying a larger house come bigger property taxes, utility bills, and a bigger mortgage. However, you are rolling all of your profit from the last flip into the next house, so your down payment is going to be bigger too. Eventually, your only increased expenses will be taxes and utilities.

Buy a fix-it house at $100,000 with 10 percent down and flip it at $175,000. Take all that money and profit to buy another one at $100,000. But this time you can afford to put 20 percent down. Just keep flipping until you can eventually pay all cash! No increase in expenses, utilities, or property taxes . . . and *no* mortgage!

HOW FLIPPING WORKS
Creating a Home and Selling a Lifestyle

My mantra for creating long-term financial security by flipping properties is "You are not selling a *house*. You are creating a *home* and selling a *lifestyle*." This book is not about buying underpriced, distressed properties and fixing them up with a coat of paint and a new stove. You are going to find a property with potential, get it for the best price, make all the needed repairs, transform your property into an exciting, warm, inviting, emotionally stimulating *home* that is exactly right for your targeted buyer—and then sell for a profit.

Create the Perfect Home with the Six Levels
of Improvements—for Someone Else

The house you fixed up is the one your prospective buyer only dreamed they could find . . . until now. You set the stage and make that dream come true. When you make improvements on all of the Six Levels of Improvements, you are increasing the "perceived value" of your flip. That's a *home* worth far more to your new buyers than the sum of the costs of the land, materials, and labor. It's their dream. That's why they are willing to pay top dollar.

You've charmed them with curb appeal, wooed them with design choices, wowed them with extras and upgrades, emotionally engaged them with lifestyle vignettes and inspired them to put themselves into this beautiful picture the minute they open the door. The buyer who is willing to pay top dollar for your flip house is doing so because he or she has no idea how to fix or renovate a home . . . or any interest in doing so. Otherwise they would be buying the house that needs some "TLC" down the block for much less money.

GETTING STARTED

Read this book, do your research, and dive in! However, you won't magically learn everything and start flipping. There are things that only hands-on experience can teach. Flipping should start out as a commitment to increase your wealth in slow increments, as a part-time activity alongside your current job and schedule. With more expertise and equity, you will be able to do more flipping projects more quickly. Your first flip is bound to be a steep learning curve, especially when it comes to evaluating property values and making on-the-spot estimates of fix-it costs.

Start going to open houses—all of them. I love this part. I have spent many Saturday or Sunday afternoons this way. You will learn about prices and pick up fix-it and design ideas by seeing what works and what doesn't through your own and other buyer's reactions to what's out there. This is wealth of information. Think of it as a school field trip, without the bus.

Jack-of-All-Trades, Master of None

I am truly a jack-of-all-trades. I have learned a working knowledge of each of the *Find It, Fix It, Flip It!* areas, but by no means am I the master of any of them. And that's OK! Flipping is an art. You don't have to get your broker's license, contractor's license, or your design degree to practice it, but you need to become a bit of Renaissance man or woman to master it.

Whatever your natural talents, there is no possible way that you could become an expert in every stage of the flipping process. Being a good "numbers" person will not guarantee that you know which set of French doors will best showcase the new deck off the master bedroom. Having a great sense of color won't help you decode the loopholes in a contract. And being the person that everyone calls when it's time to go furniture shopping has nothing to do with knowing how far you can push a reluctant seller in the heat of closing. You can't be an expert in every area. But you can take advantage of the expert advice of the flipping Dream Team you put together.

Ask Questions, Get Answers

What I am really good at is asking questions, recognizing other people's great ideas, and delegating to experts. I learned how to evaluate the progress, quality, and professionalism of each of the experts I hire.

Novice flippers and first-time home renovators take heart. Your creative vision and your willingness to learn from experts will serve you well.

A Step-by-Step Process—Most of the Time

Finding a house, fixing it, and flipping may sound like a sequential process, but it's not. For the novice, it's like throwing a big dinner party without knowing how to cook, how to shop, what to buy, and in what order to do any of it! There are areas of knowledge, specific ways of doing things, timing and scheduling issues, and aesthetics to consider. Some of these happen in a clear progression, yet all of these can happen at once. This book lays out the process in a step-by-step fashion. You will find that certain things happen first, yet you need the knowledge of other later elements to make some of the earlier decisions and choices. Not to worry, just keep reading.

IT'S NOT ABOUT "NO MONEY DOWN"

As I write, it's late at night and I have the TV on in the background. On comes an infomercial about how to get rich quick in real estate with *no money down*. I have to admit that years ago I purchased one of those courses. The entire basis for making money in real estate in those programs relies on seeking out distressed properties, foreclosure, probates, or the "desperately motivated seller." Plus you need to snap up those properties at bargain-basement prices. But wait, there's more! You do this with a litany of complicated and risky no-money-down borrowing, loaning, and financing techniques. My approach is much more conservative. I am not a proponent of no-money-down buying.

Many of the books that I have read on buying fixer-uppers rely on finding a buyer in dire financial need of cash or a property so distressed that it's for sale at least 30 percent under value. That doesn't make sense anymore. What seller, no matter how strapped or crazy or "motivated," is going to sell a property worth $300,000 for $200,000? The public has become far too savvy. All any distressed owner has to do is pick up a phone or go on a Web site to discover an appropriate value for his home. Maybe ten years ago the theory of "stealing" distressed properties could work, but not anymore.

That's why it is imperative to know how to select the right flip house with the right things wrong. And it's no longer enough to just "clean up" a fixer. You need to know how to create and sell a home and a lifestyle.

SOME FLIPPING INSPIRATION

FLIPPING SUCCESS STORY

I recently shot a story on *Extra* about a real estate investor named Jeff Beuth who was flipping a house in the Hollywood Hills above the Sunset Strip. Leonardo DiCaprio, Courteney Cox, and Christina Aguilera all live within a few blocks in this celebrity enclave. Jeff bought the house in horrible condition, used all the techniques in this book and sold it for $11,000,000.

But this isn't the best part of the story. Jeff started out on the flipping path less than ten years ago with a tiny $60,000 fixer flip in a blighted low-income area in Los Angeles. His very first down payment of $6,000 plus $12,000 to fix up the house was borrowed from family and friends. His next flips were small properties that garnered small profits of $20,000 to $30,000 each. He flipped his way up to an $11 million dollar flip home by rolling flip after flip to real estate success!

PHOTOS COURTESY OF JEFF BEUTH.

This is one of Jeff Beuth's first flips. A $60,000 fixer in a transitional neighborhood of Los Angeles. His profit was $20,000 after a few months.

Before

After

This is one of Jeff's more recent flips, a multimillion-dollar estate quite a few steps up the real estate ladder from his humble beginnings.

Jeff has at this point flipped more than two hundred houses! He did it the right way—he started small, learned from his successes, built his Dream Team, and kept reinvesting his profits. His success is an inspiration to us all.

Be Your Own Boss

If you have ever wanted to be in business for yourself, finding, fixing, and flipping houses is a natural. It is also empowering to both your financial future and your life. With any business comes responsibility, liabilities, anxiety, and stress. And no one knows what they *don't know* until they start. I certainly didn't. But thanks to my experience, you can minimize the negatives. Just utilize the tools and the tips I learned the hard way and apply the techniques I was lucky enough to learn by talking to the best people in the field. You'll have the benefit of the skills and insider knowledge you need to avoid the most common pitfalls and the insider shortcuts that will catapult you far ahead of any novice flipper. You can do this!

Two

FLIPPING ECONOMICS 101

Real estate is a business. It can also be a passion or a hobby, but first and foremost it is a business. Flipping is a numbers game. If the numbers work, then find it, fix it, flip it. If they don't, then walk away!

In this chapter I'll explain the economics of flipping. There are seven important areas you will need to understand in order to make them work for you. We'll cover:

- Why flipping works

- Crunching the numbers to a profitable flip

- The profit calculator chart, which takes the guesswork out of flipping

- Calculate your profit before you buy

- How to succeed whether the market is up, down, or sideways

- Getting your personal economics in order

- How much house you can afford—how much money you need

WHY FLIPPING WORKS

I have always been very hands-on. My friends would say controlling. I like to know what is going on around me. And I especially like to know how my investments are working for me.

The most important aspect of flipping is that you control every step of the process. This comes from knowing how to secure the best deal you can by buying a house that most people will overlook because they don't know what to do with it. Not only do you gain automatic equity (profit) from the start, you are now going to add more profit as you fix it into a Flip Dream Home!

Because you build a profit number into the price you pay for the house, you know what your profit will be in advance. And selling immediately upon completion is a sure way to avoid losses from downturns in the market.

Historically, there has always been a market for the home in perfect shape, one with all the amenities, and most important, a home with an oh-so-marketable emotional edge over the competition because it comes with a lifestyle.

CRUNCHING THE NUMBERS TO A PROFITABLE FLIP

When looking at a potential property, there are four essential questions you need to answer to even consider it as a potential flip:

1. What will the house be worth when I fix it and sell it—that is, the Final Flipped Price (FFP)?

2. How much will I spend on renovations to make this house a winner?

3. How much profit do I want to make?

4. Based on the above, what is the most I should pay for this house?

Most beginners think that if they purchase a property, fix it up, and put it on the market for $20,000 to $50,000 more than the purchase price plus the cost of improvements, they will automatically make a profit. In my experience, more times than not, they will be lucky to recoup their investment. Without knowing how to analyze a potential flip's current value and then how to estimate what it could potentially sell for after renovation, they're just guessing how much they'll make. But by accurately estimating the house's FFP, they'll *know*.

The technique that I and all successful flippers use is a very specific series of calculations that make it possible for you to determine a house's potential for profit long before you even get near the closing table. This is the tried-and-true formula I use each and every time I analyze a potential flip house—no matter which way the market is headed.

THE PROFIT CALCULATOR CHART TAKES
THE GUESSWORK OUT OF FLIPPING

THE PROFIT CALCULATOR CHART	
Estimated FFP (Final Flipped Price)	$ _____
Purchase Price of the House	– _____
Purchase Closing Costs	– _____
Estimated Fix-It Costs	– _____
Carrying Costs	– _____
10% Buffer	– _____
Sale Closing Costs and Commissions	– _____
Total	$ _____
– Capital Gains Tax	– _____
PROFIT	$ _____

The easiest way to determine whether or not a house is good flip candidate is to work through the Profit Calculator Chart. Once you learn what the entries are and how to estimate them, all you'll have to do is plug in the numbers. Enter your best-guess estimates and you'll have a very quick idea if this house is your next big moneymaker, or one you won't even remember two weeks from now!

Take a look at the components of the chart. There are eight items. Learn how to estimate these eight items and you can instantly calculate the profit potential of any house!

- Purchase price of house

- Purchase closing costs

- Estimated fix-it costs

- Carrying costs

- 10 percent buffer

- Closing costs

- FFP (Final Flipped Price)

- Taxes

CALCULATE YOUR PROFIT BEFORE YOU BUY

Having the ability to determine your profit before you buy is what sets
flipping apart from all other real estate strategies. By the end of chapter
five, "The Financial Model for Success: The Profit Calculator," you will
be able to analyze the profit potential of any house. Will you have a crys-
tal ball? No, but you will have what most beginners and amateurs don't:
The Find It, Fix It, Flip It Profit Calculator Chart.

If you're not comfortable with the final number for your profit, then
walk away. There are plenty of other properties out there. If your final
profit number is a surprisingly large amount that you would be thrilled
to have, recheck your estimates, because some of them are probably too
low! So double-check your estimates, and maybe even add in a few more
possible expenses for good measure. If you still are showing a nice profit
number, then congratulations: You have a winner!

"I Don't Know How to Estimate These Yet!"

At this point, you may be asking yourself, "How can I possibly know
what a house will be worth—the FFP—when I am finished fixing it up
and finally ready to sell?" You've realized that you have NO idea how
much closing costs or carrying costs are, or worse, how much it is going
to cost to fix up the house! Well, not to worry. You are not expected to
know at this point. I just wanted you to be familiar with the terms now as
you continue reading. We will explain them one at a time in chapter five.

How Much Profit Is Enough?

Profit is what you get after you've paid off the mortgage, all costs, and
taxes. The entire reason for flipping is to make a profit and roll it into
your next flip. But before we discuss how to calculate your profit, let's
discuss how much profit you should expect to make. This is a very

subjective topic. It depends on the cost of your flip house, and it will change at various levels of your flipping career. A beginner could be very happy with a profit of between $15,000 and $25,000 on a home purchased for $150,000. Do that three or four times and you've just created a total profit of nearly $100,000. For many, those few "small" flips can double their income.

As you progress and take on larger, more expensive projects, you can expect to earn higher profits. A higher capital investment has the potential to generate a higher profit margin. Some advanced professional flippers won't touch a property unless they know they can make $100,000—or more.

You need to decide for yourself how much is enough. How much is your time worth? Could you be making a bigger return on overtime at work, or taking on a second job? Don't be shortsighted. Putting in extra hours at work may make you some additional dollars now, but flipping has the potential to create profits, equity, and capital, and also give you a skill that can change your future—something a little overtime simply cannot do.

Profit Rule of Thumb

In the beginning you should be happy with a modest profit. If it turns out to be more, then congratulations! And if the house is in really bad shape and takes a lot of time and money, you should have to factor in a higher profit to better reward yourself for taking the higher risk.

I think a good rule of thumb is 10 to 15 percent of the purchase price in profit. In other words, if you buy a house for $200,000, you ideally would like to realize a $20,000 to $30,000 profit. That means that after you deduct all the costs on our worksheet from the sales price and deduct your portion of capital gains to Uncle Sam, you should be left with $20,000 to $30,000.

INSIDER SECRET

Create a Profit Buffer—The other reason I suggest that you shoot for a 15 percent profit is that it helps you create a profit buffer. In case expenses run over (and they always do) and carrying costs are slightly more than expected (and they always are) you will still end up with at least a 10 percent clear profit.

HOW TO SUCCEED WHETHER THE MARKET IS UP, DOWN, OR SIDEWAYS
How Real Estate Appreciates in Value

Real estate over the past thirty years has appreciated at an average of approximately 5 percent a year. More recently we have seen 10 and even 20 percent appreciation a year, especially in growth areas: major cities, oceanfront property, and states like Florida and California. When you flip a house, though, you are going to turn that 5 to 20 percent economic appreciation into a 30 to 50 percent increase in value. Not only do you benefit from the automatic appreciation gained in an up market, but through the FFF process you will turn an undervalued fixer into a comp-breaking jewel. ("Comp" is short for comparables, or houses in the neighborhood with the same number of rooms and the same kind of amenities as yours.) By adding perceived value to your flip, you break the comps, or get a significantly high price for what, on paper, may seem to be the same house.

However, the market doesn't always continue to appreciate. Like the ocean, it moves and changes. As I write this book, the market is on fire, and interest rates are on the rise. Things could cool off quickly.

In an ideal world, you would decide how much profit you want to make, determine all the costs of the purchase, fix up, carrying costs and sales costs, and then figure out what you need to purchase the house for to get the profit you want. Fix-it gurus will all tell you this is the way to go, which is great in a flat market. However, in a hot or cold market, you have to factor in the market's movements.

Factor the Market into Your Calculations

If you put the added value into the property and are trying to turn your flip house over quickly, you won't be at the mercy of the market. However, you can and must calculate anticipated up or down swings.

For example: If you are in an UP market and there is an anticipated 15 percent value increase per year and you are going to flip your house in six months, then you can afford to pay 7 percent more for the house than you would in a flat market. If the market is going DOWN 10 percent a year, then offer 5 percent less for the purchase price. The secret is quick turnover! You never need to be outsmarted by the changing market.

Hot or Upward Market

These are the signs that the market is hot:

- More buyers for fewer homes—very little inventory
- Quick sales, often before the property is listed
- Multiple offers and bidding wars
- Homes sell for more than the asking price

Cold or Downward Market

Remember the late 1980s? It gives me shivers just to think of it. That was one cold market. Homes sat for a year without offers. Inventory was endless. Buyers were nowhere. Prices sank by as much as 40 percent. Brrr.

These are the signs that a market is turning cold:

- Homes are listed and sitting for more than 120 days without offers
- Prices are low, sometimes 10 to 15 percent lower than the year before
- Big inventory

- No buyers, plenty of sellers
- Those that do make offers make lowball offers
- Repos and foreclosures galore

Normal Market

These are the signs that the market is normal or flat:

- A reasonable inventory of homes that sell within thirty to ninety days
- Sellers are willing to negotiate offers at slightly below asking
- Average increase in home values of 5 to 6 percent a year

Be Ready to Move with the Market

Whether you are going to fix and flip immediately or fix and hold, finish your fix-it phase and get the house as close to ready for sale as quickly as possible. That way, when you do a quick reevaluation of the market, and the barometers indicate a downturn is approaching, you'll be ready and able to put it up for sale and take advantage of the strong pricing climate while it lasts!

INSIDER SECRET

Don't Count on the Market—Many novice flippers go into a flip thinking, "Maybe there isn't a lot of profit margin here, but the market is going up and so will my profit." *Never count on the market to bail you out!* Expect that the market won't rise a single percentage point by the time you are ready to sell. In fact, assume that the market will probably drop 5 percent by the time you will be ready to flip. Subtract 5 percent from your FFP and use that new number for your Profit Calculator Chart. I believe it is always better to be conservative early on and pleasantly surprised later.

GETTING YOUR PERSONAL ECONOMICS IN ORDER
Credit

As you begin to think about flipping, economic housekeeping is critical. Good credit opens the door to success and bad credit can close it. Even as you read this book and begin to go to open houses, find out what your buying power is—and what you can do to improve it.

Get Your Credit Report

If you don't have a current one, get your credit report now. If there are problems, you need to know about them and address them before you apply for a loan. Get your report from any of three reporting agencies:

Equifax
P.O. Box 740241
Atlanta, GA 30374-0241
(800) 685-1111
(800) 997-2493 for residents of Colorado, Georgia, Maryland, Massachusetts, New Jersey, or Vermont.
www.equifax.com

Experían
P.O. Box 2002
Allen, TX 75013-2104
(888) EXPERIAN
www.experian.com

TransUnion LLC
Consumer Disclosure Center
P.O. Box 1000
Chester, PA 19022
(800) 888-4213 to get your credit report
(800) 916-8800 for answers to your questions
www.transunion.com

What Your Credit Report Says About You

A complete history of all your financial activities, your credit report lists your creditors, when you opened your bank accounts, what you owe and to whom, your credit limits, and your history, including late payments and any other negative information. It shows employment history, marriages, divorces, child support, bankruptcies, property liens, whose name is on what, etc. When a lender requests information, this is what they get.

Mistakes Happen

According to financial guru Suze Orman, a whopping 25 percent of those declined for a mortgage had errors in their credit report. When you spot them, it's up to you to fix them. Your credit report will come with a form titled, "Request for Reinvestigation." Fill it out, make a photocopy, and send it back. It's free. You should get a response within thirty days.

Credit Scoring

This process gives a numerical value to all aspects of your credit history, factoring in your income, your debt, and your employment history. The past six to twelve months is examined first, so it's critical to keep current with your bills. Here's how the scores break out:

- 660 or greater: Generally acceptable risk and may compensate for other less attractive aspects of your financial past

- 620–659: Motivates a closer look at potential risks and may inspire a request for credit documentation and letters of explanation

- 620 or under: This lower score may keep the best loans and terms out of reach

FICO

Fair Isaac Corporation (FICO) is a company that assigns a numeric value to your credit history and your credit habits. All creditors use this score and every credit-using American has one. It is different than your credit score—and infinitely more important! When I talked with Suze Orman, she said, "The difference between a credit score and a FICO score can sometimes be fifty to a hundred points. And 75 percent of all mortgage companies today only accept true FICO scores." Your FICO score is not just looked at for your mortgage either. *A higher score means you get lower interest rates on everything you buy with credit.* A lower score means you pay higher rates. This score is even being used by landlords and employers, so it is definitely in your best interest to know where you stand.

The Range of FICO Scores

FICO scores go from a low of 300 to a high of 850. To get the lowest interest rate on a mortgage, not to mention all other credit purchases, you need to have a score in the top range. To the lender, a score below 675 represents a greater financial risk. And a score below 500 falls into the sub-lender category. When you go to www.myFICO.com and find daily updated mortgage rates on the home page, you'll see that a higher score makes a real dollar difference. There's also a ton of other important information, starting with tips on how to fix your score.

Fix Your FICO

The best way to have a good score is to responsibly manage your credit over time.

- Stay current—Pay your bills on time.
- Get help—See a credit counselor if you are unable to manage.
- Maintain low balances—Pay those balances down!
- Don't move it, lose it—Pay off your debt, don't just move it to a new card.

What I have done and suggest that everyone do is to go to Suze Orman's amazing Web site www.SuzeOrman.com. There you will find Suze Orman's FICO Kit. This interactive program allows you to correct your credit reports, get FICO scores, and, based on your scores, get coaching on how much of a home you can really afford. It really is a great, user-friendly Web site. It has a minimal cost and will be the best investment you can make to get your finances in order.

HOW MUCH HOUSE YOU CAN AFFORD— HOW MUCH MONEY YOU NEED

The first step to find it, fix it, flip it success is figuring out how much house you can afford. You need to take a realistic look at how much cash you have to invest, how much are you able to borrow from family and friends, and how much a bank will loan you.

Once you've cleaned up your credit, and before you have even looked at your first house, you will want to have a mortgage broker do a complete analysis of your buying potential:

- How much money have you saved or can you borrow for your down payment?

- How much of your cash are you able to earmark for fix-it money?

- How is your credit?

- Based on your earning power at the moment, how large will the lender let your monthly payments be?

How Much Money Do I Need?

Every couple of weeks I get the call, "Hey Michael, I want to flip a house. How much money do I need?" Well the formula is pretty simple. But it varies by where you live, what you are looking to buy, and first and foremost, how much money you can get your hands on. I start with that question first. How much have you got to work with? Let's assume Cheryl says she has saved $35,000 and can probably get a gift or loan of $10,000 from her mom as well. That's $45,000. Well, if you're putting

10 percent down, you might think you can easily buy a house for $300,000 to flip. Wow! Except that wouldn't be right. Look at the breakdown of what you really need to do with that money:

Buying a $300,000 house with a 10 percent down payment:

$45,000	Cash
−$30,000	Down payment
−$3,500	Closing costs, including appraisal and mortgage fees (approximate)
−$12,000	Six months' carrying costs
0	Remaining for fix-it costs

Let's try a less expensive home and see if we can make the numbers work.

Buying a $200,000 house with a 10 percent down payment:

$45,000	Cash
−$20,000	Down payment
−$3,000	Closing costs
−$6,500	Six months' carrying costs
$15,500	Remaining for fix-it costs

It looks like the house that costs $200,000 or less is the more realistic place for Cheryl to start. Don't be discouraged. It is just that: a place to start. Remember, I began with $10,000 and bought my first home for $60,000. I have been able to parlay that investment into quite a considerable real estate portfolio.

Where to Get the Down Payment?

There are lots of other factors that can enhance your buying power as well. There are actually 5 percent mortgages out there and even some 0 percent down-payment opportunities too, depending on your credit score. Taking personal loans from family is also very acceptable. But I advocate only purchasing what you can actually afford! So I always suggest buying a less expensive house and flipping your way up, rather than overextending yourself. It is better to be conservative and safe than to take the risk and have to lose a house for lack of funds.

Another question I am always asked is, "Where can I get that down payment? I just don't have it." Well, a great and often overlooked source is . . . the folks. If your parents are in a position to help you, then you may not realize that they can "gift" you money each year, tax free. The old maximum was $10,000 a year. Now it is $11,000 per year, *per parent*. That's $22,000 a year that can be gifted to you tax free from your parents. If you are smart and plan ahead, two years' worth totals $44,000, a very nice start.

INSIDER SECRET

Pledging Your Deposit—Jim Gillespie, the president of Coldwell Banker Real Estate Corporation, says another great way to get that first down payment is to have a family member "pledge" the amount of the down payment in a specified "pledged" account. There are some lenders that will allow a "pledged" down payment to essentially serve as collateral against the guarantee of a down payment. That family member can still collect interest on the money, but cannot withdraw the principal until the amount is paid back someday by the homeowner.

Get a Preapproval Letter

As you read this book and prepare to start looking for properties, make yourself as economically desirable as possible. When you have cleaned up your credit scores and know how much money you have to invest, work with a mortgage broker and get a preapproval letter. The preapproval letter is your passport to profit, the calling card that turns you into a cash buyer because it tells the seller that you are preapproved for a mortgage. It is like an all-access pass to the properties in your price range. It telegraphs to a seller that you are not only qualified but prepared and serious about making a deal. You'll want one long before you make an offer because it will make your offer stronger, especially in a hot market.

Not as powerful but still useful is a prequalifying letter. It's an informal albeit professional assessment that basically says you're in good shape financially, but it is nonbinding. It is the result of a lender thoroughly checking out all the financial information you would need to get an actual mortgage, including financial history, credit history, etc. Always try to get a preapproval letter, but settle for a prequalifying letter if you have to.

Three

YOUR FLIPPING DREAM TEAM

Every successful business is built on teamwork. In order to play this game to win, you don't just need a team, you need a Dream Team. Having one in place enables you to jump on a hot bargain at a moment's notice. And if you follow my lead, you'll get a lot of their advice for free.

As we have discussed, you can't know it all. And you don't want to. Knowing how to flip a house is like being a general practitioner. My brother is a GP. He knows a lot about taking care of the general needs of his patients, but I wouldn't go to him for heart surgery! You should surround yourself with specialists because they will simply do a better job than you. In the long run, their expertise will save you time and make you money!

YOUR DREAM TEAM

- Realtor

- Mortgage Broker

- Real Estate Lawyer

- Insurance Agent

- Accountant

- Lawyer

- Contractor

- Tradesman—Electrician, Plumber, Roofer, Painter, etc.

- Handyman

When the Team Succeeds, Each Player Succeeds

The professionals who'll become your flipping team are always looking for an opportunity to be part of a successful project. Every time you flip a house, it means another job, project, or commission. You win, they win. And trust me, as you move into your second and third flips, you will be shocked at how cooperative and flexible they will become. You may well see a drastic reduction in fees and commissions.

In Los Angeles, the two Realtors on my team who work as partners have transacted around twenty purchases/sales for me, resulting in hundreds of thousands of dollars in commissions for them. They get guaranteed income and I am rewarded with their infinite expertise and outstanding service. The moment a great deal comes on the market, I know I'll receive that "drop what you are doing and grab your checkbook" phone call!

They are so gracious and appreciative of our team efforts that they have surprised me with many generous housewarming gifts, such as the shiny Sub-Zero refrigerator in my latest house. My mortgage broker has also profited handsomely. As you can imagine, he no longer charges me any mortgage broker fees, and he is always able to get me full loan approval in a matter of days. These relationships benefit everyone involved.

YOUR REALTOR
Brokers Versus Realtors Versus Agents

To be honest, it took me a long time to get this distinction straight, so you should make me look bad and learn it right away. The difference varies from state to state, but in order to list a property in most states, you must be a licensed broker. Brokers usually own the realty company and can hire agents and Realtors to work for and with them.

The difference between an agent and a Realtor is simple but important. An agent can only be called a Realtor if he or she belongs to an association of Realtors or a board. By doing this, he signs a code of ethics and is bound to them. A big advantage of working with a Realtor is that if there is an issue between your Realtor and the other party's Realtor, not only can you take their broker (boss) to task, but you can have disputes settled by the local realty board. Also, to qualify as a Realtor, an agent must participate in additional training and certification. You can work with any of them, but generally try to work with a licensed Realtor.

What a Realtor Can Do That You Can't

Realtors know the business inside and out. They have experience with each and every step of the home-buying and -selling process. They are the experts in a number of areas critical to the flip process, including:

- Knowledge of neighborhoods
- Locating flip candidates
- Knowledge of recent comps—what has sold and for how much
- Access to the Multiple Listing Service (MLS), a list of all properties for sale
- Inside-track access to properties that have not yet hit the market
- How to structure your purchase deal
- The muscle to get through escrow or being under contract
- Features that make your house competitive
- How to price your flip for sale
- Marketing your finished flip
- Closing the selling deal

Using their knowledge of neighborhoods, they find and evaluate properties. Building on their experience with what sells and how, they market them. They hold open houses. They take and make hundreds of phone calls. They prescreen and qualify buyers. They negotiate contracts. They do mountains of paperwork. They know what to do and when. They keep communications open between you and frustrating sellers. They close deals and do it all—twenty-four hours a day . . . something YOU don't have the time or experience to do.

Certainly you will develop your own level of expertise in flipping, but you'll have to find the properties first! And if you want access to all the valuable house information on the MLS or that fantastic deal that is just about to come on the market, then get your Realtor on your team right from the start.

Realty Terms You Need to Know

The Multiple Listing Service (MLS)—The MLS is a data bank that contains all the important information about properties that come on the market. It is the information you need at your fingertips twenty-four hours a day. Sure, you can go online and see listings at www.realtor.com or similar sites (and you should), but they are nowhere near as current or as thorough as the MLS. It is a treasure trove of property information you can't get anywhere else: length of time on the market, annual real estate taxes, square footage, room count, type of heating, air, roof, and special circumstances that the seller wants you to know. This information is critical to your flipping success.

In-House Listing—Beyond having access to this data bank of digital information, a good Realtor has his ear to the ground. The great ones hear about properties even before a seller makes his first call to a listing agent. Furthermore, Realtors and agents talk to each other constantly. Information is their currency, and they trade it as it suits their goals. In highly competitive markets, Realtors have "in-house" listings that never even make it to the multiples. A Realtor will announce a hot listing to the Realtors in his own home office, giving that entire home office a shot at selling the property as well as listing it, trying to "double end" the sale. Most of my best flip houses were in-house listings that I snapped up before they ever made it to the MLS.

Pocket Listings—Sometimes an agent will choose to wait several days before he puts a listing into the MLS, a common practice called a "vest pocket" listing or a "pocket" listing. This way he can find both a buyer and a seller and avoid having to split the commission.

Competitive Edge—When it comes to finding profit-making flip houses, Realtors are your competition, too. In many metro markets Realtors are buying up fixers themselves. In hot markets, I often hear Realtors say, "If my clients don't buy that house, I will." Having your own Realtor is essential to getting that competitive edge.

Concierge Services—One of the greatest benefits of working with a Realtor is the fringe benefits that a large realty office can provide. For example, Coldwell Banker offers buyers across the country a concierge service that provides a full roster of contractor and tradesman references. When you open escrow on a flip, if you do not already have your Dream Team in place, this could come in handy.

Coldwell Banker president Jim Gillespie said that utilizing their concierge service is a real benefit when buying your first fix-it house. They will present you with three to four referrals in any category of workman you require, all of whom have been scrutinized by the local realty office. These tradesmen:

- Are licensed and bonded

- Have references

- Are motivated to make you happy—because if there is a problem, they may well lose their Coldwell Banker referral

HOW TO FIND THE PERFECT REALTOR

Look for Marketing Materials That Stand Out

I am always watching for a Realtor who markets himself or herself and properties well. Pick up the local paper. Which Realtors advertise extensively? Who has great-looking ads and photos for their listings? Who seems to be doing an aggressive job of marketing their properties in the Sunday home section? Look at your mail. Is there one Realtor in particular that sends eye-catching, consistent mailings? These are all signs of a Realtor who has marketing savvy and who is hardworking and aggressive.

Flipping Experience

All Realtors are not created equal. Some specialize in representing buyers, some work best with sellers, some handle mostly condos, and some specialize in extremely high-end luxury properties. However, these two qualities are paramount:

- Flipping experience or experience with clients that have flipped properties

- Experience representing both buyers and sellers

You want a pro who specializes in flipping properties or works with people who do. You need that advantage, especially when starting out. A pro can help you see the potential in a property and then help you determine what it will take to fulfill it. The right Realtor is also an invaluable resource for finding other members of your Dream Team.

Also as important is experience with both buying and selling. You want a Realtor who will find you a property, hold your hand as you fix it, and then market your flip home for the highest profit. You need a partner who can do it all with ease. And once you have found a Realtor you like, stick with him or her and you can both succeed.

INSIDER SECRET

Internet Savvy—According to Realtor Curt Truman of Coldwell Banker Beverly Hills North, 70 percent of all buyers will start their search on the Internet even before they contact a Realtor. Make sure your Realtor has a Web site and Internet presence. It is also a great way to check out his marketing skills and style.

INSIDER SECRET

Go Straight to the Top—Jim Gillespie suggests that when looking for a Realtor, go straight to the manager of your local realty office. Tell them you want a Realtor with extensive investment experience, someone who has worked with flippers and has a working knowledge of both buying and selling. The manager will have a vested interest in your satisfaction, in keeping your business. He has an overview of all the Realtor's skills and will suggest the best one for you.

Select a Realtor You Like

If you don't like the Realtor, then chances are no one else will, either. But you say, "I may not like him, but he or she is a real bulldog and will fight for a deal." Life is too short. You are going to be spending a lot of time with your Realtor, so their style had better be compatible with yours. Do you need someone easygoing or someone aggressive? Personally, I am a self-proclaimed overachiever and I like working with someone similar, as long as they have an easygoing personality and a great sense of humor. Make sure you like them. You are going to want the people you are negotiating with to feel the same way.

YOUR MORTGAGE BROKER

Another important player on your Dream Team is the mortgage broker. Go to a mortgage broker to secure your loan rather than a bank. Here's why: They have access to many banks and lenders, not just one. Some banks don't like to lend to flippers because the bank makes its big money from you over the long-term loan. A mortgage broker will work with you, is generally more flexible with flippers, and knows which lenders will work with shorter-term loans. As part of your Dream Team, the mortgage broker will give you discounts on house number two, three, four, etc., and I can promise you the bank won't.

Unlike a bank or a credit union that offers only cookie-cutter mortgages, brokers specialize in customizing the mortgage to your flipping needs. And because they represent many dozens of lenders, they are in a good position to get you the best possible mortgage for your needs. They make money by getting 1 to 1.5 percent of the mortgage, and their fee is paid by the lender. Your only cost should be the credit report fee, which is usually around $10, and the cost of your property appraisal, which will run from $300 to $600 depending on the size of the house. Besides a great rate, your mortgage broker can get you that preapproval letter we covered in chapter two, "Flipping Economics 101," which turbocharges you into a dream buyer in a fast-moving deal.

A Mortgage Broker Has a Reputation at Stake

Unlike the online brokerages that thrive on one-time buyers, a mortgage broker's entire business is built on referrals. If he does a bad job for you, you can go to your Realtor and say, "Bob the mortgage broker did a terrible job." Bob will never get another referral again. An online brokerage, however, really doesn't have to answer to anyone! The next customer is always a click away. Working with a broker who has to answer to someone gives you a great deal of leverage.

How to Find a Mortgage Broker

As with your Realtor, the best way to find a mortgage broker is through references. Talk to your friends. If you've found your Realtor, ask them. In fact, while you're interviewing your three Realtors, ask them who they've worked with and respected.

What to Look for—and Expect

When you get him on the phone (and this should be easy or don't bother) ask for the names of banks and lenders with whom he has relationships. Find out how long he has been doing this. You want someone with at least five years of experience. Be very up-front. Tell him you are looking to purchase a property to flip, and may be doing it often. He will either love you immediately for that or see that as a negative and extra work for himself. Go for the love.

FLIP TIP

Stay Close at Hand—Look for a mortgage broker who is close by. Since you will certainly be rushing documents back and forth, the shorter the distance, the cheaper the bill for the messengers and last-minute deliveries.

INSIDER SECRET

Just Say No to Fees—If he suggests any up-front fees, say, "Thank you for your time." And move on.

YOUR INSURANCE AGENT

You need to find an insurance agent with flip experience, one who will understand your needs for various kinds of insurances, including flood and earthquake, as well as the ability to carry two or more properties simultaneously. Get references from friends, from your Realtor and your mortgage broker, your escrow officer or lawyer. And don't forget to talk to the insurance agent who carries your current car insurance. Stay away from the Yellow Pages. It's not that there's anything wrong with letting your fingers do the walking, just that your Realtor and your mortgage broker have hands-on experience and expertise. Use it.

FLIP TIP

Fix-It Insurance—Tell your insurance broker right up front that you are going to be doing fix-it work to the property so they can advise you on extra coverage for the liabilities connected with on-site tradesmen. A little extra money toward insurance could save you tens of thousands of dollars. This is not a place to scrimp.

YOUR ACCOUNTANT

You need more than an experienced professional who is good with numbers on your team. You need an accountant who has specific expertise in real estate accounting—and lots of it. One misinterpretation of tax real estate law could cost you tens of thousands of dollars!

I always confer with my accountant prior to buys and sales when flipping. That way I'll know if the income will affect my capital gains and what I need to report. An accountant who's an expert on tax laws will help you to decide when it is most advantageous to sell and when it is better to wait.

To fulfill the specific requirements, to stay on the numerous timelines, and to take full advantage of the legal tax advantages that make flipping profitable, you need an accountant who knows the ropes. One missed rung—thanks to a well-intentioned yet ill-informed accountant—can set you back.

How to Find Your Accountant

As always, I suggest you ask your home-owning friends, just in case they know someone good. But rely on the expertise of your Realtor, your mortgage broker, and your insurance agent. Among your flipping team, someone is sure to know a great accountant, and when two of them know the same professional, so much the better.

FLIP TIP

The Ultimate Question to Ask—Here's the key question to ask your accountant: Are there any circumstances where I can take my primary residence capital gains allowance prior to the two-year minimum? Answer? Yes there are: Federal tax law states that if you sell your home due to job relocation fifty miles or more from your current location, or if you need to move for health reasons, you may. If you get this answer, he or she may be your new accountant!

YOUR LAWYER

In certain states, you will also need to have a lawyer on your team. In states like New York and New Jersey, lawyers handle the closing and paperwork of your transaction. In California, an escrow company handles all the closing paper work and no lawyers are involved.

If this is the first time you are working with a lawyer, make sure you ask him or her for a one-page list of his fees before you bring him on. Unlike an escrow company and title company, whose fees are relatively standard, lawyers can still charge by the hour. If possible, negotiate for a set fee for the entire transaction.

YOUR CONTRACTOR OR HANDYMAN

Whether you choose a contractor, individual tradesman, or a handyman, these individuals have the power to make your flip a dream or a nightmare. They are an integral part of the flipping process. And you want them on your Dream Team for the long haul.

I have been working with one contractor for several years. Steven Wilder of Steven Wilder Designs and I have flipped at least ten houses together. An amazing Dream Team member, he knows that he is virtually guaranteed work with me as long as I keep flipping houses, and in return, he does an outstanding job. After so much success, he actually charges me less now than he did for the first house. He is so familiar with my techniques that he can also review a prospective house and give a ballpark bid estimate almost immediately. He always delivers the level of workmanship I expect. Even when he is not on a specific job with me, I can count on his expert advice.

In chapter ten, "The Big Fix: The Profit Improvement Levels," I will explain at length how to find a contractor, what to look for, and how to select the one that's right for you. I'll also cover subcontractors and individual tradesmen.

Four

FIND THE HOUSE WITH THE RIGHT THINGS WRONG

There really is an art to discovering a flip house that is a true hidden treasure. Not only will it need to have all the right things wrong, it will also need to be the perfect setting for lots of lifestyle upgrades, the ones that are the key to the big profit when you flip. To succeed you must develop the ability to spot that fix-it jewel, and then to think creatively when other buyers aren't. This chapter contains the techniques I use and the information you need on where to look, how to spot the right one, and which to avoid. We'll cover:

- How to tell the fixers apart

- The Six Levels of Improvements

- Fix-it levels

- Profit levels

- House-hunting tips

- Where to look: location, location, location

- How to look

- Things you can do on your own

- Other types of house-hunting opportunities

- Flip properties with income potential

LEARN TO HUNT WITH TWO SETS OF EYES

When you look at potential property, you have to see it through two sets of eyes—the eyes of a buyer *and* a seller. Through the buyer's eyes, you'll look for everything that is wrong with the property—all the flaws, the broken items, the bad features. At the same time, through a seller's eyes, you'll search for the hidden potential that amenities and upgrades will bring out. This exercise in double vision makes it possible for you to evaluate two entirely different things:

1. **Buyer's eyes:** Calculate the extent and cost of the renovations needed to determine if a house has profit potential.

2. **Seller's eyes:** Envision the completed house with all the fix-it projects completed and the house dressed and ready for sale. This vision will enable you to estimate the selling price for your flip (FFP).

HOW TO TELL THE FIXERS APART

There are houses for sale and in need of repair on every other block. How do you know which one is a potential moneymaker for you? I have found that most properties that are fixers generally fall into one of three categories—but there's only one category from which to choose your flip!

Three Types of Fixers

1. The Cosmetic Fixer

2. The Teardown

3. The Downright Ugly House

The Cosmetic Fixer

A house that just needs a bit of cleanup may look like an easy flip, but it's not. The sale price is not really discounted and there will be little room for flip profit because people are much more savvy than they used to be. Sellers and their Realtors know that with a little bit of paint and a trip or two to the home-improvement store, these cosmetic fixers are as good as new. Thus, the purchase price is not going to be much below the full market value.

Let's do the math: You buy a cosmetic fixer for $250,000. Pretty much all the houses in the neighborhood are going for that, so the seller will feel like his is worth the same, too. (He probably doesn't even think of his house as a fixer because it doesn't need much work.) You buy it, and spend $20,000 to clean up, paint, landscape, redo the floors, scour the kitchens and baths and add new appliances. Because you bought the house at market value, it isn't worth that much more than you paid for it, so you put it on the market at $300,000. Plug the numbers into the profit calculator and you see that after expenses and commissions, you just about break even. This is not what flipping is about. A cosmetic fixer is a good house for someone that wants to buy, spruce up, and stay for a while. That's not you.

The Teardown—What It Is and Why You Don't Want It

The house with "broken bones" is the money pit you must run from. When I say a house with the wrong things wrong, this is the one I mean. If a house has *major* structural, geological, or severe foundation or environmental problems, you don't want it. These will cost you. Even if you get the house cheap, the problems never go away and are sometimes impossible to fix no matter how much money you throw at them. Whatever the market, you will have to sell it for less—just like the guy who sold it to you.

Of course, any problem can be fixed. It's just a question of what it takes to fix it. Besides the expense, you'll need full permits and approval from the city inspectors for every stage of renovation. And major structural flaws can cover up underlying and costly issues. Often, it is not sufficient to just repair these problems. With significant repairs, you will have to bring the entire house up to current codes, which on an older home could run into the tens of thousands of dollars. This is a Pandora's box you do not want to open, because you will never see that money back.

Red-Flag Reasons Not to Buy a House

Structural Problems That Are Beyond Repair Economically

- Foundations that are not built on slab or concrete footings

- Major shifting due to poor foundation work

- Unsolvable drainage issues and flooding of the basement

- A bad floor plan that can only be solved by a room addition

- Bedrooms on the second floor with no bathrooms and no room to add one

- Major truss damage to the roof, causing a severely sagging roof line

- Major fire damage

- Illegal room additions that appear to be not to code, especially bathrooms

Geological Problems That You Cannot Overcome

- Severe earthquake damage

- Unstable hillside near the house

- Slipping or shifting due to soil erosion or flooding

- A house built on soil compaction (substandard by today's codes)

Environmental Problems to Run From

- Asbestos ducting

- Mold

- An old, outdated septic system

- Faulty septic system or a long sewer line to the street

- High levels of radon

The Downright Ugly House Is Beautiful to You

This is the house of your flipping dreams! It needs more extensive fix-it work than the Cosmetic Fixer. And unlike the Teardown, it has all the right things wrong with it. It has potential to be improved on all the Find It, Fix It, Flip It levels that you will learn about in this chapter. Here are some qualities that will give you an idea of what ugly means to me.

Exterior

- No current curb appeal (ugly, rundown—pick one), but lots of potential
- Great bones—good construction and architectural lines that have been underutilized or not accentuated
- Little or no landscape (my personal favorite)
- A few minor structural problems, i.e., a sagging foundation
- An abandoned car in the driveway—always a big plus!

Interior

- Dark interiors cloaked in drapery and blinds that turn off other buyers
- Upgrades needed in the house systems (electrical, plumbing, heating, air)
- Heating and air systems that have nonfunctioning vents and ducts
- Extremely dated kitchens and barely functioning bathrooms
- Rotting subfloors in the kitchen or bathroom
- A house with pets—bad smells aplenty
- Leaks in the roof and a water-stained ceiling
- Lots of small rooms, creating a chopped-up, claustrophobic feeling

Why the Downright Ugly House Is Perfect

This house is a diamond in the rough. By learning to see its potential beauty, you will get the deal that others miss. It requires vision and a leap of faith. Trust me, every time I buy a Downright Ugly House, I still think "What have I done!" but those are the ones from which I make the most profit.

To realize why this house is so perfect for a flip, you first have to understand the Six Levels of Improvements and why this house has the potential to be enhanced on every one of those levels.

THE SIX LEVELS OF IMPROVEMENTS

The Downright Ugly House has the potential for improvement on six different levels. These levels encompass all the possible fixes, repairs, replacements, and upgrades necessary to transform a Downright Ugly House into a moneymaking flip home!

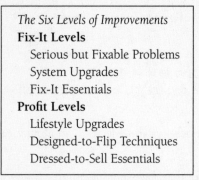

The Six Levels of Improvements
Fix-It Levels
   Serious but Fixable Problems
   System Upgrades
   Fix-It Essentials
Profit Levels
   Lifestyle Upgrades
   Designed-to-Flip Techniques
   Dressed-to-Sell Essentials

The first three levels are the Fix-It Levels—the essential, obvious improvements. Most flippers start and stop right here. But pros and insiders go on to the next three levels, the Profit Levels—and transform an *ordinary flip house* into an *extraordinarily profitable home and lifestyle*. Go for the one-two punch to profit. This is what works for me, and it will work for you.

FIX-IT LEVELS

Serious but Fixable Problems

These are the fatal flaws that send the average buyer running, but should start you drooling. Yes, they require serious professional attention. But they are also significant enough to keep a house from being snapped up by the weekend-warrior, do-it-yourself type home buyer. This leaves the field open for you. In the Downright Ugly House, you'll find Serious but Fixable Problems galore. They are big and ugly, but they are completely fixable, like a sagging foundation. These types of necessary and significant repairs force a house to be priced well below market value. And with even less competition for this house, you are really maximizing your profit potential. The problems include:

- Sagging foundation

- Major water damage from a roof leak

- Sagging roof line

- A chimney that is separated from the house

- Severe termite problems

FLIPPING SUCCESS STORY

One of my best "flip bargains" was a house whose front wall had sunken to one side. Even the front door would not open. Many unknowledgeable buyers tried to push through that crooked door and went running back out. I, however, called a foundation expert and got an estimate for the work prior to making the offer. He quoted me only $2,000. Yet I made an offer that was $50,000 below the asking price of $400,000. I got the house at $350,000. By the way, I fixed it and flipped it four months later for $749,000.

This house had a sagging front wall when I bought it for $350,000.
I sold it for $749,000.

System Upgrades

The electrical, plumbing, heat and air, and even the roof are known as the systems. Flipping pros call the system upgrades hidden costs. They are the big expenses incurred when upgrading and replacing the house systems. Replacing the roof, upgrading the electrical, replumbing and adding copper piping, and putting in a new furnace or air-conditioning are major expenses. Buyers of a flipped or newly renovated house just assume that these systems are going to be new or newly upgraded when they buy. So make sure you carefully incorporate these expenses into budget and profit potential calculations.

The Downright Ugly House is usually in need of numerous system upgrades. These upgrades allow you to negotiate the purchase price, because this is a house that requires some real improvements before it can come up to today's standards. Thus the competition for this house is less and the price should be discounted.

Fix-It Essentials

Fix-it essentials are the repairs, renovations, and upgrades that are a must-do on all flip houses: cleaning up, painting, landscaping, upgrading kitchens and baths, improving or creating curb appeal, putting in new doors, replacing lighting and hardware, adding color, new flooring, tile, appliances and countertops, and installing new cabinetry. It's all essential! We'll go through them one by one in chapter ten, "The Big Fix: The Profit Improvement Levels." You may not have to address all the items, but chances are when you spot a Downright Ugly House, you will have to address most of the following:

The Outside

- Curb appeal (landscaping, flowers, the front door)
- Exterior painting
- Pathways and driveways
- Garage door
- Outdoor lighting
- The front yard
- The backyard

The Inside

- Kitchen (cabinets, hardware, countertops, flooring, lighting, appliances, sinks, and fixtures)
- Bathrooms (flooring, cabinets, countertop, shower, sinks, lighting)
- Rooms (flooring, carpeting, walls and ceiling, painting, lighting, closets)

PROFIT LEVELS

> *The Six Levels of Improvements*
> **Fix-It Levels**
>   Serious but Fixable Problems
>   System Upgrades
>   Fix-It Essentials
> • **Profit Levels**
>   Lifestyle Upgrades
>   Designed-to-Flip Techniques
>   Dressed-to-Sell Essentials

Profit levels are the additional levels of improvements that make the difference between a breakeven or small return on your investment and a big flip profit. Not only are they your keys to incredible success in an upward or flat market, but in a downward-moving market these techniques are critical.

As the housing market becomes tighter and average home buyers become more savvy, you need to have something more to offer your potential buyers. These profit levels give your flip the winning edge even in a downtrending market. Without them your flip house will be nice, but ordinary. With them, your flip home becomes extraordinary . . . and so does your profit potential.

Lifestyle Upgrades

You need to develop that moneymaking eye for the Lifestyle Upgrades that will make you the big profits that allow you to weather any market swing. And believe me, it cuts out a lot of the competition. When everyone else is looking for a dilapidated fixer or a distressed seller situation, you are able to spot a home that not only needs some basic fix up and TLC but has the potential for some major Lifestyle Upgrades and the profit that comes with them!

Lifestyle Upgrades are born out of problems that can't be fixed with a simple replacement part. They take creative thinking, insider knowledge, and vision. You will have to think like both a buyer and a seller as you walk through a house, looking for lifestyle problems that you can solve with upgrades.

Lifestyle Upgrades = Huge Profits

Lifestyle Upgrades make the space feel livable and always inspire an emotional response. Their appeal transforms a house into a home because it epitomizes the ideal kind of lifestyle that buyers aspire to. They are the special touches buyers see in the shelter magazines and want in their own homes because they make life better or simpler or more pleasing. They include creating flow by opening up a bad layout, adding a custom master closet with shelving and space to spare, pre-wiring for the Internet, built-ins like a desk and computer station in the kitchen nook, charming touches like a window seat in the living room, and safety features like a full house alarm system. These are upgrades that will make a buyer walk through the door and say, "I can see myself living here," and write an offer for your price.

A Downright Ugly House is ripe with Lifestyle Upgrade potential. By turning these problems into Lifestyle Upgrades, you add value. Chapter ten will review each of these moneymakers in detail.

Lifestyle Upgrades

- Bad flow
- Underdeveloped living space
- A terrible view
- Little natural light
- An unwelcome entrance
- Undefined property lines
- No security system
- No backyard boundaries

- Never heard of the Internet
- No privacy
- Wasted yard space
- No outdoor living space
- Cemented backyard
- Noise
- Underdeveloped structures
- No income potential
- Borderline neighborhood
- Tiny master closets
- Hidden square feet
- Bad kitchen layout
- No home office
- Underutilized storage spaces

FLIPPING SUCCESS STORY

My "View" Upgrade That Made Me More Than $200,000—The fixer that became my Allenwood property was a rather unassuming ranch-style house that had been on the market for three months but hadn't sold. I decided to find out why. The answer was obvious once I walked into the living room. When I peered through two small windows that looked out to the backyard and pool, all I could see was a wall of overgrown twenty-foot-tall trees and bushes at the edge of the property. My heart started racing and I wrote an offer on the spot. I am usually a cool customer but I could barely contain my excitement. Even the Realtor was surprised at my enthusiasm.

Let me explain why I got so excited about a bunch of overgrown trees. I had done some snooping around the neighborhood and I knew that behind all the trees and bushes was a spectacular view of the canyon and mountains beyond. All of the houses on this winding street were built on the edge of a cliff in the Hollywood Hills. Each house's backyard literally dropped off at the far end. No one could see the incredible view because of the landscaping. But I knew it was there. And I knew what it was worth.

The day I closed escrow I had a crew in there ripping out all the overgrown landscape and gnarled trees. It was one of the most tremendous lifestyle transformations I have ever seen! I spruced up the house with the required fix-its and replaced the entire outside wall in the living room with glass sliders to capture that glorious view.

On sale day, the buyers walked in, their mouths dropped open and the offer writing began. I sold the house with multiple offers over the asking price. I had paid $375,000. I put only approximately $60,000 into it and sold it for $735,000. The $835 it cost me to rip out those trees yielded a profit of around $247,000!

This view discovery gave my Allenwood house the monumental Lifestyle Upgrade that helped make me a $247,000 profit!

Designed-to-Flip Techniques

These are the design touches that add value, increase aesthetic appeal, and make the house more profitable because they look so great. These techniques allow you to create great style that has mass appeal. I've seen these easy and affordable design elements in the homes of the wealthy and the famous as host of *Extra's Mansions & Millionaires*, and I've used them in each and every one of my flips to great success. Everything is covered in detail in chapter thirteen, "Designed to Flip," but here are some of my favorite designed-to-flip topics:

Designed-to-Flip Topics

- Creating space

- Consistency in style and materials

- Why neutrality works

- The advantage of natural light

- Today's lighting

- Paint and working with a palette

- Bringing the outside in and expanding boundaries

- The extra "brooches" that get buyers excited

Dressed-to-Sell Essentials

The house is gorgeous because you've done it all. Now it's time to give it the "emotional edge." This is the ineffable quality that turns a mildly interested prospective buyer into an offer-writing bundle of enthusiasm because the place feels like, well . . . home. From dressing the house for success to hitting the buyers where it counts—in their hearts—I cover the techniques that put your house over the top in detail in chapter fourteen:

Set the Stage The hottest trend in real estate—staging—uses furniture and accessories to make a house a home.

Vignettes Create living "still-life" snapshots of a well-lived life.

Seduce the Senses With scents and sounds and touch, you can make potential buyers feel relaxed, cozy . . . and seduced.

The Sale-Day Prep List Be prepared . . . it's showtime! Use this step-by-step checklist to make sure you've done it all, from making the countertops gleam to putting a smile on the face of every buyer.

THE POWER OF THE PROFIT-LEVEL UPGRADES

Something magical happens when both the Fix-It Level and the Profit-Level improvements are combined. Individually yes, each level of improvement adds value. But there is a synergy that happens when you put them all together. The whole really *is* greater than the sum of its parts! You have taken a house and created much more than a home. You have created an emotionally appealing LIFESTYLE. And the value of that is . . . priceless!

HOUSE-HUNTING TIPS

Now that you know about what to look for in terms of problems and how to improve them, here's what you need to know about location and some specific house-hunting tips you can use once you zero in.

Don't Get Discouraged

Be persistent. The hardest houses to get to see are usually the best buys. I am always delighted to hear that a seller or, better yet, the renter of the house has been making it difficult for anyone to get in! That means that I'm going to get a deal. Most buyers don't have the tenacity that I do. They also don't get the results that I do.

Three Times Is the Charm

I like to see an interesting property at least three times before I make an offer: during the day—to see the activity on the street, at rush hour—to check for traffic, and at night—to check for noise and safety.

Walk the 'Hood

You have to check the neighborhood out on foot. Get out of the car and take a stroll. Meet the neighbors. That's the only way you'll know about the obnoxious barking dog, the garages that are home offices or bedrooms—all the aspects of the neighborhood that will directly affect your property value, should you buy. And while you're there, chat up the neighbors. They're a great source of information.

FLIP FLOP

They Bark All Night—I bought a wonderful home in the Holly-wood Hills. Unfortunately for me, it was the one time I did not fol-low my own advice to chat up the neighbors to learn about potential problems. It caused me many sleepless nights—literally. My first night in the house, I woke to the sounds of two barking, yelping dogs that howled and bellowed until morning. I couldn't believe it. The next night the same thing happened. I later found out that the seller had been fighting with the neighbor over the barking dogs for six months. The surrounding neighbors had also been complaining, but the awful, miserable owners of the dogs just didn't care. It took me more than a year of working with L.A. Animal Control before the owners agreed to take responsibility for the problem. I was unable to put the house on the market for an entire year, because I would have had to disclose the problem, and I would have had to take a steep discount prior to resolving the is-sue. Otherwise, I would have been liable for not disclosing, just as the man who sold the house to me without disclosing it was. Had I chatted up neighbors, I would have been much less tired all year long!

A Little Charm Can Save You Money!

The more architectural detail a house already has, the easier and less ex-pensive it is to create charm. It's already there: All you have to do is showcase it. For the smaller house, look for details that you can accentu-ate. With an older house keep some of the elements, like the original tiles and maybe even some of the original cabinets. Just dress them up with new hardware. Classic architectural styles like craftsman, turn of the century, and cottage style are loaded with architectural detail. Keep the old bathroom fixtures as well, even if you upgrade the plumbing and electrical throughout. This money-saver creates a classic look.

INSIDER SECRET

If It Needs More Square Footage, Keep Looking—Avoid houses that need room additions. I never add square footage beyond the actual footprint or roofline of the house. It is just too time consuming, and the permitting process and the architectural plans and engineering involved are just too overwhelming to make a flip project worthwhile. If the house needs an increase in square footage to work, it may be a good buy for an "owner user," but not as a flip. It's fine to push a wall out and take advantage of the existing roofline and existing foundation, but not if you have to add an additional roof and foundation.

You're Not Just Buying a Condo, You're Buying a Building

The Downright Ugly Condo or Co-op is a beautiful thing, as long as the building isn't Downright Ugly, too. And when I say that, I'm not referring to its physical beauty. I'm talking about financial health. If the financial profile seems shaky, or if additional assessments for big-ticket items like new elevators or windows or a large-scale lobby re-do are needed, no matter how cost-effectively you can upgrade your unit, you'll still have to bear the cost of the building's ailing finances . . . and so will your prospective buyer.

INSIDER SECRET

Condo Flipping on a Budget—Sherry Manatay of Corcoran Realty in New York City says you can often get a great deal on co-ops and condos from buildings that are on leased land. Manhattan in particular has numerous residential buildings on leased land. It makes unknowledgeable buyers nervous, so the prices are steeply discounted. However, when flipping, it allows you to buy into a unit at a lower cost, fix it up, and then sell it at a premium. Granted, you're going to be selling it for less than units in non-leased land buildings, but then again, you also paid less for it.

WHERE TO LOOK: LOCATION, LOCATION, LOCATION

Now that you know what to look for, the question is, where to look? The tried and true adage is "buy the worst house on the best block." Of course this is true, but everyone knows it, so competition will be steep. The trick is to find the right block!

To be successful, you have to invest time in this process. Got an hour? Get out and drive around neighborhoods in your community. That's the only way you'll become aware of areas on their way up or down. Think of it as research on four wheels.

Fringe Neighborhoods and Neighborhoods in Transition

Look for fringe neighborhoods that are adjacent to a "good" neighborhood but still have a few clunkers for which good deals are possible. In these areas, once you start to fix up your flip, neighbors often get inspired and begin to appreciate their homes as well. Within a few weeks, you'll see small improvements, all of which raise the value of your flip as the neighborhood improves.

Inner-City Metropolitan Neighborhoods

Has a Starbucks just opened on the corner? Is there a trendy restaurant where a tattoo parlor used to be? These are all good signs that a city neighborhood is on the upswing. You can bet that big chains like Starbucks spend a lot of money and time analyzing neighborhood potential before they open up a new store. So go ahead, tap into their market research and be their neighbor.

Older Neighborhoods

These neighborhoods are a good source of Downright Ugly Houses, ones where the houses are a minimum of twenty to thirty years old and showing signs of age, but the lawns are kept neat and clean and show pride of ownership. Most houses are owner-occupied. There may be a few young families investing sweat equity, a sign that the neighborhood is appreciating.

Affluent Neighborhoods Are Tricky

Once in a while, you'll find a flippable house in an upscale area, but the costs are usually higher and the pool of potential buyers is smaller. If you find that proverbial worst house on the best block, then snag it, because it has profit potential built in. But not for your first flip.

Signs That a Neighborhood Has Profit Potential

Your Realtor can help you research the points below, all of which are signs you want to see. Take this list with you when you're out and about.

- Older homes, at least twenty to thirty years, with visible wear and tear
- Good schools
- Pride of home ownership
- Well-maintained front lawns
- Garbage under control
- 15 to 20 percent of houses are or have recently been fixed up
- Low crime rate
- R-1 zoning—single-family residences, not apartment buildings
- Lots of real estate activity—current listings, closed-sales, and pending ones
- More than 75 percent of the sales are to owner-occupants, not landlords
- Buyers went with conventional financing
- Accessibility to stores and services
- A strong homeowners association

FLIP TIP

Graffiti Gone—Don't automatically make a U-turn when you see a bit of graffiti. Come back in a week. If it's gone, then pride of ownership is in force. If not, think twice.

FLIP TIP

Cookie-Cutter Communities—Houses in newly developed communities are just too hard to sell because of their cookie-cutter nature. There's no way to make your flip stand out. And if you try too hard, you'll overcapitalize. They're also not old enough to need the big improvements that make profit.

FLIP TIP

Megan's Law—You may want to review Megan's Law, the law that entitles neighbors to know if there are sex offenders living in the neighborhood (go to www.registeredoffenderslist.org). This may not be an issue for you, and you may not be a supporter of the law, but unfortunately, your future buyer MAY be someone who will want to have those neighbor profiles—especially if you are flipping to a family.

FLIP TIP

Locations to Avoid—It's just common sense, but don't buy a house next to a problem that is not going to go away, like a busy mall or a graveyard or a hospital. You may get a deal, but selling will be another story. No matter how much money you throw at it, that mini-mall will still be across the street. Need I say more?

HOW TO LOOK

This is mostly where your Realtor gets to do his job. Looking for proper-ties is what he does. Finding the right one for his customers so he can profit is his calling. Besides, because he is on your team, he knows he will get the commission when you buy and will probably represent you when you sell. If you have been clear with him about your price range and that you want a flippable house that meets all Six Levels of Im-provements, have him get to work. Expect him to:

• Scour the MLS

• Talk to other Realtors in his office and other franchise offices

• Cover the bank repos, tax records, foreclosures

• Speak with potential sellers

FLIPPING SUCCESS STORY

The House Next Door—My Dream Team Realtor is always trying to be creative and one step ahead. There was a house on Charl Place that I thought would make a great flip, and I had put in an offer. Well, it went into multiple offers and the price went up be-yond what would be profitable for a flip. My always attentive and ever-observant flipping partner noticed that the house next door would be a good candidate. He knocked on the door and told the owner he had a buyer who was willing to pay around $800,000 for a house like his. The homeowner was interested. I got the "drop everything and bring your checkbook" phone call. I bought the house on the spot. His ingenuity snagged me a great flip house even before it went up for sale.

My "house next door," before and after.

THINGS YOU CAN DO ON YOUR OWN

Make it clear to your Realtor that while he is looking on your behalf, you will be looking too, and that if you find something, you will bring him in to write the offer and do the deal. This statement shows loyalty on your part and will inspire hard work on his.

Hit the Internet

The minute you finish this chapter, jump on your computer and start surfing. You aren't going to find any great deals there. The kind of hot properties you want are gone long before they hit the public realty Web sites, but you will get an invaluable education about how much or how little your money will buy. Go to www.Realtor.com and to the other sites listed in the back of the book. Plug in your zip code. Put in the minimum and maximum price range and . . . bam. You will see a very good sampling of houses in your price range on the market at this very minute. The Internet is especially beneficial in metropolitan areas like New York City, where open houses are rare. The Internet is a window on the widest cross section of properties available. Get in the habit of checking these realty Web sites, found in the appendix at the back of the book, every few days. You will see what is selling and what is sitting.

Go to Open Houses

It sounds obvious, but get in the habit of spending time each Saturday or Sunday at open houses. This is not for the hot deals, but for the education. You want to size up the competition. Check out what features and amenities buyers are impressed by or leave them nonplussed. And when you go, don't be shy. Talk to people, starting with the broker who is showing the house. This is a network-based business. Everybody loves to be in the know about great properties, great neighborhoods, or terrific agents. Get out there and mingle.

Carry a House Search Notebook

In the heat of the hunt, you may think you'll be able to remember the location and details of every house that has caught your eye. You won't. Carry a notebook that is exclusively for real estate notes. You will be surprised how many times months later you may want an address or phone number of a prospective house you jotted down. Keep them all in one place. To succeed, you'll be carrying lots of details around for a long time. Relying on your memory just won't work.

Hunting Techniques for a Hot Market

When the market is hot and inventory is low, I have gone so far as to canvass a neighborhood I like and knock on doors of houses that look like good flip candidates. I simply introduce myself and let the homeowners know that I am looking to buy a house in the neighborhood. Try it, but never insult them by making them think you have singled out their house as the worst on the block. They will often tell you who might be ready to sell among their neighbors, and if they are looking to sell, you might be able to strike a deal before they even list the property. It's happened to me. The seller saved half the commission and I got the house I wanted.

Hunting Techniques in a Down Market

In a down or cold market, you still have to work to find good deals. Also, be aware that in a downward-moving market, a good deal today may be a little high-priced next month. When prices are dropping you need to find really good deals to allow for the declining prices. But fortunately for you, down markets also mean that as the climate in which you can make flip profits based on market appreciation alone begins to disappear, so do the flippers that rely on it to succeed. As a result, there is less competition for you—because you don't.

Rentals Become Sales

Look for rental houses that appear to be flippable and find out if the owners might want to sell. You never know; it never hurts to ask. Visit www.rentnet.com for even greater inventory.

OTHER TYPES OF HOUSE-HUNTING OPPORTUNITIES

As I have said, I am not an advocate of the "no-money-down, get-rich-quick" school of real estate success. For Sale by Owners (FSBOs), foreclosures, and Real Estate Owned (REOs) have never worked for me. My time is much better spent elsewhere. I work hard, but I am not a do-it-yourselfer. I rely on professionals, starting with my Realtor.

The following are descriptions of these kinds of opportunities. If you choose to go after them, do so with the help of your Realtor.

FSBO

"For Sale by Owner" properties are often described with words like "TLC" and "handyman's delight." The ads *should* also say that you'll be dealing with a non-pro, an owner who is deeply and personally invested in the property, as opposed to his representative, a professional real estate agent. And this person thinks that they know it all, as indicated by the mere fact that they are trying to sell their house as an FSBO! If you go this route, get your Realtor involved once you've made contact. Let them do all the negotiating. It's worth the commission. Sometimes an FSBO seller will understand that it is worth it to pay half the commission than deal with the paperwork necessary to do the deal. But, in my experience, even though an FSBO may be below market price, it's not worth the extra effort you need to exert in dealing directly with an owner on all fronts.

Foreclosures

When a homeowner can't meet his payments, the lender takes the property back. When the market is hot, you can't find foreclosures. When it's bad, they're everywhere. But to find them, you have to do more legwork than I, for one, have the time to do. And, chances are you are working another job and juggling a family, as well. You have to locate a rundown property, then go to the assessor's office and find the owner. Then you have to meet him, get him to sign a quit claim deed over to you for a nominal amount of money, and then get your financing. Sound easy? It's not. Plus, you have to research unpaid second, third, and sometimes fourth mortgages, or you'll end up having to pay them off too. There goes your profit.

There are entire books and infomercials devoted to buying foreclosures, but I have found that working with a smart and motivated real estate team has secured me much better deals. My brokers have brought me at least four of my most recent flips before they had even been listed for sale. That kind of thorough and alert realty has paid off for me much more than scouring the papers and banks for foreclosures.

REOs

REO means "real estate owned." Lenders don't want the world to know that they have these properties, because it looks bad on their books. Unlike foreclosures, REOs usually offer you clear title. With foreclosures, you get a better price, but you might never really know the title history of what you are buying until it becomes a problem. This means the property could still have liens or back taxes, etc. REOs are priced higher because they have already been cleaned up and are, therefore, not the profit center you need. Your time is better spent elsewhere.

FLIP FLOP

My Wasted Weeks—Here's a story from my career that illustrates that foreclosures and REOs are not automatic profit-makers. I got a call from a flipping friend who was at the tax assessor's office, basically looking for people whose taxes were in arrears so he could approach them and get a deal. He had come across someone who was $100,000 in arrears. Because he was going after another opportunity, he gave this one to me. I got the address and spent four weeks tracking down the owner. Once I found him, we negotiated endlessly. At first he wasn't interested, then he was, then his brother wanted the house, then he didn't. This went on for weeks. Once we had verbally agreed on a price, I called my Realtor to get his input. The Realtor ran the comps, said it was overvalued and that I wouldn't make any profit. So I didn't buy it. I got caught up in the assumption that if a property is ready to foreclose, it must be a good deal. I waited all that time mistakenly assuming that any distressed property, FSBO or REO, is a steal. All I did was steal weeks of my own life from myself.

FLIP PROPERTIES WITH INCOME POTENTIAL

In this book, I am concentrating on single-family homes, because as a beginning flipper or a current homeowner, that will be your focus. However, there is no reason to overlook:

1. Duplexes—Sold as one property with two separate residences

2. Triplexes—Sold as one property with three separate residences

3. House with a guest house

4. House with a separate apartment or rentable room

Buying/flipping a multiple unit, duplex, or house with guest house is a very smart way to go, especially if you are going to do the find it, fix it, hold it for two years path. Having that additional income really helps to offset your carrying costs.

Advantages

That additional income can sometimes cover between half to all of your carrying costs. It allows you to live almost for free for your two-year period, if you are going to hold for two years. It is also a big incentive for your potential buyer, who will also see the advantage of that extra income.

Disadvantages

In short-term flipping, you will now have *two* kitchens to renovate, two heating systems to upgrade, twice the number of bathrooms, etc. You also don't want to have tenants living in the unit or units while you do the work. And if you rent immediately to a tenant, you will not have the flexibility to sell your property vacant when you choose.

I have flipped three duplexes in Los Angeles and one house with a guest house. I have done both the fast track and the fix-and-hold with them. I like them, and I like the added income. So keep an eye out for them, as well.

Five

THE FINANCIAL MODEL FOR SUCCESS: THE PROFIT CALCULATOR

THE PROFIT CALCULATOR CHART

Estimated FFP (Final Flipped Price)	$ _____
Purchase Price of the House	– _____
Purchase Closing Costs	– _____
Estimated Fix-It Costs	– _____
Carrying Costs	– _____
10% Buffer	– _____
Sale Closing Costs and Commissions	– _____
Total	$ _____
– Capital Gains Tax	– _____
PROFIT	$ _____

You've found a candidate that fits the criteria. If it fits the financial model for success, you make an offer. If it doesn't, you move on. But what are the criteria? Well, as much fun as I have and as creative the process is, the real goal is to make a profit! Thus the ultimate criterion you use in choosing a house to flip is profit potential.

As we briefly discussed in chapter two, "Flipping Economics 101," this Profit Calculator is a very specific set of calculations that is easy to use once you know how to estimate the numbers you're going to plug in. Once we discuss each of the following elements, you will be able to start entering your numbers immediately:

- The Final Flipped Price (FFP)—The cornerstone of flipping

- The secret to FFP: Know your market and your buyer

- Estimating Fix-It costs

- Carrying costs

- Capital gains taxes on your profit

- Calculate the maximum you should pay for the profit you want

---

THE PROFIT CALCULATOR CHART

Estimated FFP (Final Flipped Price)	$ _____
Purchase Price of the House	– _____
Purchase Closing Costs	– _____
Estimated Fix-It Costs	– _____
Carrying Costs	– _____
10% Buffer	– _____
Sale Closing Costs and Commissions	– _____
Total	$ _____
– Capital Gains Tax	– _____
PROFIT	$ _____

THE FINAL FLIPPED PRICE (FFP)— THE CORNERSTONE OF FLIPPING

The FFP or Final Flipped Price is the top price you hope to get for a property once you fix it. If everyone could pull this number out of the air and do this off the top of their heads, they'd all be rich. But they can't. But with well-researched information, a thorough analysis of real estate comps, the ability to visualize, my Find It, Fix It, Flip It techniques, and your good instincts, *you* can come up with a pretty accurate number.

The ability to accurately estimate the FFP is the single most important tool in your arsenal of flipping techniques, because the FFP determines two other essential values:

- How much profit you will make once the house is in perfect flip condition

- What you should pay for the house to guarantee that profit

Calculating the FFP

To determine what your house could be worth, you first need to visualize what you expect it to become. Visualize that Downright Ugly House in perfect flipped condition, with all the amenities and lifestyle upgrades that you plan to add. See it transformed by all Six Levels of Improvements. Then compare that future vision with all the comps of the other houses out there that are on the market and that have recently sold.

Comparing Apples to Apples

"Comps" is short for comparables, the list of all properties that have sold or are in the process of selling in every neighborhood. Your Realtor has access to them. But you're not comparing the house *as it currently is* to the comps. You'll be comparing the house as it will be *when it's finished.*

What to Compare

- Square footage

- Age of home

- Number of bedrooms and baths

- Amenities—pool, spa, walk-in closets, gourmet kitchen

- Lot size

- Condition—newly renovated, perfect condition, cosmetic fixer, teardown

Use the existing comps as an indicator of what the market will bear, in order to establish the top price at which you can sell your flip house. Make sure to compare your house to the houses that are as similar as possible—in other words, apples to apples.

This is another area in which your Realtor will be of utmost importance. Discuss your vision of the finished flip in great detail. Any Realtor with flipping experience can share that vision—and help you fulfill it by interpreting those comps and determining a ballpark selling price for this future beauty, your FFP.

BREAKING THE COMPS

I am very proud to say that I have "broken" the comps for every house I have ever flipped. Every time I sell a house, I price it 5 to 10 percent above anything else that has sold in the neighborhood! Why? Because not only am I creating and selling a dynamite house, I am offering a home that comes with the promise of a lifestyle.

Well, now you have a new problem, but it's a good one to have. Chances are, by using these Find It, Fix It, Flip It techniques, YOUR flipped house will be much more appealing, inviting, and exciting than any of the other houses for sale in the neighborhood. As a result, your house may and hopefully will "break" the comps, selling for more than any of its counterparts. But evaluating the comps does not set anything in stone. It just gives you a guideline. And once you come up with a target price, even though you could have the potential to sell it for 5 to 10 percent over the comps, don't bank on it. Be conservative with your FFP now, and be pleasantly surprised later!

FLIPPING SUCCESS STORY

My Okean Terrace Comp-Breaker—I found an interesting house in the Hollywood Hills. It was kitty-corner to Ellen DeGeneres's house at the time. The house was a 3,000-square-foot ranch-style home owned by a producer/writer who had turned it into a true 1980s Hollywood bachelor pad. It was loaded with electronic equipment and exercise paraphernalia, and the entire living room was covered in black rubber gym-floor matting. Although the house wrapped around the pool, there was almost no access to the pool or to the grounds.

I did all my homework to determine the FFP. I looked at the

comps, envisioned the house finished on all Six Levels of Improvements, and conferred with my Dream Team Realtors. The house was on the market for $524,000. I set my FFP at $900,000. I could see there was a lot of work to be done—but there was also a lot of potential.

As I redid the house, I incorporated all the first three levels of fix-it improvements. But the three Profit-Level Improvements made all the difference.

I added in twenty-two all-glass French doors, opening every room in the house to the gorgeous, piano-shaped pool. I put in a restaurant-style six-burner stove for gourmet cooking. I transformed the house from a dark bachelor den to an entertainer's dream home, thus creating a lifestyle. I purchased the house for $525,000, used the profit from my previous flip to fix it up, and sold it for $1,050,000 after two weeks on the market. That was nearly $150,000 over any other comp in the neighborhood! And well over my original estimated FFP.

As you can see, I utilized every available inch of my Okean Terrace property, created poolside access from every room, and transformed it into a luxurious indoor/outdoor oasis.

FLIP TIP

What's Not Selling—You can learn a lot when determining your FFP by observing not only what IS selling but observing what is NOT selling. Are its true qualities hidden? Is it overpriced for what it offers? How does it compare with your house? What is it lacking that yours won't be? Take note.

THE SECRET TO FFP: KNOW YOUR MARKET AND YOUR BUYER

What is the biggest mistake that beginning flippers and many home-owners make? It is overcapitalizing, an ugly expression when it comes to flipping. It means you have put more money INTO your house than you can possibly ever get OUT of it when you sell. It means you made more improvements and spent more money fixing up your house than the house is worth for the neighborhood or current market. But how do you avoid overestimating your Final Flipped Price and making improvements to your flip that are totally unnecessary, eat away at your profit, and cause you to lose money? When estimating your Final Flipped Price for any potential flip, it is imperative to:

- Know your market
- Know your buyer

KNOW YOUR MARKET

As you mentally renovate your flip house, charging through the house room by room, ripping out cabinets and installing recessed lights, you first need to know your market—and the neighborhood. Who lives there? Single people, working couples, and young families will tend to cluster in certain neighborhoods for obvious reasons, such as the size and price of the housing stock and proximity to schools or transportation. Look at the houses and you'll get a snapshot of who's buying there. Look at the cars for clues as well. Do you see Hondas, SUVs, or sports cars?

To know your market is also to know your competition. Do this by

going to open houses, asking questions, listening to the answers, and using your powers of observation. How fixed-up the properties are and
what kinds of upgrades they have will give you a sense of whether you
should go low-, medium-, or high-quality in your renovations and
amenities.

Knowing your price range is critical. Are you in a $200,000-home
neighborhood or an $800,000-home neighborhood? You don't want to
over-improve and be selling the only house with a newly added pool.
You won't be able to make a profit. You want your finished flip to be just
slightly better than the best house that has sold in the 'hood.

Choose the Right Materials for the Neighborhood

Naturally, you want your flip house to be the best it can be. But choose
the level of quality by knowing your target buyer and evaluating the
comps, not by what you see in shelter magazines. If most of the homes
have neat, tidy kitchens, step away from the granite and the flag-
stone . . . and head for the tile countertops and linoleum. Your FFP
won't support the higher-end materials.

However, if you are in a more affluent or transitional area and your
house is priced above $300,000, go for it. Consider the sophistication
level and the expectations of your buyer, and you'll make the right
choice.

What Does the House Down the Block Have That Yours Doesn't?

I have always been smart enough to know what I don't know. When it
comes to the fix-it process, I have continuously sought out the help and
advice of others. Your real estate agent is always a good source for ideas
about what to improve. Just ask him, "What do the houses in this neighborhood that have sold for more money have that this house doesn't
have? Is there any amenity that the average buyer in this neighborhood
will expect that this house doesn't have?" Whatever his answer, include
it in your plans.

Many of the comparable amenities would seem to be logical additions
or omissions when making your upgrade decisions. But you would be
surprised by how many beginning flippers don't do a market analysis

first. For example, in vacation areas like south Florida or Palm Springs, adding a pool is a profitable upgrade, but in the Northeast it is a waste of your flipping dollars.

KNOW YOUR BUYER

Just like in television commercials, you need to know who your target audience is. At *Extra*, the show is tailored to our target customer, which is women age thirty-five to forty-five. At the Home Shopping Network, the target is women age twenty-eight to fifty-five, with a median yearly household income of more than $70,000. By using this kind of thinking in your flip, you create profit by investing in features your buyers want. And you save money by avoiding the amenities they don't. But first you must know your buyer.

Who Is Your Buyer?

To know this, talk with your Realtor and ask the question, "Who are we planning to sell this house to?" Your first answer may be, "Anyone with the money!" That would be great, but the reality is that certain types of buyers look for certain types of houses. A single man or woman will look for a cozy two-bedroom house with a big master bath. A pair of working professionals might get all worked up over an alcove with a built-in desk and recessed lighting. A husband and wife with children will want an extra bedroom with a den and an enclosed grassy backyard. Pinpointing your target market will help you choose between investing in dramatic features such as a double Jacuzzi in the master bath or a hardworking feature like built-ins in the smaller bedrooms. As a result, you will reach your goal: a quick sale at the highest possible price.

TYPES OF BUYERS

You can't be all things to all people. Don't try to make the house work for everyone. You just can't. You want to be as broad as possible, but on target. Make these decisions up front with your Realtor.

There are many different kinds of buyers, from single moms to families with live-in in-laws. What they have in common is that they all want a wonderful home. The target-specific upgrades you can make are always based on what the neighborhood will bear, i.e., whether you are improving a low-end home or taking a property to the medium high-end level. Here are four of the most common kinds of buyers and what they look for:

1. A Single First-Time Buyer

is usually a renter moving up into home ownership, and wants a perfectly presented home. Since a huge percentage of renters are women, it's no surprise that they represent a large percentage of first-time buyers. The house needs to be spotless, have great curb appeal and a warm and welcoming feeling with a few amenities, but be basic enough to be affordable. Lifestyle Upgrades such as a home office and a security system are appropriate in these low- to medium-range brackets.

2. A Working Couple

is looking for a brand-spanking-new, well-maintained home with an extra private/working space for each individual, his-and-hers sinks, a well-outfitted closet, and neighborhood-appropriate upgrades.

3. A Family

with more than one child wants a fabulous house with the extras for the way they live, like a great room or an open plan kitchen/dining room, ample storage in each of the bedrooms, upgraded laundry room, and a separate master suite or area for the parents.

4. Retirees or Empty Nesters

are a growing portion of the population. After cashing out of their longtime family homes, they are often looking for a simpler lifestyle in a home with lots of amenities, such as a gourmet kitchen and a Jacuzzi in the master bath. They also look for smaller, more manageable backyards and low-maintenance landscaping. Upgraded security systems are also in demand. If you are flipping in Florida, Arizona, or Southern California, these buyers will be plentiful.

FLIPPING SUCCESS STORY

Targeting My Buyer—The story of my Spaulding house is a good example of how to target your buyer. It was a cute craftsman—three small bedrooms and 1,800 square feet in the heart of Los Angeles. When I lived there, I designed it for a single person and converted the three bedrooms into two larger bedrooms and a larger master bath, replacing the third bedroom with a den. But when I was ready to flip it, I realized I needed to convert the attic into a third bedroom so I could open my potential universe of buyers to include young couples with a child. By moving a few non–load bearing walls, I created a luxurious bedroom/master bath for myself. And by adding an upstairs bedroom when it was time to sell, it worked perfectly for a young couple who were ready to adopt!

The Woman Decides and the Husband Writes the Check

As out of step with the times as this may seem, it is true more often than not. Keep the woman in mind as you improve. Give her amenities in the kitchen and perks in the master bath and she'll be sold before her husband can say, "Let's think about it."

The Buying Power of Single Women

Jim Gillespie, the president of Coldwell Banker Real Estate Corporation, gave me some very valuable information. Over the past several years, one in five new home and condo purchases have been made by single women. That's 20 percent of the market. Give these important potential buyers careful consideration.

ESTIMATING FIX-IT COSTS 101

THE PROFIT CALCULATOR CHART	
Estimated FFP (Final Flipped Price)	$ _____
Purchase Price of the House	–_____
Purchase Closing Costs	–_____
Estimated Fix-It Costs	–_____
Carrying Costs	–_____
10% Buffer	–_____
Sale Closing Costs and Commissions	–_____
Total	$ _____
– Capital Gains Tax	–_____
PROFIT	$ _____

Can you really estimate these fix-it costs before you make an offer? Not only CAN you, you are going to HAVE to if you want to accurately access a property's profit potential. But don't worry. You aren't expected to be able to do more than guess at the costs on your first estimated fix-it costs budget. Right off the bat I am going to say that making that first ballpark estimate is not easy. That's OK—think of your first flip as a crash course in estimating renovation costs. This first flip has a steep learning curve. But once you master the art of estimating fix-it costs you will have a winning edge: the ability to make the educated quick decisions and move quickly on the hot real estate deals.

ESTIMATING YOUR FIX-IT COSTS IS A FOUR-STEP PROCESS

Step 1: Visualize Your Finished Flip

The key to fixing up a property is to have an overall plan. Before you make an offer, sign a contract, or lift a hammer, you have to have a finished vision for your flip, one with as much detail to it as possible. The very first time you see the property, imagine each room in its upgraded state as you walk through the house. Embellish your vision each time you have access or drive by.

Step 2: Selecting the Improvements That Maximize Your Profit

Once you have evaluated the neighborhood, the other houses on the market, the quality of materials and amenities these neighboring houses offer, and have a basic idea of who your target buyers are, it's time to start making lists!

To create an accurate budget you need to review all the possible improvements you plan to make. Chapter nine, "The Big Fix: The Fix-It Improvement Levels" and chapter ten, "The Big Fix: The Profit Improvement Levels," will walk you though your flip house room by room to identify all the possible repairs, replacements, and fixes you will need to make. Each of the Six Levels of Improvements will be detailed, giving you a clear understanding of all the necessary fix-its and upgrades.

Step 3: Put Together Your Fix-It Hit List

Once you have identified all potential fix-it projects, organize them using the Fix-It Hit List. I have put together a Fix-It Hit List Worksheet (page 193) for you to use for every potential flip house you review. As you'll see in chapter eleven, "Your Fix-It Hit List: Costs and Budgets," you will continuously update and refine this list throughout the project. Your Fix-It Hit List, the basis for your first budget, will be your bible. Carry it with you every time you look at a house. Refer to it. It's like having the answers to the test. Photocopy it ten times. Make notes about every flip candidate. Believe me, by the time you look at your third house you will not remember which one had the leaky roof, which one had the missing floor boards, or which one had the bad add-on porch . . . you get the idea!

FLIP TIP

Throw in Everything . . . *Including* **the Kitchen Sink**—The only way you will be able to create an accurate ballpark estimate of your renovation costs is to include them all on your list. Then check it—and include some more.

Step 4: Gather Your Costs and Create Your Budget

With the Fix-It Hit List in hand, you will be ready to start to gather estimates. Chapter eleven will review all the methods I used to get ballpark costs and estimates. You'll also find a list of the most common fix-it projects and their ballpark costs, an entire section on the right sources for estimates, the challenges of getting contractor estimates before you have made an offer on a house, and other great sources for costs. There are also sample costing charts from the *Marshall & Swift Home Repair and Remodel 2005 Cost Guide,* one of the leading cost estimating publications in the country, used by contractors and tradesman.

THE PROFIT CALCULATOR CHART	
Estimated FFP (Final Flipped Price)	$ _____
Purchase Price of the House	− _____
Purchase Closing Costs	− _____
Estimated Fix-It Costs	− _____
Carrying Costs	− _____
10% Buffer	− _____
Sale Closing Costs and Commissions	− _____
Total	$ _____
− Capital Gains Tax	− _____
PROFIT	$ _____

PURCHASE PRICE

The purchase price is obviously what you pay for the house. Use the price the sellers are asking now. If you think you can get the house for less, run the numbers again with your dream price and see how much that changes your final profit figure.

PURCHASE CLOSING COSTS

This includes all the expenses incurred to purchase the house: appraisal fees, buyer's broker fees, loan application fees, loan broker fees, loan points, termite inspection reports, and structural inspection fees. These tend to average around half a percent of the purchase price. Chapter eight, "How to Survive Escrow and Come Out a Winner," reviews these in detail.

FLIP TIP

Don't Count the Down Payment—Make sure you don't make the mistake of including the down payment amount into your calculation. It is not an expense, and you get that down payment money back when you sell.

CARRYING COSTS

Carrying costs are any of the costs incurred to pay for the property for the period of time that you own it. If you buy a property and think it will take six months to fix it and flip it, estimate for the full six months of carrying costs. Don't forget the approximately two months you'll be in escrow or under contract after you have an accepted offer on the property—a total of eight months of carrying costs.

A ballpark carrying cost estimate including taxes, insurance, utilities, homeowners insurance, fees, etc., is 45 percent of your mortgage payment. It will vary, but it's a good conservative place to start. Thus, if your mortgage payment is $1,700 a month, estimate that all your additional carrying costs will be approximately $765. So the house will cost you $1,700 + $765 = $2,465 each month.

Carrying Costs Normally Include:

- Property taxes
  - State
  - Local
- Insurance
  - Homeowners
  - Flood
  - Fire
  - Earthquake
- Utilities
  - Water
  - Electric
  - Gas
  - Trash fees
  - City/county sewage fees
  - Homeowners dues (condos)
- Mortgage interest payments
  - PMI

Property Taxes

Property taxes vary from state to state. Your Realtor, your insurance agent, and your mortgage broker should all know the number by heart.

Insurance

Insurances costs include all the types of insurances that you will need for your property, including homeowners, fire, flood, and earthquake.

To do a ballpark calculation of your average insurance costs, figure $35 a month for every $100,000 of the purchase price. A $300,000 house will cost you $35 × 3, or $105 a month. Flood and earthquake will vary by region. Have your insurance agent give you a ballpark figure over the phone.

FLIP TIP

Mortgage Interest Carrying Cost—Only include the cost of your mortgage interest into this calculation. Any money that is automatically applied to principal, although this will be very little in your first year of mortgage payments, is actually reducing your loan amount and will come back to you when you sell.

PRIVATE MORTGAGE INTEREST—PMI

If you put down less than 20 percent on a property, your lender will require that you pay private mortgage insurance, or PMI, to make sure they are covered in case you default. Your PMI premium is usually paid on a monthly basis, separately from your mortgage. You pay it until you build up to 20 to 22 percent equity, and it's not tax deductible. Ouch. But if a lower down payment is what makes it possible for you to get into a property, then PMI is just the cost of doing business. Eventually, you'll use the profit from your flip to get into the next one with 20 percent down, and avoid it altogether.

THE 20 PERCENT BUFFER

The 20 percent buffer can be best explained by one of my Fix-It Truisms: my "20 Percent Rule of Renovation"! **It will always take 20 percent longer and cost 20 percent more than you originally planned!**

So always add in an additional 20 percent of the cost to your renovation estimate and add an extra month or two of carrying costs. Because no matter how experienced a flipper you are, costs always overrun.

Sale Closing Costs

Closing costs are considered sale costs—the fees, charges, and expenses incurred by the sale of the property. I review them all in chapter eight, and I cover which ones are real and which ones are "junk" fees. Whether in escrow or under contract, once you identify these unnecessary fees, you will negotiate to have them removed!

Your biggest expense at closing will be the Realtor's commission. The standard throughout the country is 6 percent of the sale price. The simplest formula I use to estimate all sale closing costs is 7.25 percent of the sale price. This seems to be a good ballpark estimate for all the costs, including the Realtor's commission. Thus, on a $300,000 sale, your closing costs would be $300,000 × 7.25 percent = $21,750.

CARRYING COSTS ALLOW YOU TO LIVE FOR FREE— LIKE I DID

Here is the other thing I love about flipping: I hated the thought of having to pay for where I live. To me rent is money thrown down the drain. The thought of carrying a mortgage on a house seemed so extravagant. And it didn't help that my father was always yelling, "If you want to be an actor, you can't afford to burden yourself with high overhead living expenses, like a mortgage. You should live at the YMCA." My father equated the financial stability of being an actor with that of joining the circus. I knew there had to be a way to reduce my living expenses and still not live like a gypsy sharing a common bathroom at the Y.

When I moved to Los Angeles, I wanted to come up with a way out of the rent-or-mortgage-payment trap. I found a house and planned to fix it and flip it. Once I had done the initial demo and the house was almost in livable condition, I moved in. That way, I could still deduct the mortgage carrying cost in my profit formula even though I was living in the house. I eliminated any personal housing expense for myself by mooching off my flipping carrying cost, which I was already paying as part of a business expense anyway! I lived for free— and you can too.

FLIP TIP

Give Yourself a Room—If you do live in the fixer, have at least one room and a working bathroom that you can not only lock but seal off from construction dust. I have managed quite nicely for months by doing this. It's a great way to conserve your capital. Once you have flipped a few houses, you will have more flexibility. Now I always wait until the house is nearly or completely done before I move in, even if I have to rent back my sale house for a few months until my new one is livable! Eventually, you'll never have to live through a fix-it stage again, but if you must, it is doable.

CAPITAL GAINS TAXES ON YOUR PROFIT

THE PROFIT CALCULATOR CHART

Estimated FFP (Final Flipped Price)	$ _____
Purchase Price of the House	– _____
Purchase Closing Costs	– _____
Estimated Fix-It Costs	– _____
Carrying Costs	– _____
10% Buffer	– _____
Sale Closing Costs and Commissions	– _____
Total	$ _____
– Capital Gains Tax	– _____
PROFIT	$ _____

Once you have established that there is profit to be made, you will need to calculate how much you will have to pay in capital gains taxes. Until you subtract the amount you'll have to pay in taxes, you won't really truly have your profit. How do you determine what Uncle Sam gets and what you get? In chapter fourteen, "Time to Cash Out!: How and When," I will explain to you in detail all the tax requirements and the ways to work within the tax system to pay as little tax as necessary—or, and in many cases, to pay NONE AT ALL. But here are five tax rules to take advantage of:

TAX RULES TO TAKE ADVANTAGE OF

1. Keep up to $500,000 tax-free profit if you and your spouse/partner hold your primary residence property and live in it for two years or more.

2. Keep up to $250,000 tax-free profit if you are single and hold your primary residence property for two years or more.

3. Pay no capital gains if you move from your primary residence in less than two years, if you qualify for special circumstances.

4. Own the home for one year and a day, and pay significantly less long-term capital gains tax than the day before!

5. Roll It Over. By utilizing the Federal 1033 tax-deferred exchange program, you can sell a property and roll your profit into the next one . . . no matter how short a time you have owned it . . . and pay NO tax on it!

By understanding the tax laws and loopholes I review in chapter fourteen, you will be able to tailor your flips to maximize your profit and keep as much of it as possible. Timing your flip sale properly can save you tens of thousands of dollars, which you can use to increase your equity and speed you that much faster toward your financial goals.

CALCULATE THE MAXIMUM YOU SHOULD PAY
FOR THE PROFIT YOU WANT!

OK, now that you understand the basic calculation for determining the profit potential of a house, the second most critical calculation you will need to make is the maximum purchase price you should pay to garner the amount of profit you predetermine up front. In other words, if you want to earn a $25,000, $30,000, or $50,000 return for your flip efforts, you will need to find a flip house that will garner that profit amount. Here's how:

A seller usually thinks his or her home is worth just what they are asking for it. And that's OK. The real question is, as a potential flip property, what is the property worth to you? Is the selling price one that will allow you to create the profit you want? Well, there's an easy way to find out!

Let's turn the **Profit Calculator Chart** upside down and rename it!

TARGET PURCHASE PRICE CALCULATOR CHART

Estimated FFP (Final Flipped Price)	$ _____
The Profit You Want to Make	– _____
Purchase Closing Costs	– _____
Estimated Fix-It Costs	– _____
Carrying Costs	– _____
10% Buffer	– _____
Sale Closing Costs and Commissions	– _____
Capital Gains Tax	– _____
TARGET PURCHASE TO PAY	$ _____

Decide How Much Profit to Make

The other way to calculate a house's flip potential is to settle on a ball-park figure of how much profit you want to make on that house. In other words, you are actually going to be able to decide how much profit you want to make on a flip house. You will then find the house that you can purchase for the price that will give you the profit you want. You simply factor your profit into the purchase price calculation.

Using the profit chart, you determine the FFP—Final Flipped Price, and then subtract your predetermined profit, and all the remaining costs, just as you did with the Profit Calculator Chart. The final number is the Target Purchase Price you should pay to create the profit you want. Trust this figure. If the seller won't agree to your Target Purchase Price, then just walk away—and keep looking. But if you can get it at that price, you've found your moneymaker, with your profit already built in!

Six

BECOME A FLIPPING SLEUTH

GET THE INFO YOU NEED TO GET THE DEAL YOU WANT

You have now zeroed in on a prospective flip. You have identified that it meets all the major requirements to be your next project:

- It's Downright Ugly

- It has strong potential for value increase on all Six Levels of Improvements

- Your FFP (Final Flipped Price) will be just slightly higher than the most current top comps in the neighborhood

- The Profit Calculator Chart shows a comfortable potential profit number

- The Target Purchase Price Calculator Chart estimated a purchase price within reach from the current asking price

- It's located in an improving or already improved neighborhood

Congratulations, you've found a winner! You've done your homework. You have done the math and, based on our formula, you have established that this house is affordable, improvable, and sellable (at a profit, of course); therefore it is flip-able.

The next step is to buy the house for the best possible price. You need to secure the house at your Target Purchase Price or better. But how? If the seller's price is above your Target Purchase Price, you need to arm yourself. To win this battle you are going to need the Inside Scoop.

THE INSIDE SCOOP—WHAT'S NOT IN THE LISTING

It's time for you and your Realtor to find out everything you can before you make an offer! There is no need to develop psychic abilities. Just become a flipping sleuth. Get the inside scoop, the information that you can't get from reading an MLS listing, the details that you will use to make your offer the best it can be.

The Inside Scoop is everything you can find out about why this house is on the market and just how motivated the seller really is. Only then will you go into the process of making the offer, negotiating and renegotiating the deal with a winning advantage. If "information is power," this will put that power on your side of the bargaining table:

- Know your seller—are they motivated?

- Ten questions home sellers don't want you to ask

- Find out the house's history

- Chat up the neighbors

KNOW YOUR SELLER—ARE THEY MOTIVATED?

People sell houses for a wide variety of reasons. They may want to move up. Their family may be getting larger or smaller, or they may be having unforeseen personal or financial problems. Because of a situation beyond their control, the seller may need cash now. These conditions make sellers flexible and/or desperate, or—as we say in the business— "motivated." As heart-wrenching as they can be, these life-stage, personal, or event-driven factors make a seller highly motivated and give you leverage and power:

- Divorce

- Death in the family

- Job loss

- Job relocation

- Advanced age or illness

- The purchase of another house has created a need to sell

- Sellers are upside down in their mortgage and owe more than it's worth

TEN QUESTIONS HOME SELLERS DON'T WANT YOU TO ASK

Every property has some little quirks that the seller hopes you don't discover. Some are minor. Others could even impact the marketability of the house when you sell it, costing you big profits. In a perfect world, owners would fess up when they fill out the property condition disclosure form that many states require. I am a huge proponent of disclosing everything and being completely honest when selling a house. Unfortunately, not all sellers operate under these same standards.

Below are the ten questions home sellers don't want you to ask. You probably won't get to ask them yourself, so your Realtor will have to do the sleuthing. If the seller's real estate agent is any good, they'll make sure that you never come face to face with their client. As a matter of practice, real estate agents have the sellers leave the property during showings so that they won't hover over prospective buyers, but also so they don't reveal information that would help the buyer negotiate a better price.

1. **Why are you selling?** People have lots of reasons for selling. What you want to know is how motivated they are. Simply put, bad news = seller motivation = better price. We're talking about big life changes—a sudden or nasty divorce, chronic illness or infirmity, job loss, or, on a more positive note, relocation for another opportunity. Then there's the possibility that they are already in escrow on another house, which creates financial pressure that you can leverage.

2. **What did you pay and how long have you owned the house?** People love to brag about what a good investment they've made. If their home has gone up in value, they're excited about it. They feel smart. While it's not smart to tell you, they just might. Also, the homeowner who has owned his house for many years has built up

quite a bit of equity by both paying off his mortgage and because of any appreciation in value. He may have more flexibility to come down in price than a seller who has only owned the home for a short time and will be walking away with much less cash out at the time of sale. It never hurts to ask.

3. **How do you like the neighborhood?** Unless there is gang graffiti on the burned out house next door, the homeowner will tell you it's a nice neighborhood. But this question opens the door for you to query further about barking dogs, loud neighbors, kids repairing cars in the street, etc. Hopefully, they may slip and give you some indication.

4. **Have there been any crimes in the neighborhood?** Whatever the answer, probe further, and ask about house or car break-ins, petty thefts, or gang presence. Obviously, this is important information.

5. **How old is the roof?** This can be a tough one to get answered. A cagey seller may say, "I'm not sure, I just know it doesn't leak." The correct follow-up is, "In the time you have owned the house, have you put on a new roof?" And if not, then ask if they have a contact number for the former owner. Chances are if they have owned the house more than seven years, you are getting close to needing a replacement. Most composite shingle roofs have a seven-to-ten year lifespan. Tile or slate roofs last much longer. Your Realtor will be able to give you a ballpark idea. The more you can pin them down, the easier it will be to ask for a full or partial roof credit after your inspection.

6. **When was the last time the furnace was cleaned?** The correct answer is, "Once a season." What it tells you beyond the obvious state of the furnace is the kind of attention the seller has given to overall upkeep of the house and systems.

7. **Has there ever been a violent crime in the house? Are there any kind of unworldly goings-on?** It may sound ridiculous to ask either question, but here's why you should: In many states, an owner is required to disclose if a murder, suicide, or violent crime has taken place in the house. Also, some states even require a

disclosure of "paranormal" activity. Whether or not you believe in poltergeists, you need to make sure there is nothing about the house that will make it impossible to sell. If not, even if you buy it, fix it up, and go to flip it in six months, a prospective buyer could chat up a neighbor who could mention "poor Mr. Jenkins and that awful double murder." And the last you'll see of him is his car pulling away from your formerly very appealing curb.

8. **Are the local schools good?** If the schools are good, the seller will tell you so. If they're not, they may claim ignorance. Either way, your Realtor should know the real answer. Unless you are absolutely sure that you'll be selling the flipped house to a childless couple, this is important.

9. **What is your deadline to sell?** If a seller is on a timetable, it can work to your advantage. They may want a short closing or a long one. They may want to sell the house because the market is hot, but need to stay and rent back because of work or the school calendar. Or, conversely, they may prefer a long escrow in order to avoid taxes by hitting a certain date. Knowing to offer that rent-back can be a powerful negotiating tool.

10. **What's the one thing you won't miss about this house?** This is an open-ended question that can prompt the owner to share something they shouldn't. Asked casually, it can yield a piece of the truth that you can use to your advantage, either as a negotiating tool or as a basis for walking away.

FIND OUT THE HOUSE'S HISTORY

How Long Has This Property Been on the Market?

The complete sales history of the property will also help you gauge the seller's motivation. It allows you and your Realtor to customize your offer based on what has not worked in previous offers. Also, if the property has just been listed on the MLS, the seller will have one frame of mind. If it's been languishing on the market, he may be much more motivated. If it has just fallen out of escrow, he may be into another house already and ready to deal.

Have your Realtor try to find out the following:

- How long has the property been on market?
- How many offers have been made?
- Have any been turned down? Why?
- Were any previous offers accepted?
- Has the property fallen out of escrow?

INSIDER SECRET

How to Read Your Seller's Mind!—I *always* ask my Realtor to contact the selling broker *prior* to making an offer. Realtors will often resist this. It is extra work for them and sometimes a bother, but trust me, it will save you thousands! Insist that your Realtor have a nice conversation with the seller's agent to find out as much as he can about the seller, the seller's needs, any previous offers, and what kinds of deal points the seller will respond to favorably. Your Realtor should then close the conversation with, "So, if I can get my buyer to write an offer, what do you think will get your seller to accept?"

As there is no written offer on the table, a selling agent is under fewer obligations of privacy and may reveal quite a bit more information than he can once an offer is on paper. You can now customize your offer. This is like having the answers to a test! You have just eliminated at least one round of offers and counteroffers, and you are guaranteed not to offer more than was necessary, possibly saving you tens of thousands.

The Seller's Bottom Line: What Would You Take If I Gave You All Cash?

OK, until you've flipped a number of houses, you aren't going to be able to make an all-cash offer. But by asking this question, your broker can learn a lot about the seller's flexibility and maybe even find out their bottom line.

If the answer is "The asking price" followed by "Take it or leave it," then the seller is obviously not motivated. If they appear even mildly interested, your real estate agent can throw in the idea of a short escrow or a long escrow, learning more about the seller's flexibility or hidden agenda.

CHAT UP THE NEIGHBORS

People love to be in the know. If you are friendly and respectful, all you have to do is walk down the street and talk to the neighbors to find out a wealth of information. Tell them you're thinking about buying the house, and since you're a potential neighbor, they'll be sizing you up too, creating some common conversational ground. Ask how long they've lived there, how they like it, etc. You can ask them all the questions your Realtor should ask the seller. With very little prodding, they will tell you about everything from messy divorces to the mall that's going in next year to barking dogs.

Seven

WRITE A WINNING OFFER

I am a big believer in the idea that someone else's success is not something to envy or covet. I look at another man's success as a road map and as an inspiration for my own. I try to observe what others do to succeed, and then apply those techniques myself. This has worked for me and can for you, too.

In all my years of successfully finding, fixing, and flipping properties, I have always believed in the idea of the win/win outcome for both sides. Nowhere is this truer than when making an offer. At the most fundamental level, one person wants to sell, one person wants to buy. Once the terms are agreed upon, voilà . . . win/win. If one party is miserable with the final terms, no one wins. The deal will ultimately fall apart, unravel or turn ugly, causing you aggravation and costing you time and money in the end.

Making Deals the Wrong Way

I worked with a company a few years ago that was partnered by a little man I will call Brant. Not only was he small in stature, he was small in integrity and soul, too. He took great delight in squeezing every last dollar out of any business deal he negotiated. It was not enough for him to make the deal and a profit. He needed to know that the other party felt like the loser. Needless to say, within a few years I watched this little man fend off lawsuit after lawsuit from those he had squeezed and his company eventually fell apart.

My point is that your success in flipping and building your own wealth is not based on someone else's loss. When you act with honesty and integrity everyone wins—especially you.

DEAL-WINNING STRATEGIES

The offer is nothing more than your terms and conditions for purchasing the property. It is a starting point that includes the price you want to pay, the contingencies that must be met, the terms, and the down payment. All of these elements can be finessed to create a win/win situation if you learn to use them as bargaining chips. Your goal is to make an offer that is irresistible. Components include:

- Price

- Deposit

- Down payment

- Contingencies

  - Inspection

  - Loan approval

- Terms

  - Length of closing

  - Which title escrow or lawyers to use

  - Rent backs

  - Home warranty

  - Closing costs

Here are the tactics that make you look like a dream buyer, the strategies you can use to get what you want: an accepted offer at the price you want and the terms you are comfortable with.

PRICE

You've determined the Final Flipped Price (FFP). You did your Target Purchase Price calculation, so you know what you want to pay in order to get the profit you want when you sell. That will be the maximum price you will pay for the house. Start your negotiations with that in mind.

Never Want It Too Much

You found the Downright Ugly House of your dreams, the one you wanted, the one that will make everything right. You must have it, right? Wrong. It's just a property. There will be others. Make your best offer, play it out, but don't ever get attached. Part of negotiating from a position of strength is being willing to walk away. If the numbers don't work, let go and keep looking. There's another deal out there. If you're stuck on the one that got away, you'll miss it.

HOW MARKET UPS AND DOWNS INFLUENCE YOUR OFFER STRATEGIES

Sellers always want the most they can get. And you will always want the house for less. But whatever the asking price, the market's direction will determine your offer strategy.

Making an Offer in a Downward Market

When the market is heading south, I look for properties listed at a little more than I want to spend because I know the real price will be at least a little less. When buying in a downward-moving market, the challenge, as we saw in the 1990s, is that it's hard to know where the bottom is. A good deal this month may not be a good deal in six months—all the more reason to bargain hard and flip the property as quickly as possible.

When the market is moving downward at 10 percent a year, factor that into your offer. If you figure in the fact that in a cold market your FFP will be 5 to 10 percent lower in four months, then you can make a downward market work in your favor by offering 5 to 10 percent less. If you can't get the price that will withstand the temperature when you turn around and sell in four months, give it the cold shoulder and walk away.

Be Careful When Lowballing the First Offer

When someone sells their house, they are selling a piece of themselves. This house is the setting of their life. For the seller, its value includes what it represents, not just what it lists for. As a result, residential real estate transactions are emotional. Lowballing, especially in a hot market, can get you off on the wrong foot. Be smart. Be reasonable with your initial offer. You may not even get a chance to negotiate if you've offended the other party out of playing the game.

FLIP FLOP

The One That Got Away—In my early days of flipping, my Dream Team Realtors called me about a cute little house in Hollywood that was about to go on the market at $303,000. It was a fixer, and at that price, it was a very good deal. Well, I thought, OK, I'll pay $303,000, but I want to first see if I can lowball and get it for less. My Realtors warned me not to lowball, but I offered $270,000, figuring they would come back and close the deal at $290,000. Well, they did, but with someone who came in at $290,000. They were so offended by my low offer that they refused to sell it to me at any price! My Realtors remind me of this story to this day!

Making an Offer in a Medium Market

In my experience, in a normal market, homes can be had for 3 to 7 percent under the asking price. In a cold market, I've seen sellers take 10 percent less—and more. This is another reason why you should never make your Target Purchase Price offer first.

Making an Offer in a Hot Market

When you go on a walk-through and see the competition with their pens drawn, writing offers on their agents' backs, you know you're in a hot market. Forget lowballing. If you've done your homework and you know the comps, you may have to be willing to act immediately. In a hot market be prepared to pay full price and be ready to jump on it. Once you've done a few flips, you have the experience it takes to know a good thing when you see one. But even in a situation this competitive I would never ever offer more than your Target Purchase Price.

DEPOSIT

There is always a risk with a deposit. Here's what you can do to lower it.

- **Write the check, hold the funds.** Make the offer with the caveat that the deposit will not be made until the sellers accept it.

- **Put up a smaller deposit.** Some states have suggested or contracted deposits of 3 percent.

- **Increase your deposit later.** Make a smaller initial deposit but include language that states you'll increase it once the contingencies are all removed.

DOWN PAYMENT

Many sellers feel that the bigger the down payment, the more financially able the buyer. This is not necessarily true, but in a hot market, especially in a multiple-bidding situation, this posture can make you more attractive. And the more you flip, the larger the down payments you will be able to make, making you look even better in a buyer's eyes.

FLIP TIP
Offer 20 Percent Down—If you can do it, this will put you at the head of the pack in a cold market. In a hot market, it may well be the cost of entry.

Why No Money Down Makes Me Nervous

There are many ways to borrow, to carry notes, and to use "creative" financing options that involve coming up with little or no money down.

Even when flipping, meaning you won't be holding a property for very long, I always recommend at least 10 percent down. In a volatile real estate market, it's too risky to have NO equity in your property.

If you purchase a home with "creative" financing and decide to live there a while or to hold, you could be in deep financial trouble. Many of the no-money-down programs promote borrowing money at high interest rates for short periods. However, if you need to hold onto a property due to personal problems or a sudden downturn in the market, you are going to be paying big monthly payments and maybe even be forced to sell the house at a loss. I always want to leave my options open—and so do you. The Find It, Fix It, Flip It method is more conservative. That's why it works for the long haul, not just for the fast profit.

CONTINGENCIES

Contingencies are negotiating tools that can be used with great success. They give you a way to walk away without consequence. The key is to find out what the seller wants and give them something in return that makes no difference to you. Include only the ones that protect you, not the seller.

The most common contingencies are the inspection, the disclosures, and then the mortgage contingencies. If you don't like what you see, you have the right to take your deposit back and move on. In fact, in California, where the market is insanely hot, buyers have three days to make a decision after they see the inspection and the disclosures. Aggressive buyers make offers on properties they have not even seen in order to tie them up, knowing they can use this contingency to walk away.

Clearly, the universe of smart buyers has figured out that it's a jungle out there, and that contingencies are a powerful guerrilla tactic. But use them judiciously, keeping as many in as possible without loading down the offer. In your purchase agreements you will want to include the following:

Contingent Upon Inspection

The idea of having a certain amount of time to make an inspection is standard in most real estate contracts. After your inspection, you give the seller your list of problems, current and potential, along with the opportunity to fix them, make a price adjustment, or give you a credit back. As the buyer, the burden is on you to have your inspection and present your list in a timely manner. Otherwise, you waive the right to this particular contingency.

Contingent Upon Financing

This is another way to make sure you can walk away from the deal if you can't get the financing you want. Not only are you off the hook, you also get your deposit back. Not only would I not make an offer without a loan contingency, I would make sure that I don't have to take a loan that's not in my best interest just because there's a contingency that says I have to take a loan. You can do this by stipulating the maximum interest rate you will be willing to pay for your mortgage. Once again, it is standard and usually involves a time in which the buyer must make reasonable efforts to first get a loan and then present a copy of the loan commitment in writing to the seller.

You will usually have seventeen to twenty-one days to get approval. You don't have to alert the seller that it is finalized and approved until the final day of your contingency period. But you don't want to miss your deadline either.

INSIDER TIP

Use the Mortgage Terms to Keep You In or Out of the Deal—
Especially when interest rates are rising, pay close attention to the interest rate you say you will accept. Always put in a rate and terms that are as low as possible. In other words, if you will not be comfortable paying a 7 percent rate on your loan, put 6 percent as the top rate to pay in this contingency. However, remember that if you are flipping, it's OK to pay slightly more for the loan if you have to. You won't be holding it for very long. But to give yourself leeway to get out of the deal, keep a tight cap on the terms to which you agree.

Contingent Upon Marketable Title

This means the seller must prove that the title is insurable by producing a title report or commitment. Even if there are problems, if the seller can fix them before the deal closes, the contract holds.

Too Many Versus Not Enough Contingencies

Every contingency that you add makes your offer look weaker because it makes it that much harder to close. Lawyer-negotiated deals can get loaded with contingencies very fast. Lighten up and make sure you really want what you're asking for. Otherwise your seller may look elsewhere.

However, you take a huge risk when you offer a contract with no contingencies. You can also win big. But if you lose, you forfeit your earnest money if you decide not to go for it. I just don't feel comfortable doing it. I like fall-back options.

TERMS

Length of Escrow

This is one of the great negotiating tools. Customizing the length of escrow to suit the seller's needs can often seal the deal with a higher-priced offer. A seller will generally want a fast closing, usually thirty days. If you have all your ducks in a row, and your Dream Team in force, you will be able to do this—and snag yourself a great deal in the process.

Real estate agents make their money right after closing, so the sooner you close, the happier they will be. With two offers on the table, why wouldn't the agent encourage his client to take the one with more money up-front and a shorter closing over a higher offer?

Other times, a seller may need a longer close. Perhaps they have to hold the property to a certain date for tax reasons, but want the security of knowing the property is already sold. Be a Flipping Sleuth. Know what they need—and give it to them!

Choice of Escrow Company and Title Company

Your Realtor will have favorites because every Realtor has a relationship with an escrow company and a title company. Name your own choice in the offer—especially if you have a relationship with them and they are part of your Dream Team. However, a good negotiating ploy is to let the seller have their pick—providing you get something in exchange in the counteroffer!

Home Warranty Policy

This is a wonderful way of getting some protection from the seller that ensures the systems, appliances, plumbing, and electrical in the house are working and operational. However, as you will be buying the Downright Ugly House, you know up front that most of these things are not operational or are going to be replaced, unless there is a pool and pool equipment to be covered or a roof you were NOT planning on replacing. You could waive the request for this, saving the seller approximately $500. Ask for it in your initial offer, knowing you can pull it off the table in counteroffers for something in return!

Rent Back

Renting back is what happens when you buy the property and the former owners become your tenants for a set period of time. You will hold their rent money back for the sale of the property. This is a great way for a seller to close the property, and get his cash out of the sale and have time to get ready to move. This can be a great negotiating tool if you want to get a better price on the sale. (Hint: You do.)

Closing Costs

"Who pays what" is another way of structuring the deal and gives you some negotiating room in a counteroffer situation. Certain states already have standard practices in place as to who pays what, but it never hurts to ask, especially in a counteroffer situation.

SIX THINGS TO INCLUDE THAT WON'T BOTHER YOUR BUYER BUT WILL BENEFIT YOU!

1. Request a copy of all permits to be provided at time of inspection

2. Request disclosure statements to be provided at time of inspection and the ability to approve or disapprove

These first two items give you the opportunity to examine the facts and then really investigate them while on premises. It's like having the answers to the test right before a big exam! You can walk away if you don't like what you find.

3. A full disclosure of problems and approval of the disclosures

4. A walk-through before closing to confirm that nothing has happened since inspection

5. The return of your deposit if the seller backs out

6. The right to assign

As buyer, you want to assign the contract, if you so choose. By adding your name as buyer with "and/or assigns," you can sell off this great deal to someone else before you even close, if you choose. If there is language that forbids assignment without the seller's permission in the contract, then cross it out.

PRESENTING THE OFFER

In addition to the offer itself, there are two letters to include in your offer that will make you a Dream Buyer to any seller. One is a window on your financial ability that demonstrates your creditworthiness. The other is a window on your soul that shows that no one could appreciate this beautiful home more than you.

THE LETTER OF PREAPPROVAL

As we discussed in chapter two, "Flipping Economics 101," the preapproval letter you asked your mortgage broker to draft when you started looking is now going to be put to use. Being preapproved by a mortgage broker for a set amount truly puts your best financial foot forward. It means that the lender preapproves you for a loan, in essence turning you into a cash buyer. It is much better than being prequalified, which just means you check out financially. It is your all-access pass to a fast deal—because you are good to go.

THE "PLEASE LET ME BUY YOUR HOUSE" LETTER

I know, I know, you are thinking this is soooo cheesy. But let me share a story and then you decide for yourself. A professional real estate investor friend of mine, who specializes in flipping, had his house on the market. The house went into multiple offers with three similar offers on the table. Two of the offers came with very heartfelt letters explaining how much they liked the house, would love to live in the neighborhood, loved the view, etc. Even though my friend is a seasoned professional, he was actually put off by the buyer who *didn't* send the letter because the others did—and he sold to one of them. The moral is to write a sincere letter about who you are, and to highlight the qualities about the house you really like. Be creative—after all, you are buying a Downright Ugly House!

PUT A TIME LIMIT ON SIGNING

If a seller lets your offer sit, they may be waiting for a better one. A weak agent might accept that. Don't. The best way to combat it is to include a deadline for acceptance in the offer. Set a twenty-four-hour deadline in which the sellers must act, either to accept, reject, or counter your offer. It forces them to do something or lose you as a buyer.

The Hotter the Market the More Elusive the Seller

Sellers go out of town just when the offer is made. It's a common ploy. In a hot market, this technique can generate multiple offers. In these days of faxes, e-mail, cell phones, and FedEx, everyone can be available—if they want to be. Your Realtor's job is to be persistent and to get a response to your offer.

INSIDER SECRET

Another Offer's Coming—Another reason a selling agent likes to take his time presenting an offer to his seller is that the longer it takes, the longer he has to tell others that "there's an offer on the table—it will have to go into the multiples—so you had better up your offer." I know this is common practice and when I go to sell a flip, I do the same thing, and so will you. But when buying, don't fall victim to this technique.

WHEN LOSING THE DEAL CAN BE A WIN— THE BACKUP POSITION

I have won big in backup situations where there has already been an inspection and the house falls out because there are problems that an average buyer can't handle. In this situation, I have the advantage of jumping in to save the day when the buyer is already frustrated and just wants to sell and get out. It puts me in a stronger negotiating position.

By making an offer you have automatically put yourself in a backup position when someone else gets the deal. In a situation where there are multiple offers, you can be first, second, or even third backup. It costs you nothing. You don't have to put out any money, yet you are in line to get the property if the current buyer falls out. Plus, buyers love backup offers because it puts pressure on the accepted offer to negotiate quickly, knowing that there is a line of prospects standing on the front porch, hoping he'll fail. There are four things to include in an accepted backup offer:

BACKUP OFFER MUST-HAVES

1. **Thirty-Day Time Limit** The longer it takes to complete the transaction, the greater the chance the two parties have to work through their differences. A time limit will force the hand of your competition, which may make them unable to close the deal.

2. **Right of Refusal** This is the beauty part. You're not bound to take the property, but once they've accepted it, they are bound to ask you first.

3. **Get the Terms in the Agreement** Lock those sellers in to you. Make sure that they are obligated to sell to you within a certain period of time at the agreed-upon terms if the property becomes available.

4. **Extra Bonus for the Backup Buyer** Legally, the sellers have to disclose any problems that the first-position buyer uncovered, the ones that made them bolt! As a result, you will know the property's recently uncovered flaws ahead of time.

FLIPPING SUCCESS STORY

Double Backup Success—In the red-hot Los Angeles market, a friend lost in a bidding war on a very desirable property. Six weeks later, when the winners fell out of escrow because they were scared off by what looked like a problem with the main sewer, my friend was suddenly the buyer of choice. A quick visit by a sewer expert revealed that the problem was eminently fixable. She asked the seller to pay for what was now a fully disclosed problem. They did. She bought it, fixed it, and flipped it at a profit—all because she stayed in the game by making a backup offer. Not only was she smart enough to be in a backup position, she also knew enough to get that sewer expense credit from a now-anxious seller.

Never Stop Negotiating

The offer process is full of opportunities to incrementally improve your position. From the very first offer to the counteroffer to the inspection, every shift is a chance for more solid footing. Every parry is a chance to thrust. I never take no for an answer. I always come back with a way to keep the ball in play. In my experience, there is always a way to amend, add to, and increase or tweak an offer while keeping it a win/win for everyone.

Eight

HOW TO SURVIVE ESCROW AND COME OUT A WINNER

THE ESCROW PAPERWORK

What is escrow? As defined by the Escrow Institute of California, an escrow is "a deposit of funds, a deed or other instrument by one party for the delivery to another party upon completion of a particular condition or event." It assures that NO funds or property will change hands until all of the instructions in the transition have been followed. In English this means someone is selling, someone is buying, and escrow makes sure the exchange of monies and paperwork are done properly.

The name of the entity that facilitates this transfer and the process of exactly how this is done varies from state to state. Many West Coast states have actual escrow companies that handle all the paperwork and distribute all the funds. Washington, D.C., and Maryland use settlement offices or settlement agents. In New Jersey and New York, lawyers and real estate agents handle all the paperwork, as well as the exchange of the funds and the title. In these cases, once an offer has been accepted and your buyer's deposit has been handed over, the property is considered to be "under contract" rather than "in escrow." No matter what it's called, the process to be accomplished and the timeline remain the same. For simplicity I will refer to it as the escrow process, except where noted.

UNDERSTANDING THE PROCESS WILL SAVE YOU THOUSANDS

I merely stumbled across some of the money-saving tips and simple explanations of some extremely complicated processes you'll find here. Others I figured out through trial and error. The rest I learned from the pros. But now *you* get it all in one place—and it will save you hours of stress and lots of money.

Escrow is full of legal language and very specific terminology. It can be daunting, to say the least. The greatest lesson I can teach you is that if you don't understand a term or a process, *just ask*. I do it all the time. Make it your business to find out why things are done in a certain manner. See this escrow as a process you can master, not merely endure, and you'll have a whole new knowledge base to use when you go to *sell* your flip.

THREE-RING CIRCUS

The escrow process is truly a three-ring circus. There's something going on in every arena—yet it all relates. Avoiding costly oversights and finding ways to save money that most novice flippers overlook or leave unattended is very difficult. But when you know what to look for and how to stay on top of it, it can be done.

Think of yourself as the ringmaster and a highly skilled juggler, jumping back and forth between the three rings. Your job is to keep all the balls in the air. When it goes smoothly, everything comes together at closing for the big finale: making the sale happen!

THE THREE SIMULTANEOUS ESCROW ARENAS

- The house inspection

- Securing the mortgage

- The escrow paperwork

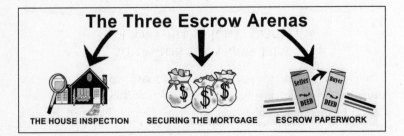

The Three Escrow Arenas

THE HOUSE INSPECTION   SECURING THE MORTGAGE   ESCROW PAPERWORK

Escrow Timeline

The key to mastering this circus is timing! With so many things happening at once and in three different arenas, without a timeline of events it's next to impossible to stay on track. That's why I like to put together a calendar of target tasks and dates—it helps create order out of chaos. Having a big-picture timeline is so helpful when setting your escrow task priorities. As we review each escrow task, refer back to this calendar to see just where in the timeline it falls.

Thirty-Day Purchase Escrow Timeline

January					
Mon	**Tues**	**Wed**	**Thurs**	**Fri**	**Sat / Sun**
1 PURCHASE AGREEMENTS SIGNED	2 ESCROW OPENS! SCHEDULE INSPECTION	3 BEGIN MORTGAGE PROCESS SEND IN DEPOSIT	4	5 REQUEST ESTIMATED CLOSING COSTS	6/7
8 REVIEW DISCLOSURES, PLOT MAP, PERMITS	9 INSPECTION MEET WITH CONTRACTORS, TRADESMEN	10	11 NEGOTIATE INSPECTION FINDINGS	12 CREATE WORKING BUDGET	13 / 14
15	16 APPROVE TITLE REPORT	17	18	19 MORTGAGE CONTINGENCY EXPIRES MORTGAGE APPROVAL DUE	20 / 21
22 REQUEST ESTIMATED CLOSING COSTS	23	24 HOMEOWNERS INSURANCE SECURED	25	26	27 / 28
29 REVIEW ESTIMATED CLOSING COSTS	30 TRANSFER DOWN PAYMENT INTO ESCROW	31 FINAL WALK-THROUGH OF PROPERTY	ESCROW CLOSES! CONGRATULATIONS		

THE HOUSE INSPECTION

The house inspection is one of the flipper's most powerful tools. It is an essential part of the process that protects you in four different but equally invaluable ways.

HOUSE INSPECTION BENEFITS

1. **Know Your House from Top to Bottom**—This is your chance to bring in a knowledgeable professional inspector who will fully inspect and analyze the property from top to bottom. The inspector goes over every system, every crawl space, and every door and window to find all the defects you couldn't possibly have identified while house-hunting.

2. **Have a Way Out**—The inspection contingency in your purchase agreement gives you time to consider and reconsider your purchase. It buys you an extra seven to ten days to decide if this property is truly the profit-making flip you hoped it would be. If for any reason you find something physically wrong in the inspection, you can walk away—without penalty.

3. **Refine Your Budget**—Inspection is an opportunity to review and refine your Estimated Fix-It Costs Budget with your inspector, a contractor, or tradesmen.

4. **Renegotiate Your Deal**—Inspection allows you to continue to negotiate. Within three to five days after the inspection, you may request that the seller fix any problems discovered, from the serious to the simple, give you a cash credit toward the cost of the repairs, a credit toward closing costs, or reduce the price of the property to reflect the repair costs. If they refuse, you can walk away.

HIRING THE INSPECTOR

Finding your inspector is not that difficult. Most real estate agents usually have several they like to work with. Here are the qualities you want:

- **He is licensed.** Not all states require this. But try to find one that is a member of the American Society of Home Inspectors (ASHI) at www.ashi.com.

- **He is tough.** You want someone who is meticulous and points out every little problem. It is to your advantage to have a long list after he's finished.

- **He lets you tag along with him during the inspection**.

- **He has a working knowledge of renovations.** Ask ahead of time if you will be able to ask him repair questions as the inspection is in progress.

- **He writes up the report on the spot.** That's what laptops are for.

- **His fee is reasonable.** Your real estate agent will know what's standard in your locale. $250 to $450, including the written report, is average.

Inspect with the Inspector

Always follow the inspector as he works his way through the house. Don't sit around and gab with the Realtor. Watch and ask questions. His knowledge is invaluable. I tag along with my notebook in hand and say things like, "Oh really . . . how much might this cost to repair? Is it major? Is that really serious or is it fixable?" This is the best crash course in fix-it and renovations you can get!

Write down what he says as he does the inspection. Once he puts it in the report, it becomes set in stone and subject to legal problems if something is contested, so he'll tend to soft-pedal what he puts in writing. In person, he'll often give you the worst-case scenario.

INSPECTION TARGET SPOTS

Working through the inspection with the inspector allows you to make additional refinements to your Estimated Fix-It Costs Budget based on his expertise. Carry your budget with you and jot down notes as you go. Here are the critical areas that your inspector will shed some light on, literally:

Foundation

This may be your only opportunity to peer under the house. Use it. What kind of foundation are you dealing with? Is it built on wood footings with a cement base, a stone foundation with a basement, a cement slab, or is it a raised foundation with a crawl space? Each one has pros and cons.

There are regional tendencies. The East Coast and Northeast tend to have basements. Coastal areas and states like Florida and earthquake-prone states like California rarely do. Houses there are often built on cement slabs, which can be a real challenge if you want to make any plumbing changes to move sinks, toilets, showers, or gas-burning appliances. Factor in those costs.

Attics

- Determine if you can convert the attic—a profitable Lifestyle Upgrade. Your inspector will know the local codes and height requirements and may be able to give you a quick answer, saving you big money on an architect or structural-engineer consultation.

- Check the insulation.

- Look for signs of roof leaks.

- Examine any visible heating and air ducts.

Plumbing

- Test the water pressure. Turn on several faucets and flush a toilet or two at the same time. If the water pressure drops, plan to do some re-piping.

- Does the water heater look big enough to handle a small family? Ask the inspector—he'll know.

- Is the piping plastic, copper, galvanized, or lead? Is it in the walls or in a clement slab? If it's a slab, factor in increased costs.

Heating and Air

- How old is the system?

- Any rooms missing vents or ducts?

- If the systems are eight years of age or older, they may be a problem about to happen, or something you may have to replace before you flip.

Flooring

Don't be afraid to snoop in the closets. I always carry a small pair of pliers with me so I can pull back a small corner of the wall-to-wall carpet in the back of the closets and see if there is hardwood flooring underneath. If there is, that's money in the bank.

Nonconforming Use

Converted garages, sun porches, or add-on bedrooms can increase square footage, but when done without permits, they can also add headaches when it's time to make them legal. You may be better off ripping them down rather than bearing the cost of permitting something you didn't build before sale.

FLIP TIP

Come out with a Closet—In order to be legally considered a bedroom, there must be a closet in the room.

Moisture, Mold, and Toxins

- Check for moisture in any basement or below ground-level areas. Moisture is an indicator of the potential for a mold problem—if there isn't one already.

- Check for asbestos if the house was built prior to 1975. You may find it on insulation around ducting, water heaters, and pipes. It is accessible and can be removed by an asbestos specialist and replaced.

OTHER INSPECTIONS YOU MAY NEED TO COVER YOUR . . . ASSETS

Don't assume that if you hire a home inspector, he will tell you everything you need to know about the house. Home inspectors are very careful not to take on liability for issues that are outside their area of expertise. Which means the overall basic home inspection is your first step. Because you will be reselling this house to a discerning buyer, you need to make sure you do all the inspections *now* that a new buyer may do *later*.

- **Chimney Inspection**—Your regular inspector may not do this, but if there is any question of stability or structural damage, have a chimney specialist do a "chimney cam" and run a small video camera down the chimney to see it from the inside.

- **Geological Inspection**—Especially for hillside and cliffside properties, or in flood areas, a geological inspection can unearth a severe drainage or ground-shifting problem—and save you thousands.

- **Sewer Inspection**—A sewer expert can use a "sewer cam" to discover serious expense incurred when there are cracks or breaks in the sewer line from the house to the street—especially on properties that are heavily landscaped, where root growth can crack and clog the pipeline.

- **Termite Inspection**—This is sometimes done by the buyer and sometimes by the seller. Whoever does it, make sure all the recommended work is taken care of!

FLIP FLOP

A Sewer Backed Up the Whole Sale—Rudy, a beginning flipper, did not get a sewer inspection when purchasing his 1920s Spanish Hollywood Hills property. He spent hundreds of thousands of dollars fixing, upgrading, and dressing the home. He landscaped, added retaining walls, a front-yard gate, and all the amenities on this gorgeous finished flip. His buyer offered full price and Rudy turned away many offers after that. Come inspection day, the buyer arrived with a sewer-line inspector and his "sewer cam." They found numerous cracks and severe shifting in the sewer line, which were about to cause major problems at any moment. Of course the buyer insisted that it be replaced. It cost Rudy $20,000 to dig up his gorgeous front yard, do the repair, and then replace the beautiful landscaping. He could have refused and lost the sale. But by law he would have to disclose the problem to any other future buyers and drop the price or fix it anyway.

The moral of the story: inspect, inspect, inspect—because your new buyers will!

FOUR THINGS TO DEMAND PRIOR TO INSPECTION

1. The seller's disclosure settlement

2. Permit history

3. Plot map

4. A condo or co-op's financials

Disclosures

Most states require sellers to present a disclosure statement. Depending upon local precedent, this disclosure is presented anytime after the presentation of the offer by the buyer, sometime during escrow. It is usually a preprinted form itemizing all the possible areas of the home that may be in need of repair or are defective. The seller is obligated to include all known problems, outstanding permit issues, any problems with neighbors, or even the fact that a serious crime has been committed in the home. It also includes environmental problems such as the presence of radon or lead paint. The disclosure offers no warranty. It is only a statement of facts as known by the seller. But without it, a seller or broker may be liable when and if preexisting problems pop up. It is an invaluable tool as you begin to develop your list of potential fix-it projects and cost out your renovations. Get it prior to your inspection—at the latest.

FLIP TIP

Get It Up Front—I always ask for the disclosure statement to be presented upon acceptance of my offer. That way I know what problems to look for in the upcoming inspection. If the seller discloses a serious roof leak, you will know to bring your roofer to the inspection for an estimate.

Request a Permit History Before Inspection

Ask for a presentation of all permits on the property before inspection so you'll know more about what you're looking at—and for—during inspection. Some seller's Realtors don't like to do this, while others will happily comply. If the seller won't do so, get them yourself. Your Realtor will advise you on how to obtain them. You want to know if that room addition was done with a permit and if the roof was installed by a professional or a handyman.

The consequence of not doing this can be expensive. If you decide to do work and apply for a permit and there is a history of which you are not aware—such as an unapproved permit that has been floating around since an old room addition—you'll have to pay to bring it up to code. If it wasn't done right in the first place, you'll have to redo the original job. The only way to be sure is to see the permits yourself.

Request the Plot Map

Always request a copy of the plot map. If there is a question, do a site survey. You would be surprised how many times the property lines are not exactly where the sellers think they are. A confirmation of the actual lot lines can go either way. I have discovered extra land—a big boon when I went to sell. Another time I was very disappointed because a big section of the property was on a city easement and I was unable to develop the back yard.

Condos and Co-op Financials

You will want to review the financials of a building with your Realtor prior to doing an inspection. Why? An inspection costs you money. And if a building's financials are out of whack or you discover an impending assessment, you may want to walk away before you invest the cost of inspection.

HOW INSPECTION DISCOVERIES GET YOU A BETTER DEAL

Never Stop Negotiating

Your inspection report will always be full of problems and repairs large and small. After all, that's why you are buying the property! Between the inspection report and the seller's disclosure statement, you will have a handful of repairs and problems ranging from minor to serious. But these problems can start making you money even before you own the house if you use them to negotiate a better deal.

How to Get Money Back and Start Making a Profit Now

Even when purchasing a new home, the savvy buyer knows to open negotiations all over again after the inspection. Remember, thanks to your inspection contingency, you can walk away from the deal without penalty if any issues are revealed in either the disclosure or the inspection report. But don't walk just yet. Negotiate a better price instead. During the contractual time period, usually within five days after inspection, have your real estate agent submit a list of the repairs to be made or credited for their value.

For example, if the hot-water heater is completely rusted out and ready to keel over, and you knew you were going to have to replace it anyway, you included the expense in your Estimated Fix-It Costs Budget. You can still ask for it to be replaced, or better yet, get a credit for the $550 repair cost, reducing your fix-it cost by $550 and increasing your profit!

Bigger problems can create even greater rewards. Even though you budgeted for a new roof, ask for the credit. The buyer is now put on notice that if you are not credited the $9,000 to replace the roof, or the price is not reduced accordingly, you have the option to walk away.

THREE REASONS WHY THESE SELLERS WILL AGREE TO A CREDIT BACK

1. Once a problem is discovered, revealed, or identified, by law the seller must disclose it to any other buyers. They will *have to* deal with it. And chances are the next buyer will ask for the same credit or price reduction anyway.

2. Inspection credit requests usually come almost two weeks into the escrow process. During that time your seller is already making moving plans and assuming the deal will go through. It is in their best interest to make the deal work and give some concessions, rather than start all over again.

3. Most sellers' Realtors don't want to start from scratch, find a new buyer, and put together a whole new deal. It's double the work for the same commission. So the sellers' Realtor will be giving them an extra goose to come up with some concessions.

FLIP TIP

Take Your Time—Wait until the last minute to submit your request for credits or repairs. The longer the property has been tied up and off the market, the more pressure on the seller to meet your demands.

FLIP TIP

Don't Over-Negotiate—Don't get TOO cocky—in a hot market, a seller may call your bluff if he feels he can get more money. You might over-negotiate yourself out of a deal.

INSIDER SECRET

The Best Offense Is a Good Defense—Remember all of these techniques for continued negotiations and ways to get a better deal. Because when you go to sell your flip, they will be used against you! But don't worry—chapter seventeen, "Let the Selling Begin," is full of safeguards that counteract these techniques.

SECURING YOUR MORTGAGE

As the inspection negotiations are in progress, you as ringmaster need to jump into ring number two and get your mortgage secured. In chapter two, finance guru Suze Orman advised you to check and upgrade your credit scores to obtain the best possible interest rate. And I instructed you to meet with a mortgage broker to be preapproved and to establish how much mortgage you can qualify for. With all of that done ahead of time, this next stage of the mortgage process will be a breeze.

A Mortgage Broker Is a Flipper's Best Mortgage Source

As we reviewed in chapter five, a mortgage broker is your best resource. They understand the flipping time frame and have access to many banks. Best of all, they can customize a mortgage to fit the specific needs of flipping a property, whether you're on the fast track—flipping immediately after completion—or on the slow and steady path, flipping after two years when the capital gains threshold has been met.

FOUR KINDS OF AVAILABLE MORTGAGES

There are many different types of mortgages. I'll review four of the most common, and then explain how a Perfect Flip Mortgage combines the best of them all.

1. Fixed-Rate Mortgage

Just like the name implies, the interest rate in this mortgage is locked in and won't change. This can be a thirty-year or a fifteen-year. A low rate is an advantage for a homeowner, but you are not a homeowner, you are a home flipper. If you are flipping the house any time within the next two years, you do not need the security of a locked-in fixed rate for a long period. The higher interest rate that comes with it is a waste of money for you.

2. Adjustable-Rate Mortgage

There are many variations of an adjustable-rate mortgage, or ARM. But the common denominator is that the interest rate and payment can change over the term of the loan. It can start low, which helps you qualify when rates are high, and then adjust in a short period of time.

3. Fixed-Rate Adjustable Mortgage

This is a mortgage whose initial rate stays the same for anywhere from six months to five years, and then adjusts. This loan has benefits, some of which we will incorporate into our Perfect Flip Mortgage.

4. Interest-Only Loan

This is a loan that can be either fixed-rate or adjustable. Either way, you only pay the interest on the loan each month. You never pay anything toward the principal. In traditional home ownership this is a terrible loan, because most homeowners continue to pay only this amount and never pay off any principal. In thirty years, you have paid hundreds of thousands of dollars in interest, and still own the original loan amount. But if you are flipping, it is a great cost savings.

THE PERFECT FLIP MORTGAGE

To create the Perfect Flip Mortgage, your mortgage broker reviews your timeline goals for the house. If you plan to flip it right away or hold it for two years, let him know. He will take the best elements from each type of mortgage available and combine them with the best terms. This is where his expertise gets you the mortgage you need for the most favorable cost, tailored exactly for the period you need it.

Components of the Perfect Flip Mortgage

- **Adjustable-Rate mortgage**—An adjustable rate is one of the main components of the Perfect Flip Mortgage, offering a much lower interest rate than the fixed.

- **Six-month teaser rate**—Adjustable-rate loans often offer the first six months at reduced interest rates. This is a real cost savings if you're on a fast track.

- **One- to three-year fixed adjustable**—This gives you a locked-in low rate for one to three years, after which the rate rises. If I plan to keep a house for a full two years, I usually go for a three-year fixed, just to give myself some breathing room.

- **No prepayment penalty**—This is essential. You want to be able to pay off your loan as soon as you flip the house and sell. Make sure your mortgage broker builds a no-prepayment-penalty clause into your loan at the beginning of the process.

- **Interest-only option**—This allows you to pay even less per month—the amount of interest on your monthly payment—and no principal. This is great for short-term loans to lower your carrying costs. But I do not recommend it if you are keeping the house for more than two years.

- **No points**—A point is the up-front cash amount you are asked to pay based on a certain predetermined percentage of your entire loan amount. You generally have the option to pay from one to two points up front. The higher the point amount you pay up front, the lower the interest rate. For long-term mortgages this makes sense. But for a short-term flip you won't hold the property long enough to recoup the interest savings you will gain. Paying a slightly higher interest rate is worth not having to come up with additional cash up front.

- **A low-doc or no-doc loan**—This loan requires significantly less documentation than other kinds, requiring only checking account, savings, or income tax statements. It makes it easier if you are self-employed. It also comes with a higher interest rate and often higher points.

THE PERFECT FLIP MORTGAGE VERSUS THE TRADITIONAL MORTGAGE

By tailoring your mortgage to fit your flipping needs, you can save thousands of dollars in capital expenditures. Take a look at this three-year adjustable rate, interest-only mortgage. There is no prepayment penalty and no up-front points to pay. It is being compared to a standard thirty-year fixed-rate loan, also with no points.

Two important points to note:

- This comparison assumes an 80 percent loan with 20 percent down. The difference in savings would be even higher if we only put 10 percent down, because there would be additional PMI costs to pay.

- The interest rate is different for each loan. This comparison is based on actual loan rates for each of these at the time of this comparison. The adjustable rate will have a lower rate than fixed, which helps to add to your savings.

THE PERFECT FLIP MORTGAGE VERSUS THE TRADITIONAL MORTGAGE

VALUE: $300,000
Down Payment: $60,000
80 percent LTV

Loan Type	Loan Amt.	Rate	Payment	Total One Year
Standard Mortgage 30-Year Fixed	$240,000	5.875%	$1,420	**$17,040**
Flip Mortgage 3-Year Adjustable, Interest-Only	$240,000	5.125%	$1,025	**$12,300**

A One-Year Savings of $4,740

By selecting the Perfect Flip Mortgage, you have saved yourself nearly $5,000 your first year. If you were doing a "find and hold" for two years before flipping, you would have saved nearly $10,000 in capital outlays.

FLIP TIP

Lock in Your Rate—When rates are on the rise, it's good to get a lower rate locked in, but make sure the time it's locked in for matches the length of your projected closing. If rates are going south, there's no point to locking in. But if you do, protect yourself with a "float down," so that if they do start to drop you can float down along with it.

Saving Big Money on Mortgage Fees

Make phone calls and ask mortgage brokers about their standard fees. Any fees paid to the mortgage broker for their service are paid by the lender, not you. Your only up-front cost should be the fee for your credit report, approximately $10, and your appraisal fee, approximately $300 to $500, depending on the size of the house. Run away from a mortgage broker who wants a fee from you.

Because of the Real Estate Settlement Procedures Act (RESPA), the lender you choose must by law give you an estimate of the costs. Read it. If you think it's a "junk" or added fee, ask that it be taken out immediately. In the next section, we will review both expected and unexpected fees.

ESCROW PAPERWORK

Once an offer has been negotiated, there are numerous escrow instructions to be carried out. You need to be involved and on alert. And you the buyer need be to ready. Rex Berkebile of Escrow Exchange West in Beverly Hills says, "The biggest mistake buyers make is that they don't read every document carefully and ask questions. They could learn so much and actually save time and money if they would immediately check documents and respond quickly."

Buyer's Escrow Responsibilities

- Submit your deposit

- Complete your inspection and negotiate any concessions from the seller

- Review and approve the title report

- Request and review estimated closing cost statements

- Secure your mortgage

- Remove the contingencies

- Select and secure property insurance

- Prepare and transfer your funds to escrow

- Sign the final closing documents

Submit Your Deposit

Get it in on time. And make sure the funds are good. If the check bounces the seller may walk away. I know I would!

Complete Your Inspection and Negotiate Any Concessions from the Buyer

As mentioned earlier, after inspection, notify the seller of any requests or credits back. Once they are negotiated and your Realtor writes them up and submits them to escrow, review them to make sure they are exactly what you negotiated.

Review and Approve the Title Report

The title report is done by a title-search company. It shows who really owns the property. This title search has to be done to make sure the title is clear of liens, back taxes, or any other judgments against the seller. Review it to see if there are any restrictions on the property regarding use or development, such as height restrictions or an easement that could keep you from developing certain parts of the property.

FLIP TIP

Historical Issues—If you discover that the property is part of a "historical overlay zone," meaning that it's been designated by the city, state, or federal government as having historical significance, you will need to get any planned renovations approved by a review board. If you are planning on making lots of changes to the front, add in extra approval time to your carrying costs.

Secure Your Mortgage or Financing

As we discussed earlier in this chapter, securing your mortgage preapproval is your responsibility. Having all that approval done prior to making an offer makes your life in the escrow process much more manageable. Work with your mortgage broker to select your mortgage as soon as possible. Getting all your mortgage paperwork signed and into escrow by your deadline is a must.

Make sure to request a review of your loan fees. You will find these in the Estimated Closing Cost Statement you'll receive during escrow.

FLIP TIP

Date Your Documents—Make sure to sign and date a document titled the 4506 Lender Form. It allows a mortgage company to request and review your federal income taxes for up to three years from the date. Some lenders will ask you not to sign. Don't listen to them. You do not want your tax returns available for indefinite scrutiny.

Remove Your Contingencies

You will need to make sure you remove your major contingencies, such as inspection and mortgage, by the cutoff dates. I always wait until the last minute to remove my contingencies. This is your last chance to back out of a deal without penalty. Warning: Don't miss a deadline! Keep an eye on your calendar.

Select and Secure Property Insurance

Check with your insurance broker to make sure this property is insurable, *before* escrow. Is it in a flood plain or an earthquake zone? Is there some other existing condition that makes it uninsurable? You must know. Get your insurance lined up and secured as soon as the escrow is opened. Don't wait until the last minute. Most lenders require your insurance to be in place before they issue the mortgage. Make sure you start this process right away. It gives you time to shop around and save some money. There are big variations in the pricing of insurances, and you want to have the time to compare prices.

FLIP TIP

Combine Your Insurances—Have your insurance broker put your auto and homeowners policies with the same carrier. You can get a big discount for the whole package.

HOW TO SAVE MONEY ON CLOSING FEES

Every transfer of funds and property comes with fees, whether through an escrow, a settlement company, or a lawyer. Most are valid and necessary, but when you know what to look for, you unearth a plethora of what are known in the business as "junk fees" or "garbage fees."

You will save yourself thousands of dollars when buying or selling if you review and analyze each and every fee charged to you. I know this sounds daunting, but it's not. And if you use this first purchase as your learning opportunity, you will eventually be able to spot these junk fees at a glance.

WHAT IS THE ESTIMATED CLOSING COST STATEMENT?

The Estimated Closing Cost Statement issued to you just prior to closing makes it easy to review closing costs. By law, it lists all of the closing costs associated with your transaction. It includes all of the one-time closing costs, such as title-transfer charges, Realtor commissions, recording fees, etc. It also includes an estimate of "recurring fees," such as your first month's mortgage payment, your first payment toward property taxes, your first six months to one year of homeowners insurance, etc. It's all there.

The Insider Secret to Unlocking the Estimated Closing Cost Statement

You are not going to settle for the customary *one* estimated closing cost statement. You are going to request a total of *three* along the way.

1. Ask for a preliminary estimated closing cost statement right after you open escrow or go under contract. This gives you a basic idea

right up front of what fees you have to pay. You can start to question which ones are valid and which ones are junk fees. These first estimated closing costs will be just that—very estimated. The escrow officer or lawyer will not yet know what many of the fees such as mortgage fee and taxes will be, but it still gives you a basic idea.

2. After the inspection and confirmation of your mortgage approval, ask for an updated version. You'll see all the funds you are going to need to close, as well as any suspicious fees or items you believe may be negotiable.

3. The Final Estimated Closing Cost Statement should come a few days before closing. Review it immediately! Keep time on your side. Do not wait until the day before closing to question fees. All parties involved will be scrambling to tie up loose ends and will not have the time to give you the service you need.

JUNK FEES: ONES TO LOOK FOR—AND GET RID OF

"If it walks like a duck and quacks like a duck, it's a duck!" Well, some fees are not all they are quacked up to be. They are junk. If you see the ones listed below, scrutinize them and *ask* if they are necessary or negotiable.

Mortgage Loan Fees

- Application fee—This can sometimes be saved.

- Assumption fee—This can be too high.

- Courier fee—Ask for details.

- Points—Are they what you agreed to?

- Lender's attorney's fee—Ask to have this removed.

- Lender's title insurance—This can be too high.

- Extra costs for appraiser's photography—This is just silly.

- Fee to receive a copy of your loan schedule printout.

- Origination fee—This can often be waived.

- Download document fees—These can often be waived.

Title fees

- Courier fee—Ask for details.

- Download document fees—These can often be waived.

Escrow Fees

- Courier fee—Ask for details.

- Document preparation fee—This is often too high.

- Escrow charges—These can often be too high.

- Impound setup—This is an extra fee.

- Loan tie-in fee—Try to negotiate this away.

- Underwriting review fee—Try to get this waived.

- Warehousing fee.

- Writing and managing documents fee—Ask to have these re-moved.

- Sub-escrow fee—Ask to have this waived.

Miscellaneous

- Realtor commission—Make sure it's accurate.

- Closing review fee—Ask to have this waived.

- Document drawing/signing fee—This is often too high.

- Padding—This should come back to you and is only used as backup money.

To give you an idea of what to expect, here is an actual estimated cost statement from a house purchased for $631,500.

BUYER'S ESTIMATED CLOSING COST STATEMENT

Property: 123 Dreamhouse Lane   **Date:** March 8, 2005
Buyer: John Doe   **Closing Date:** March 17, 2005
Escrow No.: 02-701560-S8

	Debits/Credits
Financial Consideration	
Total Consideration Deposit	631,500.00
Deposit	18,300.00
Deposit Credit	845.00
New 1st Trust Deed	505,200.00
Loan Information	
(Charges $2,296.79)	
Appraisal Fee	275.00
Credit Report	24.66
Tax Service	79.00
Processing Fee	395.00
Underwriting Fee	400.00
Flood Certificate	18.00
Interest at 5.6250% from	
03/17/2005 to 04/01/2005	1,105.13
Prorations/Adjustments	
Taxes at $524 10/semiannually	
from 03/17/2005 to 07/01/2005	302.81
Other Debits/Credits	
Estimate Insurance	1566.12
Estimate Messenger	70.00
Estimate Wire	25.00
Estimate Notary	80.00

Title/Taxes/Recording Charges

ALTA Loan Policy Fee $506K	640.00
Policy Endorsements to Title Ins. Co.	200.00
Sub-Escrow Fee to Title Ins. Co.	65.00
ALTA Inspection Fee to Title Ins. Co.	50.00
Recording Grant Deed	30.00
Recording Trust Deed	150.00

Escrow Charges

Escrow Fee	1,274.00
Loan Tie-In Fee—1 loan	250.00
E-mail docs per loan (if applic)	75.00
Refundable Padding	600.00
Funds required	115,029.72
Total	**$639,174.72**
	$639,174.72

This Is an Estimate Only and Figures Are Subject to Change

The written estimated closing statement is read and approved by the undersigned and is in compliance with the allocation of costs in the Residential Purchase Agreement and Joint Escrow Instructions and/or subsequent instructions in the above numbered escrow.

_____

John Doe

FLIP TIP

Recurring Costs—Make sure to review and question all costs that are applied to your recurring costs: your first month's mortgage, property taxes, and homeowner's insurance. These are sometimes over- or underestimated by the escrow officer. They are called recurring costs because even after you close, you will continue to pay these fees monthly or yearly.

INSIDER SECRET

Don't Freak Out—Escrow expert Rex Berkebile advises buyers and sellers not to "freak out" when they first review their statement. Escrow companies intentionally estimate high to make sure they are in the black at closing.

INSIDER SECRET

The Bigger Loans Have More Fee Flexibility—Mortgage broker Rob Cohn of Capital One reminds us that since a mortgage broker is paid a commission based on the size of the loan, the bigger the loan the more flexibility he has to waive or reduce some fees. On small loans, especially $100,000 or less, there is very little room for the broker to "absorb" some of your fees. Always ask, but don't be upset if he can't.

Have Your Funds Ready and Transferred to Escrow

Get money ready to be transferred and plan ahead. You'll avoid paying penalties for withdrawing funds from other investment accounts if you plan ahead. This could save you big bucks. And you'll sleep better.

Sign the Final Closing Docs

In a formal closing as part of escrow, you will be asked to sign all documents either at the escrow office or with a closing agent. The buyer and seller usually do this separately. If you are "under contract," you will be called in to attend the actual closing, and the buyer and seller will sign the contracts in the presence of their lawyers. You all sit at a big table in the conference room—or at your dining-room table in some cases. And in certain states a title insurance company does the closing, in addition to doing the title search and selling title insurance. The dance of escrow concludes with a flurry of Post-its with little arrows on them, endless initialing, and the occasional inking of thumbs. The escrow officer or attorney executes and delivers the deeds, you sign all the loan docs, the funds are collected and disbursed and recorded.

FLIP TIP
When the Divorce Isn't Final—If you are separated but not divorced, you can not purchase a property without the signed consent or quit claim deed of your soon-to-be ex. Don't wait until closing day to try to get this settled. It won't happen that easily.

FLIP TIP
Never on a Friday—Always schedule a closing on a Wednesday or Thursday. Last-minute items often get delayed. Closing on a Wednesday allows for a day or two extra, just in case. That still leaves time to get your fix-it workers on the job on Monday.

SEVEN FLIP TIPS FOR A SMOOTH CLOSING

1. Get your estimated closing costs three times during escrow and review. Don't wait until the last week.

2. Stay on the escrow company to make sure the seller is staying on schedule.

3. Remove contingencies in a timely fashion. If you are asking for repairs to be made, the seller won't want to start repairs until your contingencies are removed.

4. Stay in touch with the mortgage broker. Have all your bank statements, pay stubs, and records ready to go at a moment's notice.

5. Don't miss a deadline or leave a document unsigned. It could cost you your purchase.

6. Review every document sent to you and return it immediately. Time is of the essence, and you need to be ahead of schedule at all times.

7. Don't plan to take possession of the property on the day of closing. In fact, don't schedule anything for at least two days after the preferred closing date. Things always go wrong, and escrows are often held up.

Part Two

FIX IT

Nine

THE BIG FIX: THE FIX-IT IMPROVEMENT LEVELS

Now that you have learned what you need to know to FIND your property, you need to know what the heck to FIX to make it a moneymaker, and what to skip to save some big bucks. Your Downright Ugly House has the potential to be fixed on all Six Levels of Improvements. You need to understand why there are six levels, and how each one brings your house closer to creating the perfectly finished and profitable flip home. But first, you have to know your house and understand more about cost and return. We'll cover:

- Know your house

- Cost versus return

- The Six Levels of Improvements

- The Fix-It Levels

- System Upgrades

- Fix-It Essentials

- The outside

- The inside

KNOW YOUR HOUSE

Before you start ripping out those cabinets or digging up the lawn in your newfound Downright Ugly flip house, you need to analyze and get to know just what style of house you are going to fix. Before you create this silk purse out of a sow's ear, you had better know if it's a Gucci, a Birkenstock, or a Prada to begin with.

Identity Crisis—Your House Knows Best, So Work with It

All houses, however humble, are built in a certain architectural style. Work with it, not against it. Do not try to turn a fifties Ranch into a Center-Hall Colonial, a Mid-century into a Spanish hacienda, or a Country Cottage into a Santa Fe Ranch. It just won't work. The proportions will be wrong. The windows, doors, trims, and facade won't work together. And worse, it won't sell for top dollar because it won't feel right. Go with what you've got and make it the best it can be.

The Best Renovation Is Often a Restoration

If you ever have the opportunity to bring a house back to its original architectural style, do it. You will be rewarded. Just as you can't ever really disguise the style of the house because the elements are always still there, bringing them back to the forefront is not only far less expensive than trying to hide them, it simply makes the house feel "right." It's an intangible upgrade that brings big returns.

Easy Architectural Styles

Mid-century and modern are easy architectural styles to work with. Thanks to their very clean lines, they don't need a lot of expensive detailing, and they always look sexy and sophisticated when lit well and dressed with a minimum of furnishings.

COST VERSUS RETURN

There is not always a direct relation between exactly how much you put into a renovation and exactly how much you will get out of it.

Charts describing the cost versus return on common home-renovation projects can be found in many magazines and on the Internet. Review the improvements item by item and you'll come to the conclusion that a fix-it is a losing proposition, because the dollar-to-dollar value of improvements is only an average of eighty cents on the dollar. That means if you spend $1,000 to replace the windows on your flip house, when you sell you will only recoup $800 of the value. The same goes for a bathroom fix up. Spend $5,000, and if you are lucky you will maybe recoup $4,900 of your money. Well, wow, that doesn't add up.

PERCENTAGE OF COST RECOVERED CHART

Cost data from HomeTech Information Systems, a remodeling estimating software company in Bethesda, Maryland

	National Average 2003
Deck Addition	104.2%
Siding Replacement	98.1%
Bathroom Addition, Mid-Range	95.0%
Attic Bedroom	92.8%
Bathroom Remodel, Upscale	92.6%
Bathroom Remodel, Mid-Range	89.3%
Window Replacement, Upscale	87.0%
Window Replacement, Mid-Range	84.8%
Bathroom Addition, Upscale	84.3%
Family Room Addition	80.6%
Major Kitchen Remodel, Upscale	79.6%
Basement Remodel	79.3%
Master Suite, Upscale	76.9%
Master Suite, Mid-Range	76.4%
Major Kitchen Remodel, Mid-Range	74.9%

OVERCOMING THE COST VERSUS RETURN CHALLENGE

Individually, item by item, renovations don't add up to much profit. But when you put them all together with vision and creativity and include the Profit Levels of Improvements, you create an emotional edge that says to your carefully targeted buyer, "This is not just a house, but a lifestyle." The whole package is far more valuable than the sum of its parts!

And here is the other factor that allows this cost versus return to work in your favor. You know up front that you are going to do these renovations. You know that you need a new roof, or have to replace all the cabinets. You are factoring in those expenses long before you buy the house and then building them into the purchase price. You are not buying at market value and then adding the expense on top to give you a small return on your invest per item. You are subtracting the expenses from the purchase price to begin with, giving you a full return on your costs *plus* all the added value of the transformation that the sum total of these upgrades creates.

THE SIX LEVELS OF IMPROVEMENTS

The Six Levels of Improvements encompass all the changes you are going to incorporate to make this property profitable. Some things are structural, some are cosmetic, some are Lifestyle Upgrades, and some are Dressed-to-Sell Essentials, the finishing touches that give an emotional edge and create a lifestyle. They encompass all the possible fixes, repairs, replacements, and upgrades necessary to transform a Downright Ugly House into a money-making flip home! Identify them, execute them, and you will create a flip house that a buyer will be thrilled to pay top dollar to call home.

The Six Levels of Improvements
Fix-It Levels
    Serious but Fixable Problems
    System Upgrades
    Fix-It Essentials
Profit Levels
    Lifestyle Upgrades
    Designed-to-Flip Techniques
    Dressed-to-Sell Essentials

Each one of the fixes you perform on each one of these levels needs to meet these three requirements:

- Increase value of the home from a *buyer's* standpoint

- Increase marketability of the home from *your* standpoint

- Increase profitability of the home from *your bottom line's* stand-point

Why Three Levels Just Aren't Enough

Understanding all Six Levels of Improvements and incorporating them into your flip is the key to flipping success. The first three levels are the Fix-It Levels, the essential improvements that every flip house must incorporate. Most flippers start and stop right here. Statistics show that dollar for dollar, a break-even return is what you can expect on improvements. And that's what most flippers get, or if they are lucky, a little more. Where the beginning flippers and the get-rich-quick gurus stop, the pros and insiders continue. They incorporate the additional three Profit Level Improvements and transform an ordinary flip house into an extraordinarily profitable home with the promise of a lifestyle.

In an upward-moving market, these three levels will guarantee you the big profits. In a downward-moving market, as novices fall by the wayside, they can keep you in a winning position and maximize your cash-out. And, if you are selling the house you live in, you especially need to use these techniques to recapture the equity that a softening market has eroded!

THE FIX-IT LEVELS

Let's begin with the first of the Fix-It Levels, problems that are serious but fixable.

SERIOUS BUT FIXABLE PROBLEMS = PROFIT IN YOUR POCKET

A house in poor condition and in need of substantial repairs can still be well worth your while. In fact, solvable problems are what make you money. Find a house with a sagging foundation, significant termite problems, or water damage from a leaky roof. Make your initial offer with a subject-to-inspection clause as discussed in chapter seven, "Write a Winning Offer." After the offer is accepted, and during the inspection phase, your inspector will identify issues that need to be corrected. If

they are big, you will immediately bring in a professional—a contractor
or structural engineer—to assess the situation, advise you on what steps
to take and how much they will cost to make sure the house is struc-
turally sound. You then negotiate with the seller to either fix the problem
themselves, give you a credit toward closing costs, or lower the selling
price to reflect the expense. At this point, if they say no, the "subject to
inspection" clause gives you the power to walk. But if they say yes, then
you have some profit before you even start your fix-it phase!

Turning a Deal-Breaker Problem into a Deal-Maker Solution

The trick to dealing with any of the major structural issues, once you
have an accepted offer and are in escrow, is to try to get the seller to have
them rectified prior to closing. That way, if they discover the repair job is
bigger than anticipated and a Pandora's box has been opened, *they* are
responsible and will have to have it fixed and signed off on by the city.
Knowing to ask for those things helps to move a house from the teardown category and turn it into a Downright Ugly beauty. And you will
be richly rewarded for your efforts. Here are a few of my favorite Serious
but Fixable fixes:

Sagging Foundation

If the frame of an old house has shifted, wood foundation braces can be
jacked up and re-supported relatively inexpensively.

Sagging Roofline

To the untrained eye, a sagging roofline can be frightening. But the key
to fixing any of the Serious but Fixable Problems is to call an expert to
see if it really is a problem. Get an estimate from a structural engineer or
a good contractor, but don't tell the sellers what it is. I promise you, it
will be far lower then what they imagined, or they would have had it
fixed. Negotiate for a credit or a price break, or ask them to fix it.

A Chimney That Is Separated from the House

This looks daunting, but in reality, knocking down an existing brick or stone chimney and replacing it with the same or, better yet, a new metal-lined and stucco-framed chimney, is not that expensive. I did it for approximately $4,000 after I bought the house for a very discounted price, unlike the prospective buyers who walked away.

Major Water Damage from a Roof Leak

Water damage can be an ugly mess, featuring fallen or sagging ceilings, discolored walls, and the ever-popular smell of mildew. But unless you find wood rot during inspection, it is not that hard to fix and will cost far less than the big discount in price you get when the other buyers go running! Chances are you are going to replace or fix the roof anyway. Fixer houses rarely have a shambles of an interior and a brand-new roof. So the only additional cost you will incur is new drywall or plaster for the ceilings and possibly several extra coats of a stain-covering paint.

FLIP TIP

Termite Damage—Most lenders won't issue a mortgage if there is termite damage, so the seller will have to repair the damage to sell the house to you or anyone. That money will not come out of your budget.

FLIP TIP

Always to Code—When you make significant repairs, make sure they are done to code and with permits to avoid any long-term liability issues. Keep this in mind when estimating Serious but Fixable repair costs.

The Six Levels of Improvements
Fix-It Levels
   Serious but Fixable Problems
 • **System Upgrades**
   Fix-It Essentials
Profit Levels
   Lifestyle Upgrades
   Designed-to-Flip Techniques
   Dressed-to-Sell Essentials

SYSTEM UPGRADES

These are the systems that keep a house running. Sometimes called the bones of the house, they are often referred to as hidden costs, because replacing the roof, upgrading the electrical, re-plumbing and adding copper piping, a new furnace or air-conditioning are major expenses that are never "seen." You will often hear a prospective buyer coo over the granite countertops in the kitchen. But you will rarely hear one say, "Wow, look at those new copper pipes!" The bones are not "sexy" upgrades or flashy big-ticket items, but they are absolutely essential to your future profits. So make sure you incorporate the cost of upgrading them into your Estimated Fix-It Costs Budget. The systems are:

 • Electrical

 • Plumbing

 • Heating and Air

 • Roof

 • Windows

Electrical

Check the electrical panel. If an older home has modern circuit breakers instead of the age-appropriate fuse box, it has been upgraded. You may still have to add in more capacity, but that is much less costly. Most upgraded houses of around 2,000 square feet need approximately 200 amps. A really big house (3,500 to 5,000 square feet) may need up to 400 amps.

Plumbing

Turn on all the water. Does it get hot? How long does it take? What is the water pressure like when you flush a toilet? Make sure the piping is consistent throughout. In Los Angeles, we always replace the plumbing with new copper piping, using companies that specialize in full re-plumbing and can do the entire house in a matter of days. Per your inspection you will know exactly what the plumbing issues are. Allocate their costs and throw in a little extra, too.

FLIP TIP

Plumb It All at Once—Make sure to use the same plumber for all the plumbing work in your house. If a plumbing company is coming in to re-plumb all of the main lines, make sure his price includes the final installation of all the rest of the work, like connecting the new sinks, showerheads, and appliances—a huge money-saver.

Water Heaters

Water heaters should always be new, or nearly new. Use a flashlight to look for any rust on the bottom. Ask your inspector if they are vented and placed properly according to code. In California they need to be strapped to the wall for earthquake protection. Also confirm that they are of adequate capacity. Most Downright Ugly Houses will need a downright larger water heater.

FLIP TIP

Add a Hot-Water Recycler—This simple device that your plumber can add to your water heater will continuously sense the temperature of the water in your pipes and circulate fresh hot water whenever necessary, so that when you turn on the tap, it's hot. Talk about a nice selling point. You can also put it on a three-dollar lamp timer so that it only recalculates during peak usage hours to save on utility bills.

Heating and Air

If central air is standard in the neighborhood, make sure it cools the whole house, is updated, and is working well. Sometimes all it needs is a good cleaning or new filters. If it's not already a feature, you must add it in order to command top dollar. And whatever the weather, test the heating system, as well.

FLIP TIP

Double Ducting—If you already have ducting in place for your heating system, it's relatively inexpensive to add in central air because it uses the same ducts. Central air is a lifestyle upgrade with a big profit potential.

INSIDER SECRET

Turn Up the Temp—One really smart technique I always use is to upgrade the thermostats in the house with the newest technology. (Right now it's digital display.) Even if the heating and air are merely in good working order and not new, this will give the impression that you spared no expense.

Roof

You will probably have to install or at least repair the roof. Local roofers will know the codes and specifics as to whether a completely new roof is needed or if you can you just lay a new one on top of the old one. It is a big job, but it really is necessary. You'll want to present a buyer with a relatively new roof. And believe it or not, one that is visible from the street, i.e., not flat, is actually a real selling feature. By choosing a color that goes with the paint and trim, it dresses up the house and screams "well-maintained" to prospects.

Windows

I list windows with the system upgrades because windows are a recurrent element throughout the entire house and should be consistent in style. There is nothing more devaluing to a house than mismatched windows—some wood or cheap aluminum, others painted shut. Most important are the windows in the front. They should be consistent and match the architectural style of the house.

FLIP TIP

Dress Up the Old—It's actually very inexpensive to make the windows look new. First, make sure they are functioning properly. Sand or chisel off extra layers of paint. Then, using a spray like WD-40, lubricate them so they open and close smoothly. The final touch is to simply replace all the hardware (hinges and locks). This inexpensive step will completely transform the look of the windows.

> *The Six Levels of Improvements*
> **Fix-It Levels**
>   Serious but Fixable Problems
>   System Upgrades
> • **Fix-It Essentials**
> **Profit Levels**
>   Lifestyle Upgrades
>   Designed-to-Flip Techniques
>   Dressed-to-Sell Essentials

FIX-IT ESSENTIALS

Fix-It Essentials are the repairs, renovations, and upgrades that are a must-do on all flip houses. You may not have to replace or upgrade every item. But you need to know what buyers expect, so you can repair, replace, and upgrade with profit potential in mind. You analyze the cost of the problems up front, build the cost of fixing them into your purchase price, and voilà . . . profit when you sell!

Bad First Impressions Can Add Up to a Good Investment

These are the fixes that are the most noticeable, and are usually obvious even to the novice flipper. You need to be able to spot them, and then know what to do with them. Learning to trust your instincts and develop an essential fix-it eye is crucial to your flipping success.

Develop Your Essential Fix-It Eye

You have an address in your hand. You drive down the street looking at the house numbers, thinking "Hmmm . . . 221, 213 . . . Oh it's this next one! Argh! Awful color . . . oh no, that's not it . . . There it is—219 Maple!" OK. Now freeze!

This next step is crucial. You are seeing the house for the first time. I want you to remember exactly the first three negative feelings or impressions you have about this house. For example, your first three reactions might be:

Negative #1. The house feels so bare.

Negative #2. It looks cheap and really tacky.

Negative #3. The neighbors are too close.

Once you've identified your first impressions, quickly analyze the problems that create that first impression:

Problem #1. The house feels bare because there is almost no landscaping.

Problem #2. It looks cheap and tacky because the front door is cheesy, and the front windows are aluminum and don't match the original upper-floor wood windows.

Problem #3. Nothing separates it from the house next door or defines the yard lines.

Now, decide on a fix-it solution for each problem:

Solution #1. I could plant flowering bushes next to the house, put white roses along the walkway, and plant a green lawn.

Solution #2. I could install a new solid-looking front door and give it a good glossy paint color. I can replace the aluminum windows with some substantial wooden windows in the original architectural style.

Solution #3. I could put in fencing or hedges along the sides of the house to help block out the neighbors and take command of the property lines.

Congratulations! You have just learned how to see a home with a professional flipper's eye. You identified your *negative feeling* about a house, analyzed the *problem* that created it, and found an essential *solution*. Now do the same thing throughout the property, and room by room!

THE OUTSIDE

The Appeal of Curb Appeal

The first impression that a potential buyer has of your flip house will prompt them to explore further or drive away. And you never get a second chance to make a first impression. That's why curb appeal is so critical. As superficial as this may sound, most people shop for homes the same way they date. A pretty face will get you in the front door. Curb appeal is the single most important component to your Find It, Fix It, Flip It strategy. Why? Eighty percent of your qualified potential buyers will make their decision to look at your flip based solely on the look of the front of the house in a drive-by or from a photo. Curb appeal is your most powerful marketing tool!

Landscaping

Landscaping is transformational. When done properly it can make an ugly house inviting and a beautiful home even more spectacular. It can dress up any property and distract from or hide a multitude of sins. A lush and inviting front yard with lots of green works wonders. And make sure to plant any bushes or ornamental trees immediately when you start your fix-up process. This gives them time to grow in so the landscaping has a more mature look. The more established your front yard looks, the better.

FLIP TIP

Bigger Is Better—Spend a extra few dollars to plant more mature trees and shrubs. If you were going to buy a few five-gallon shrubs, buy fifteen-gallon ones instead. It's a little more money, but the result is well worth it. I always allocate a few thousand dollars for landscaping in my budgets. Many flippers overlook this valuable opportunity to create instant curb appeal, but it is the best money you can spend, and it is never lost on a buyer.

Flowers

A bed of colorful petunias, impatiens, or tulips in the front yard is a must for spring, summer, and fall house sales. I love consistency, so I like to choose one color and stick with it. For the design-challenged like yours truly, go with all white. It always looks good, really pops out against the green, and is a sophisticated look.

The Front Door

For a house or condo, dressing up the front door is essential. These individual items may seem obvious, but together these small, inexpensive changes and often overlooked details give a welcoming and finished look.

- Paint the front door with an accent color
- Replace old door handles and locks with new shiny ones
- Install a new brass kick board
- Add new decorative light fixtures that match the style of the house
- Add classic house numbers
- Add a lovely welcome mat to match the style of the house
- Add a shiny new mailbox
- Add a new doorbell and doorbell plate
- Two flowering potted plants on either side of the door are also a must

With a condo, work within your condo guidelines and make it look as inviting and special as possible.

Exterior Painting

Painting is nothing less than transformative. It is the one fix-it that can create the greatest value with the least expense. Every surface that is not in good condition should be patched, prepped, and then painted. The paint job must be perfect. All walls and wood trim need to be updated, using the three-color combination of complementing colors that I will discuss in chapter thirteen, "Designed to Flip."

Pathways and Driveway

Repair or build a welcoming pathway to the front door. Repair or replace broken or cracked cement or line the existing pathway with brick or a row of flowers on low shrubs. Remember, everything the buyer sees as he approaches your house must look inviting and perfectly maintained. The same holds true for the driveway. It is part of the first impression, and cracks and oil stains won't do. A water power-washer can often take care of the oil stains. Cracks require re-cementing.

FLIPPING SUCCESS STORY

Check This Out—My Allenwood flip had a terribly cracked and ugly driveway. And unfortunately, it was the main feature of the front of the house. So I got creative and for very little extra expense I turned a design disaster into a design element. I had the driveway re-cemented with diagonal squares, with grass in between. Laying in the sprinkler system between them and planting grass made for a beautiful effect.

The Allenwood flip was a huge challenge—zero curb appeal and no privacy. A little creativity, a few walls, and a simple but interesting driveway design brought this ugly seventies Ranch into the twenty-first century.

Garage Door

Make sure it looks great, especially if the garage door is visible from the street. When you are selling a lifestyle, there is no such thing as "just a garage." Replace the existing door if need be, and repair or replace automatic openers. Give it a fresh coat of glossy paint in an accent color for architectural detail.

Outdoor Lighting

Make the house look fantastic at night! Once a buyer is interested, he will usually drive by multiple times to review the house himself or show friends and family. Accent lighting will really dress up the house at night. Look for the fantastic new low-voltage lighting kits that give a dramatic finished look, are easy to install, and are very inexpensive. Don't miss this "brilliant" opportunity to entice your buyers!

FLIP TIP

Light It Up—Use up-light low-voltage lighting at the base of your new landscaping to create wonderful light and shadow patterns. It's very dramatic and creates an instant designer look for the cost of some low-voltage lights (approximately $39 to $89).

To improve the look of my Palm Springs Bogert flip exterior, I spent $39 for the lights and $35 for the two plants in front of the wall—a total of $74 for priceless nighttime buyer-snagging curb appeal!

Take Possession of Your Front Yard

With real estate so expensive and land at a premium, I like to do better than to provide $100,000 worth of real estate just for the neighbor's dogs. Add value by defining and separating the front yard from the hustle and bustle of the neighborhood. For instance, a lovely low wooden fence wrapped by wisteria vines creates a barrier and adds a visual appeal to the property. It also helps to visually expand the scale and depth of the property, adding a significant sense of value to the house for very little money.

FLIP TIP

Match the House—If you add a decorative fence, low hedge, or low stone wall, make sure it is in the same architectural style as the house. Don't add a white picket fence to an old Spanish-style hacienda, or a river-rock wall to a modern-style home.

A low fence in front of my Orlando Avenue flip recaptured the front yard—and captured a higher sales price.

The Backyard and Grounds

Plant right away. And get those sprinklers in immediately if you're in the part of the country that uses them. The longer new landscaping has to grow before the buyers arrive, the better it will look. The only reason to wait to get planting is if your fix-it plans include major work that will cause your contractor and tradesman to use the yard as their work area and temporary dumping ground.

THE INTERIOR

The two most closely inspected and anticipated rooms in a house are the kitchen and the bath. They need to look their best. And they will eat up the biggest chunk of your Essential Fix-It budget. Statistically, as politically incorrect as this is, these are the rooms that women are most interested in—first and last. A dynamic and well-appointed kitchen will dramatically increase the value of your flip. This is the room where you'll want to add some extra "brooches" or perks to really grab attention. The same holds true for the bathrooms, and especially the master bath. Let's analyze what needs to be done and what a buyer will expect.

Low, Medium, or High—Decide Before You Plan

Before you start planning, you must consider the market and decide to target a low-, medium-, or high-end home buyer, as discussed in chapter five, "The Financial Model for Success: The Profit Calculator." A kitchen fix-it can range from the simplest of brush ups, with a paint job and a better grade of appliances for around $2,000, to $50,000 worth of granite countertops and luxury appliances. For our purposes, let's target a medium-level buyer. Throughout the interior fix-its I will make special mention of insider tips for all three levels as well.

THE KITCHEN

There's always something new in the world of kitchen improvement. By staying on top of the latest trends and technological improvements, your flip will offer buyers the best kitchen in their price range. The first question is how much to spend. I believe you can do a very stylish kitchen for a very reasonable amount of money. Some designers recommend that you budget 10 percent of the price of your FFP to be used for the kitchen alone. That means a $250,000 house commands a $25,000 kitchen budget. I disagree. I have never spent that much on a kitchen in a home of that size—not even close. And the cost simply does not escalate proportionately as the cost of the house rises.

LOW/MEDIUM KITCHEN FIX-IT

Here's a list of what I would renovate or improve:

- Improve cabinet doors

- Improve countertops

- Improve sink, faucet

- Add garbage disposal

- Add new appliances

- Replace flooring

- Paint

- Add or improve lighting

Low-End Kitchen Makeover for Under $3,500

You can do a very economical, low-end kitchen makeover for under $3,500. The key is to work with what you have and use these cost saving tips:

Repurpose the Existing Cabinets

If the existing cabinets are of good quality wood and still in good working order, you are in luck. This is one of the first things I check when I walk through a prospective kitchen. There are three ways to repurpose old cabinets and save thousands:

- Professionally spray paint them
- Re-laminate them
- Add new doors and drawer fronts

Spray Paint

Have all the cabinets cleaned and lightly sanded, then have a painter come in to spray them. Don't try to do this one yourself. This is not about getting a couple of spray cans of paint, either. A good spray-paint job can transform ugly cabinets, making them look factory-new. You can't get the same look by painting or rolling the cabinets. Unless you are flipping an extremely low-end property, you want them to look pristine. Spraying is not any more expensive when done by a professional painter. And it's sometimes LESS expensive!

I used this exact cost-cutting technique on a high-end property in Los Angeles that sold for $750,000. I spent about $400 on the cabinets!

My Allenwood kitchen Fix-It was an inexpensive, Low to Medium Fix-It, with a much higher perceived value. I painted the existing cabinets, replaced the upper-cabinet fronts with glass panels, added new cabinet hardware, put in the new appliances, and painted!

Re-laminate

For already laminated older cabinets, a face-lift will work wonders. They can be re-covered with a wood or vinyl veneer. There are many companies that specialize in kitchens. Again, it's a great way to get a great look on a budget.

New Doors and Drawer Fronts

Another trick is to replace the cabinet doors and drawer fronts. This can completely transform old cabinets, especially if you want to add a little more design style to the kitchen. Just have the new doors and drawer fronts made and then spray out the old frames with the new fronts.

FLIP TIP

Glass Panels Are Fabulous—I love glass paneling on the top cabinets. If you are going to have new doors made, this is a good chance to have these done to add a very high-end look, even on a low-end flip.

New Hardware

Home remodeling superstores carry a great selection of door hardware. Get one that complements your architectural style. Don't scrimp here. This is what I call a brooch, an added touch that makes the whole room work! Also remove and replace all the old painted-over hinges with shiny new ones. It's time consuming, but very inexpensive. And it makes a huge difference.

Professional flipper Jeff Beuth did this very inexpensive yet dramatic kitchen makeover, with little more than new countertops, new cabinet hardware, appliances, and a bright and cheerful linoleum. He had the existing cabinets and walls sprayed-out.

Countertops

Depending on the type of house, you may get away with Formica. There are lots of new looks for this old standby. And older houses, especially those built from 1910 to 1950, look good with tile. Just promise me that when you have the tile laid, you keep the spaces between the tiles as tight as you can. The less grout, the better.

My trick is to go for granite. At $40 a square foot installed, which is way more expensive than the standard-issue plastic laminate, granite comes to around $3,600 for ninety square feet. But in a low-end project, granite countertops are a monstrous value upgrade, a selling point that you will use later to market your house. I know what you're thinking—

you could never budget for that. But think again, measure carefully, and head for a materials yard. Or go to a big home store that buys it in bulk, which makes it 20 percent cheaper than a couple of years ago. Granite is within your reach if you follow these four tips:

1. Get the least expensive granite available, usually the light gray.

2. Buy three smaller leftover pieces, rather then one large piece. I don't mind having an extra seam in the countertop if it means I have upgraded this little fixer to granite.

3. Have the kitchen and the bath countertops replaced with the same granite materials. This allows you to take advantage of otherwise wasted pieces.

4. Do not do a "bull nose" edge. Go with the simplified squared-off finished edge. The installation is much cheaper.

Keep the Plumbing Where It Is

Moving plumbing to accommodate the rearranging of sinks, ovens, stoves, or the dishwasher is a big expense. Try to keep those pipe-connected elements where they are.

Flooring

As an inexpensive alternative to porcelain tile or hardwood, I have seen some really great vinyl flooring on the market lately. It is inexpensive and can be laid by an installer for a reasonable fee. I love some of the new textured ones. Head to your home-improvement center and look around.

This was one of Jeff Beuth's first flips. With a purchase price of $60,000, this house had a very tight budget. Paint, linoleum, and new Formica countertops were just enough to land him his target buyer.

Kitchen Lighting

Get rid of the fluorescent lighting. I don't mean to offend anyone, but it's just plain ugly and no one looks good under it—especially your prospective buyers. Use recessed lighting if your ceiling can accommodate it. An electrician can put in four recessed "cans" for about $250.

MEDIUM/HIGH-END KITCHEN FIX-IT

The difference between a Low/Medium and a Medium/High-End kitchen renovation is mostly the upgraded choices, such as more expensive materials, cabinets, and appliances. The overall work is about the same. Here's where I'd put my money, in addition to the low-end fixes already mentioned:

- All new cabinets
- Upgraded countertops
- Island with second sink
- Under-cabinet lighting
- Built-in appliances
- Multiple dishwashers
- Tile or hardwood flooring
- Kitchen brooches

Cabinets

OK, cabinets are a big expense and a big portion of your budget. The best-case scenario is that the cabinets are salvageable. But more often than not, when you are doing a higher-end renovation, you may need to reconfigure them to add in larger appliances and more amenities than originally came with the house. You also may be expanding the kitchen by opening up some walls. You will need more cabinetry and, hopefully, an island as well. Since all your cabinets must match and be of the same quality, out with the old and in with the new. White milk or textured glass panels in the upper cabinets are a natural for this higher-level renovation.

Countertops and Backsplashes

Countertops and the materials you choose vary, depending on the price and level of the home. You will never see Formica in a high-end home, and you won't often see granite in a low-end flip. Low-end choices include laminate, Formica, tile, and granite squares. Medium and high-end prices demand granite, travertine, and other more sophisticated surfaces. Whatever the price range, I try to avoid using too much tile on countertops. I hate grout! It always stains and is impossible to keep clean and sanitary. And as I've said before, keep the spacing between tiles to a minimum.

Appliances

All the new home remodeling and lifestyle shows, like my show *Extra* and *Extra's Mansions & Millionaires*, have raised the bar of buyer expectations, perhaps a wee bit unrealistically when it comes to the kitchen. Fortunately, appliance manufacturers have begun to create great-looking, lower-priced lines. With a little research and some smart shopping, you can find high end–looking appliances at low-end prices. The GE Profile line, for example, is well styled, comes in the popular stainless finish, and is moderately priced. It pays to spend a few dollars more on terrific-looking appliances.

FLIP TIP

Built-in Beauty—Built-in appliances are a cost-effective way to add tremendous value. On the low-end upgrade, you can build in a beautiful microwave for less than $100 above the cost of a regular countertop model. And with a custom framing kit, you can add it into existing cabinet space. On a medium to high-end flip, the new built-in refrigerators are a must. Until recently, only the very high-end appliances such as Viking and Sub-Zero did built-ins. But now, many manufactures are creating wonderful, moderately priced models. A built-in fridge transforms a kitchen, making it feel larger and making your buyer itch to write that offer.

Sinks and Fixtures

Not just for washing your pots anymore, sinks have become a lifestyle fashion statement! I do like the porcelain ones the best, because they don't scratch the way the stainless-steel ones do.

Installation style is the great divide. With a low-end kitchen, go with a drop-in sink. Because it literally drops into the hole in the countertop, the installation is less difficult and therefore less expensive. On a higher-end home, install under the counter–mounted sinks. They are sleek and sophisticated, more expensive to install—but worth it.

Get the best possible faucet, one with a pull-out spray attachment or a gooseneck with a detachable head. It is a necessity AND a brooch. The difference between good and great is only $50 to $75. Stick to one consistent fixture finish, because mixed finishes can look like patchwork.

FLIP TIP

Inches Count—Measure very carefully before you buy appliances or cabinets. You need to know the height of the walls from floor to ceiling. When measuring, make sure to take the thickness of the new countertop into account. I made that mistake once and had to have all the new electrical wall sockets and switches moved up. It was a costly error.

Floor Plan

Are there triangular traffic patterns between the refrigerator, stove, oven, sink, and dishwasher? There should be, because that's how you create flow. Is the dishwasher next to the sink? It should be, because otherwise you create a mess every time you walk across the room with a dripping dish in your hand to get to the dishwasher. To save money I once put a dishwasher in the counter opposite the sink. I cleaned up drips on the floor for two years. Never again.

FLIP TIP

Get Free Advice—Check out the larger home-improvement centers for computer-based free design services to help lay out your kitchen. I spoke with Natalie Dalton, Manager of Design-At-Home Services for the Home Depot EXPO Design Center. She explained that the EXPO Design Center offers expert advice as well as professional design services for full-scale projects. Their professionals are at the leading edge of today's decorating trends, and their services include one-on-one client assistance as well as in-home consultations, complete project management, and installation services.

Medium/High-End Kitchen Lighting

In addition to recessed lighting, you will want to add some other light sources. Under-cabinet lights create light and drama. These thin strips of light are an instant lifestyle upgrade.

FLIP TIP

Prewire—When installing new cabinets, prewire for under-cabinet lights FIRST. The wires are hidden and the electrician can install one dimmer switch for all.

Flooring

Kitchen flooring is very important. The trend now is to expand the kitchen and open up the floor plan into adjacent areas. Defining where the kitchen ends and the rest of the house begins can create a flooring problem. In many of the open floor plans I have used, I solved this problem by ignoring it—and continuing the hardwood floor from the adjacent room right into the kitchen. It opens up the space even more, visually creating a larger kitchen area . . . always an emotional lifestyle enhancement. When that isn't possible, keep the floor color and tone similar to any adjacent flooring. Visually, this helps the flow and creates an expansive and open feeling.

THE MASTER BATH AND BATHROOMS

The mere mention of the words "master bath" should make you take a breath. It is the most challenging room in the house to renovate because every single tradesman will have some hand in the master bath fix-it. It can be a nightmare to design, schedule, and incorporate major changes into a very small room in a very short time—and all in the proper order, of course. However, on the positive side, a dramatic, amenity-filled, inviting master bath gives you the emotional edge and upgrades that will make you big profits. Builders today are making the master bath and closet areas larger than the bedroom itself. When doing a flip, unless you are doing major reconfiguring, you are constrained by the size of the original bathroom. Here's how to make the most of it:

Low-End Bathroom Fix-It

The key to doing a low-end bathroom fix-it is to save as much of the existing bath as you can and replace what is simply not salvageable. It can look more expensive if you keep several things in mind:

Tiling

Tiling is a costly job. Is the tile in bad condition overall or dated with bad color, or is it just the grout that is old and discolored? If the tile is salvageable, but the grout is the real problem, scrape off the top layer, apply premixed, stain-proof grout directly over the existing grout, and voilà—for less than $100 your tile looks like new. You have saved thousands in labor and materials, and it is guaranteed to last for twenty years!

INSIDER SECRET

Higher Counters—Highly sought-after residential designer Brian Little suggests that to give a bathroom of any price a high-end look, raise the countertops to the five-star hotel height of thirty-six inches. Your buyer will want to "check into" this high-end residence.

Cabinets

Just as in the kitchen, keep the existing ones but have them professionally spray painted, re-laminated, or refitted with new doors for a fresh, affordable makeover.

Countertops

Try to use leftover granite pieces from your kitchen. Otherwise, go with tile. Just promise me you'll keep the space between tiles as small as possible. The less grout the better.

Don't Move Plumbing

Keeping the sink, toilet, shower, and tub in place will be a huge cost savings. On a low-end property, don't move or replace the bathtub. It's a big job, especially on the second floor. For a high-end fix-it, consider replacing it with a Jacuzzi. To trim the bathroom budget, a process called resurfacing can transform an old scratched tub for around $350. Epoxy-like gloss paint sprayed onto old tile, bathtubs, and sinks works wonders. It is applied by a professional tile resurfacer and comes with a five-year guarantee.

The Shower

For a separate shower stall, if the tile is in good condition, re-grout and you are good to go. If it needs replacing, do it when you redo the countertops or floors.

Sinks and Fixtures

Sinks should look fresh and new. You can find attractive porcelain drop-in sinks for around $45. Even on a low-end fix, try to find enough room for his and hers sinks. It's a nice bonus if you can do it without moving many pipes.

Accessories

Install all new towel racks and other accessories. Built-in medicine cabinets are a must. They save space and add extra storage. Ditto for in-wall toilet-paper dispensers.

Lighting

Save money by making the most of your existing light sources. If you have lights in the wall above the sink, find the best wall mount that perfectly matches your architectural style. This is good place to spend a little extra money. And again, try recessed lights. Fluorescent lighting is an instant turnoff.

Toilets

Most old toilets are salvageable unless they have to be replaced to conform to local "low-flow" standards. Simply get a new toilet seat with new fittings and you are done. Oh, yes—only white toilets, please. You do not want them to stand out!

FLIP TIP

Floor on the Diagonal—If you have to retile your bathroom floor, it will appear larger if you lay the tile on the diagonal, as opposed to running squarely parallel with the walls.

FLIP TIP

Frameless Glass Shower Enclosures—Consider losing the tub altogether and create a big walk-in shower with a tiled seat. It looks great and saves fix-it money, too. It's cheaper than having to replace the tub and tile around it for the shower.

MEDIUM/HIGH-END FLIP

The two major differences between the low- and high-end bathroom fixes are quality of materials and the size of the rooms. The medium/high-end bathroom calls for more expensive materials for countertops, floor coverings, and accessories. Frameless doors are expected, as well as higher-end toilets and faucets.

THROUGHOUT THE HOUSE

Floors

Hardwood—Always refinish hardwood floors. And have a professional floor-finisher do it. Wait until all the other fix-it projects are done and do your floors last. You don't want tradesmen messing up your perfect new hardwoods.

FLIP TIP

Shine It On—I always use a high-gloss finish on the final floor redo. Yes, it will look like a bowling alley at first, but it will dull down pretty quickly. Ask for at least two if not three coats of polyurethane high-gloss finish!

Carpet—Go for neutral tones in brown and beige. It may seem boring, but other than paint, nothing gives you more bang for your buck. Choose a half-inch pad, and please, select a carpet with twenty-seven-ounce density. Anything less will feel cheap and tacky—and it's not much more money to be cushy underfoot!

Walls and Ceilings

Popcorn is great at the movies, but you don't want to see it in your home. Popcorn is that awful blown-on texturing that was used so frequently in the seventies to cover seriously cracked or stained ceilings. Nothing dates a house more than that stuff, short of a disco ball and black-light posters. Get rid of it. And do it first. It is messy as all heck, because it has to be wet to be scraped off . . . yuck.

While your ceilings are being replastered it is also a good time to check for cracks and holes in the walls. Have them all done at one time. And if you are doing new drywall anywhere, just remember that once they start to sand the drywall plaster, it is a sandy mess. If you are living in the house at the time, make sure you seal off your living areas before the workers start to sand!

Painting

Paint is an absolute Fix-It Essential. Color can be *so* dramatic and effective, and paint (including labor) is *so* inexpensive for the transformation it provides. Painting is the final phase, and we will cover the correct finishes and my never-fail Three-Color Technique in chapter thirteen, "Designed to Flip."

Ten

THE BIG FIX: THE PROFIT IMPROVEMENT LEVELS

You've gone through the house and identified the first three of the Six Levels of Improvements. You've figured out the Fix-It Levels, the stuff you have to do, the fix-its that everybody does.

If your prospective beauty has all the Downright Ugly qualities you dream of, you should be pretty excited at this stage, especially if this is your first flip. Now it's time to move up to the Profit Levels, where successful flippers make the investment that makes the difference. If your flip house can be improved by the Lifestyle Upgrades discussed in this chapter, then you've got a winner.

These same improvements will help keep you in the profit mode when a volatile market is on a downward swing, because they make your property stand out in an increasingly competitive field. They also maximize the value of the house you live in, whether you're flipping or just protecting your investment through these Lifestyle Upgrades.

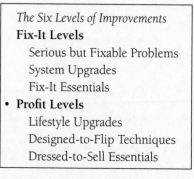

The Six Levels of Improvements
Fix-It Levels
    Serious but Fixable Problems
    System Upgrades
    Fix-It Essentials
• **Profit Levels**
    Lifestyle Upgrades
    Designed-to-Flip Techniques
    Dressed-to-Sell Essentials

LIFESTYLE UPGRADES = HUGE PROFITS

Lifestyle Upgrades are the creative, emotional, intangible improvements that return huge profits compared to their cost. They do nothing less than transform that house into a home! Some houses don't appear to be in bad condition, they just appear to have no appeal. They don't look like a place anyone would want to *live*, because they lack emotional appeal or "livability." Lifestyle Upgrades create the emotional response and feeling of livability that buyers are naturally drawn to.

You need to develop that moneymaking eye for the Lifestyle Upgrades that will make you the big profits. This cuts out a lot of the competition that simply misses the potential that your trained eye is learning to see. When everyone else is looking for a dilapidated fixer and a distressed-seller situation, you will spot a home that needs some basic fix-it and TLC and has the all-important potential for Lifestyle Upgrades.

LIFESTYLE UPGRADE WINNERS

- Bad flow
- Underdeveloped living space
- The worst view
- Very little natural light
- An unwelcome entrance
- Undefined property lines
- No security system
- No backyard boundaries
- Never heard of the Internet
- Noise
- Undeveloped structures
- Hidden square feet

- Bad kitchen layout
- No outdoor living area
- Cement yard
- No income potential
- Borderline neighborhood
- Tiny master closets
- No home office
- Underutilized storage spaces
- No privacy
- Wasted yard space

Individually, improving these problems are just that, improvements. But collectively they take needs, like "I need a closet," and elevate them to wants, like "I want a closet with custom shelving." They tug the heartstrings of the buyer because they represent a dream come true: a home that looks great and, more important, feels great. It starts with a grand entrance.

A GRAND ENTRANCE

An entrance is something you make. So make the entrance to the house as grand as possible. And I mean entrance not only as a noun, but as a verb. No one wants to walk straight up to a front door and then right into the living room. This is your chance to give your buyer a feeling of "arrival." I was given this advice years ago, and it has made me a lot of money: Always visualize your potential buyer walking up to your front door in the rain. If the house has no front covered porch or overhang above the door to protect him from the elements, by the time the door is opened, he is soaking wet and you have lost the sale! Then, picture him stepping straight into a living room and onto the carpet with no transition area from the outdoors to the indoors. This is not the way to welcome a buyer.

All you have to do to change this picture is create an overhang or small covered porch. It provides a feeling of welcome. It adds curb appeal and a charming detail. I did this on my Spaulding house. The front door was flush with the front wall and totally exposed to the elements. I created a pitched, overhanging partial porch. I went to a salvage yard and found original 1915 columns for around $100 and used them to make this new overhang feel original and restored, as opposed to redone.

Creating a front porch for the Spaulding house instantly created a welcoming entrance and a feeling of arrival.

GO WITH THE FLOW

Does the house have a foyer? An area just off the front door, even if it is only a six-by-six-foot area that separates the front door from the living room, gives a feeling of transition that changes how you experience the rest of the house. And flow, the way the house transitions from room to room, is critical.

Good flow is priceless, because it makes a house feel like you belong there, that there is room for life to happen there. It has a feeling of potential. Bad flow makes a house feel, well . . . wrong. These are not obvious repair items like a leaking roof. A home with bad flow feels claustrophobic and chopped up. The living room may seem pinched off or the kitchen has only one entrance and is shoved off into a corner of the house. The bedrooms have no access to the outside or are at the end of long, narrow hallway.

Will the flow of the house suit your buyer? If your target buyer is a family, will you be able to create open living spaces and "blow out" the kitchen to create a great room? If it is a two-income couple, can you create private space for each one to juggle both their home life and home work space? Is there easy access from the kitchen to the garage or outside? And direct access to the backyard from the kitchen for barbecuing or outdoor entertaining?

The trend today is open spaces and common-area rooms. The days of the sequestered kitchens and separate breakfast rooms cut off from the dining room are gone. People live differently. The family centers in the kitchen. Look for homes in which you can move a few non–load bearing walls and turn a cubbyholed labyrinth of separate rooms into a home of open spaces where each room flows seamlessly into the other.

FLIPPING SUCCESS STORY

Opening Up to Possibilities—My Spaulding house, built in 1914, had one of those arcane floor plans with small, closed-off rooms and no flow. It was perfectly designed for its original period but wrong for today's lifestyle. The kitchen was closed off from the rest of the house in the back corner. I removed some non–load bearing walls, opened up the kitchen into one big room and created a wonderful flow. It transformed the house, opened it up, and made it appear so much more spacious.

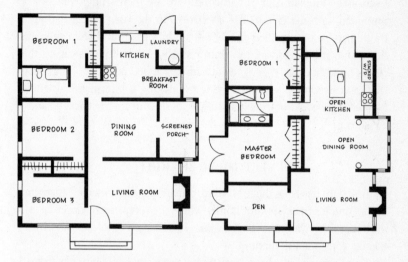

You can see from the before-and-after floor plans that all the rooms were opened and made to feel more spacious. The kitchen is now larger, yet no actual square footage was added—just rearranged.

Adding the island to this newly open space was a major Lifestyle Upgrade. A family can now gather and entertain comfortably in what was once a claustrophobic, closed-off series of small rooms.

MAKE THE KITCHEN DELICIOUS

Even if the kitchen isn't in bad condition, are there things that can be improved with the layout? Are appliances in the right place? Is there a traffic pattern or a traffic jam? By moving things around you can create flow—and profit. Add all the charm and functionality you can to this room. In addition to everything already discussed about cooking, make this room ready for advanced living by making it information-friendly. Maybe add a cookbook shelf, a built-in desk with Internet access, and a TV screen.

LET THERE BE LIGHT

Natural light has been the most transformational design secret since time began, and it's free! Look for homes where the rooms seem closed in and dark. Look for ways that windows can be enlarged or added. And by all means, consider a skylight.

A one-story house that is dark and gloomy can be totally transformed by putting skylights in the kitchen, the living room, and the master bathroom. I have often read that adding a skylight or celestial window does not return dollar for dollar on your investment. That may be true on a strict cost versus return analysis, but that does not factor in the emotional appeal of a sun-washed, light-filled space.

When buyers walk into a sun-drenched kitchen, with sparkling appliances reflecting the warm light, they immediately see themselves in the scene, lingering over the crossword puzzle on Sunday, or sending their happy children off to school as Mom and Dad stay for a second cup of coffee—or both. You get the idea. Natural light is simply magical.

If you have a two-story home and the kitchen has no roof access, then a skylight at the top of a stairwell on the second floor can also be very dramatic. Light flooding down the stairs creates the feeling that the second story is bright and inviting—and that life there will be, too.

FLIP TIP

While the Roof Is Off—Most flip houses need new roofs, and the perfect time to add skylights is right before you repair the roof.

MAKE ROOM FOR A VIEW

Is every window blocked by overgrowth? Are there trees and shrubs obscuring what could be a gorgeous view? Do rooms look out to an ugly backyard, or worse, into the next-door neighbor's bathroom window? By either removing or adding landscaping, can you create an emotionally pleasing vista out every window? Also, no matter where you stand in the house, you should be private. If that means planting a tree directly between the house next door and your living-room window, do it.

There's a reason that estates have walls or hedges. By defining the space in a way that is aesthetically pleasing, you can create the sense of a private oasis. This adds value, no matter how small the lot size.

Home Office Area

Is there unused space under a stairwell, or an odd-shaped alcove? Adding a home office in an otherwise unused corner or cubbyhole is a very inexpensive way to achieve a fantastic Lifestyle Upgrade. Add high-speed cable wiring and telephone line while you are in the fix-it process and you've created a Lifestyle Upgrade that creates a big emotional impact—with little expense.

Underutilized Storage Space

Creating storage space is another low-cost improvement that increases profit because it "feels" great. Look for an area under an outdoor stairwell you can enclose. Or build shelving in the garage. Space is precious—and valuable.

Underdeveloped Living Space

Is there an unused attic space that could be evolved into a bedroom, office, or study? Is there a beaten-up screened-in porch that could become a proper sunroom or incorporated into the actual living room or den? Underutilized outdoor areas beneath an existing roof overhang can be enclosed easily to increase square footage. A weatherized and sealed basement can become a den, workroom, playroom, or office. Is there a wall that can be extended out to the edge of the roofline? Just make sure it blends seamlessly with the original house. A room addition that looks like an addition or an add-on is better left off!

MASTER THE CLOSETS

One of the most important upgrades you can make in homes built before 1970 or so is to master the master closet. Until the 1970s, they just didn't make walk-in closets. But they are a must for today's savvy home buyer. Older homes may have wonderful details and charm, but rarely do they have big master closets, not to mention walk-ins or his and hers walk-in closets. Use these three techniques to create master closets where you lack the space.

- **Steal space from the master bedroom.** If there is room, sacrifice a few feet along one wall to create a wall of closets with sliding louvered or mirrored doors, depending on the style of the house.

- **Push into the adjoining room.** If you already have a closet, open it up to the side and take space from the adjoining room. Create a smaller den or home office in that room.

- **Create a master suite.** If the room count permits it, there are three small bedrooms on one floor, and you have identified your target market as a single person or young married couple with a child, take over some of the space in that third bedroom and use it to expand both the master bath and the master closet to create a luxurious master suite. You give a buyer a degree of luxury found in much larger homes for the price of a smaller residence. Get creative; you may even have the room to include a home office in your newly divided space!

No matter what size the master closet is, make it a study in organization. The $300 to $600 it costs to do a basic walk-in closet system with three rods, six shelves, and five drawers is worth every penny. These systems create order out of chaos and make a buyer who has never had one feel like a movie star. Upgrade with jewelry drawers and pull-down shoe racks and your most pampered prospects will be impressed.

What? No Security System?

Look for houses with no security systems or outdated ones. It's an easy plus to add. In fact, many companies will install the entire system for free if you agree to a one-year contract for monitoring. They are often worth up to $1,000. You will have to have to disclose to the buyer that they have a one-year contract for monitoring, usually priced around $19 a month. I have done this on every flip, and the buyer is always happy to have the alarm-monitoring service.

Never Heard of the Internet

Are there cable wires running across the floors, speaker wires shoved under carpets and tacked to the walls, and telephone lines with old, outdated jacks? Do you see big cables running from the pole in the back-yard and hanging down across the driveway? To me, this house has potential to come into the Internet age with in-wall wiring and Internet cables and jacks. Also, wireless Internet eliminates the need for much of the cable wiring. And cable companies will run cable wires underground from the utility pole for a nominal fee.

Speakers, on the other hand, still have wiring, and if you are going to be doing any ceiling or wall rehab, install some in-ceiling or in-wall speakers now. You can fill the house with music while your potential buyers stroll around chomping at the bit to write that check!

Garage

Garages are not just for cars, they're an extension of the living space. Neat and clean is just the beginning. Get a hanging wall starter kit with eleven hooks, a wire basket, and a shelf. For $200 you'll give buyers the idea that the garage has storage capacity and style.

PUSH THE INSIDE OUT—EXPANDING YOUR BOUNDARIES

Living space is not defined by the interior walls of your house. It actually starts at the sidewalk in front of your house or the hallway outside your apartment or condo and extends out to the edge of your property. Whether you have a balcony or a backyard, you'll want to push the inside out.

The perfect home for me is one in which every room has some access to an outside area. OK, I live in Southern California, so that's easy for me to say. But balconies, backyard patios, porches, and even the front steps are valuable living spaces that are all too often ignored. By developing your condo balcony, the cement patio on the other side of the sliding glass door, and the front steps and front porch, you create a sense of expansiveness and an emotional appeal.

Take a walk around the perimeter of the house. If there is ANY space off a bedroom or kitchen door or front porch, then you should incorporate it into your living space to expand out and bring the outdoors in. It is one of the first things I do when considering a potential flip.

FLIP TIP

Creating Patio Space—If you have room, replace the windows on first-floor bedrooms that face the side or back of the house with a set of French doors. The small deck or patio you create will feel like an addition—for a fraction of the cost.

FLIPPING SUCCESS STORY

All Hands on Deck!—Take a look at the before and after outdoor expansion I did on my Spaulding house. I added four sets of French doors, then built decks on the side and back of the house, creating 50 percent more usable living area and a hefty increase in value. Plus room for a Jacuzzi!

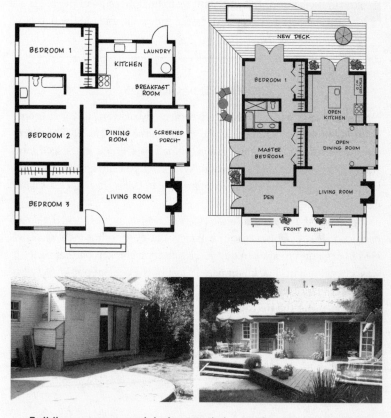

Building a wraparound deck created almost 50 percent more usable living area. Adding French doors to each room at the back of the house made it easy to enjoy.

FLIPPING SUCCESS STORY

A friend, Brian Cranston, star of *Malcolm in the Middle*, lives in a lovely Colonial-style home in Los Angeles. He told me that he loved his home, but that he'd always felt a bit confined in it—until he developed the outside space. It made all the difference in the world. He built a rose-covered white picket fence in front of his property and hedged in the sides. He claimed every available inch of property and added patios for an outdoor living room, an oasis in the heart of the city. With a minimal investment, he made his private living space start at the sidewalk and doubled the house's usable space.

CEMENTED BACKYARDS

Finding a house with a completely cemented backyard is a gold mine. For only the cost of demolition you can have the majority of the cement removed. Install a sprinkler system, some top soil and grass seed, and you'll make a major transformation. Whenever you can add in grass and landscaping, do it, especially in metropolitan areas. It creates a higher perceived value.

I purchased a flip on Orlando Avenue in Los Angeles. It had a small backyard with a pool next to the garage. But every other inch was covered in cement. On a warm day you could fry a chicken on that patio. It was an awful sight. I jackhammered most of the cement out for very little money, had it hauled away, and then planted a lawn, again for very little money. But the transformation was amazing!

This Orlando Avenue Lifestyle Upgrade is a perfect example of very little money spent creatively for a huge profit. The makeover cost less than $5,000 but transformed a dreary backyard into an oasis in the heart of the city.

UNDEFINED PROPERTY LINES

Does the house just sit in the middle of the lot? Are there no definite property-line delineations? Are there no fences or hedges separating the house from its neighbors? No sweet white picket fence in the front yard with a lovely morning-glory vine draped lazily across? Great! This plain-Jane house has the potential to be a beauty.

Houses that have exposed backyards are unsettling for most buyers. All you have to do is fence and hedge your backyard to make it feel "safe," a priceless selling point in these times.

CREATING PRIVACY

In metropolitan areas or where the home is close to the street in a busy neighborhood, another value-adding idea is to plant a full-height (six feet) hedge at the front of the property. This also allows you to create security by installing a gate that either locks or has a buzzer system. But make it a wrought-iron gate, so you can see though it, creating a charming sense of mystery. If you hide the front of the house with a solid hedge, you actually lose curb appeal.

Setbacks Create Drama and Interest

Don't build a fence or a wall or install a hedge right at the sidewalk. By leaving three to six feet and planting flowering plants in front, you create a setback that gives you drama, curb appeal, and privacy. Most city ordinances have strict restrictions on the height of walls and fences at the front of the property. Get around it with this technique.

CAPTURING UNUSED YARD SPACE

Once you add a hedge, you create a usable private courtyard that you'll want to access from the house by installing French doors in a front room. Add an outdoor fountain and seating and you'll appear to have more square footage and additional living space for minimal expense. This also creates more light inside the house year round, no matter which way it is facing.

Is It Noisy in Here?

Where is the neighbor's pool equipment or central air-conditioning condenser? Is there traffic noise? With double-paned windows, extra insulation on one side of the house, or added landscaping as noise buffers, these problems can be seen but not heard.

UNDERDEVELOPED EXTERIOR STRUCTURES

Do you see a toolshed or outdoor storage space? Good. I see a separate home office, a play room, an exercise studio, or a greenhouse.

UNREALIZED POTENTIAL FOR ADDITIONAL INCOME

Are there ways you can improve the property to create a cash flow for the potential buyer? These include creating a rental unit in the garage or adding an outside entrance in order to make a mother-in-law unit or a rentable office suite. If the property is in a congested area, is there rentable garage space? Is this a property that could be used as a location for television or movie filming? By playing up these income-producing possibilities, you can get a higher price.

On a very small budget, I maximized the existing structure by splitting the garage to create an outdoor office space. This added enormous value—and a great-looking outdoor destination.

ADDING SQUARE FOOTAGE—EXPAND CAREFULLY

I never add square footage beyond the actual footprint or roofline of the house. It is just too time consuming, and the permitting process, architectural plans, and engineering involved too overwhelming to make it worthwhile. If the house needs work to increase the square footage, it may be a good buy for an owner/user, but not as a flip.

UPGRADING THE NEIGHBORHOOD

You may not think it's valuable to worry about anything beyond your property line. But that is where successful flippers take advantage of a potentially monstrous Lifestyle Upgrade profit: improving the neighborhood.

Every neighborhood could use a little upgrading, and the more you help it along, the more your property value rises. Here's an example. I bought a cute craftsman home on Spaulding Avenue in Hollywood in a neighborhood in transition. The streets were crowded from the businesses using the neighborhood for parking. And while there wasn't a street tree in sight, there was a hooker on every corner. The neighborhood made the news when Hugh Grant was arrested there. My new neighborhood was famous!

However, I saw a lot of potential. It was right in the heart of Hollywood, with wonderful 1920s craftsman homes. During my renovation I got together with other concerned neighbors and formed a homeowners association. The rest is history. Within six months we got resident permit parking for residents and solved the parking issue. We convinced the city to set up a satellite police station on one of the corners, which took care of the hookers. Hugh Grant was never seen again. We got each homeowner to contribute $50 and planted 165 street trees in our eight-block area, and we filed for historical preservation status.

That neighborhood is now one of the hottest in Hollywood, and house prices have increased five times over their pre–neighborhood upgrade value. It was so successful in such a short period of time that I was featured in the *Los Angeles Times* for spearheading the transition.

Upgrading the neighborhood can often add as much profit to your flip as the actual fix-its to the house itself. So get neighborly!

Amid Transience, Historic Homes Endure

■ Architecture: An 8-block neighborhood of 75-year-old dwellings has been granted landmark status by a Los Angeles cultural heritage panel.

By KATHLEEN KELLEHER
SPECIAL TO THE TIMES

In a verdant pocket of Hollywood, just south of Sunset Boulevard, is a slice of "Mayberry R.F.D." Americana.

"This is a neighborhood where everyone comes to walk their dogs, where older people take their constitutionals and where women

walk with their baby strollers," said actor Michael Corbett, who lives in the neighborhood southeast of the intersection of Fairfax Avenue and Sunset Boulevard. "To be in L.A. and to be in a little neighborhood like this is really something."

And despite the ever-changing character of transient Los Angeles neighborhoods, this melange of Colonial, Spanish, Italian and Craftsman architecture now seems certain to remain. After a five-year battle with the labyrinthine city bureaucracy, Corbett and a handful of other residents have gotten the eight-block Hollywood area declared a Los Angeles landmark by the city's Cultural Heritage Commission.

The newly won status, which

became official this spring, means that all 160 single-family homes in the designated spot must maintain their original facades and stay true to the structure's architectural period.

Residents "started talking about [the area] becoming a historical landmark to fight encroachment and because we wanted to preserve one of the few single-family housing residential zoning] neighborhoods left in L.A.," said Corbett, best known for his role as David Kimble on "The Young and The Restless," a soap opera character who fell into an industrial trash compactor a year ago. "Now, no one can come in and tear down a house and build a different structure . . . or plant a hedge without

Please see HOMES, 4

CAREY GROEN / Los Angeles Times
Actor Michael Corbett restored this 1914 Craftsman-style house.

LOS ANGELES TIMES   WS / THURSDAY, JULY 7, 1994 / PAGE 3

INSIDER SECRET

A Permit You Can Live With—Most cities will issue you a general homeowner's improvement permit. This will allow you to do most of your fix-it work with your contractor or directly with the tradesman. It is a much more lenient permit, but you will still be able to present a signed-off permit to a prospective buyer.

The Six Levels of Improvements
Fix-It Levels
  Serious but Fixable Problems
  System Upgrades
  Fix-It Essentials
Profit Levels
  Lifestyle Upgrades
• **Designed-to-Flip Techniques**
• **Dressed-to-Sell Essentials**

DESIGNED-TO-FLIP AND DRESSED-TO-SELL

Lifestyle Upgrades make a huge difference in the world of flipping. They are the finishing touches that transform your house and give you the emotional edge. The two Profit Levels yet to be discussed—Designed-to-Flip Techniques and Dress-to-Sell Essentials—each deserve their own chapter, but you won't get to them until you work through your fix-it budget, have your contractor, and get your job underway. So let's turn to costs and budgets.

Eleven

YOUR FIX-IT HIT LIST: COSTS AND BUDGETS

This chapter covers costs of all the improvements you want to make to the property—the Fix-It Hit List to help organize them, how to get estimates, and how to build them into your ever-evolving budget. It includes charts that describe standard renovations and more. We'll cover:

- Your Fix-It Hit List

- Estimating and getting prices

- Marshall & Swift charts for pricing and estimates

- Creating budgets

YOUR FIX-IT HIT LIST

From the moment you set eyes on the Downright Ugly House, you must assess all the fix-it repairs that need to be done. It can be especially overwhelming for the novice flipper to know what to look for, what to identify, and what to fix, replace, and upgrade.

This is the Fix-It Hit List that you will use as a worksheet to keep track of everything that looks like it needs attention or has potential for improvement. It lists all the possible fix-its on each of the Six Levels of Improvements. It is also the basis for and the backbone of the Contractor's Hit List and, eventually, all three of your budget phases.

THE FIX-IT HIT LIST

Address _____

Description: Style _____

Bedrooms _____ Baths _____ Square Footage _____ Age _____

Garage _____ Attached _____ Detached _____

Item	Good	Repair	Add/Replace
SYSTEMS			
Electrical System			
Panel			
Amperage			
Age of panel			
Plumbing			
Main line			
Sewage line			
Septic tank			
Main line clean-out			
Copper lines			
Hot-water heater			
Heating and Cooling			
Central air			
Forced air			
Heating and air			
Foundation			
Bolting			
Re-supporting			
Cement slab			

Item	Good	Repair	Add/Replace
INTERIOR			
Kitchen			
Plumbing			
Sink			
Faucets			
Garbage disposal			
Soap dispensers			
Countertops			
Cabinets			
Hardware			
Appliances			
Refrigerator			
Oven			
Cooktop			
Dishwasher			
Freezer			
Hood			
Ice-maker			
Microwave			
Trash compactor			
Electrical			
Lighting			
Under-counter lights			
GFIs			
Outlets			
Switches/Dimmers			
Flooring			
Carpet			
Vinyl			
Tile			
Hardwood			
Subfloor			
Windows			
Skylight			

Item	Good	Repair	Add/Replace
Master Bath			
Vanity/Cabinets			
Countertops			
Plumbing			
Sink			
Shower pans			
Shower head			
Bathtub			
Jacuzzi			
Toilet			
Bathtub enclosure			
Shower doors			
Wall tile			
Floor tile			
Repair subfloor			
Accessories			
(towel racks, etc.)			
Medicine cabinet			
Electrical			
GFIs			
Switches/Dimmers			
Light fixtures			
Mirrors			
Windows			
Bathroom 2			
Vanity/Cabinets			
Countertops			
Plumbing			
Sink			
Shower pans			
Shower head			
Bathtub			
Jacuzzi			

Item	Good	Repair	Add/Replace
Toilet			
Bathtub enclosure			
Shower doors			
Wall tile			
Floor tile			
Repair subfloor			
Accessories (towel racks, etc.)			
Medicine cabinet			
Electrical			
GFIs			
Switches/Dimmers			
Light fixtures			
Mirrors			
Windows			
Walls			
Ceilings			
Powder Room			
Sink			
Cabinet/Pedestal			
Toilet			
Electrical			
Lighting			
GFIs			
Accessories			
Tiling			
Flooring			
Living Room, Dining Room, Den, Hallways			
Fireplace mantel			
Electrical			
Lighting fixtures			

Item	Good	Repair	Add/Replace
Recessed lighting			
Outlets			
Dimmers			
Skylights			
Light fixtures			
Crown molding			
Windows			
Flooring			
Hardwood			
Tile			
Carpet			
Master Bedroom			
Flooring			
Hardwood			
Carpet			
Lighting			
Closet organizer			
Bedrooms			
Flooring			
Hardwood			
Carpet			
Lighting			
Closet organizer			
Laundry			
Plumbing			
Sink			
Faucet			
Cabinets			
Countertops			
Washer/Dryer			
Laundry chute			

Item	Good	Repair	Add/Replace
Attic			
Insulation			
Structural reinforcement			
Vents			
Basement			
Sump pump			
Windows			
Moisture issues			
Lighting			
Storage/Shelving			
EXTERIOR			
Exterior General			
Roof			
Gutters			
Chimney			
Aluminum siding			
Stucco walls			
Wood siding			
Windows			
Screens			
Exterior doors			
French			
Sliding			
Glass			
Wood			
Pool			
Spa			
Curb Appeal			
Front door			
Mailbox			

Item	Good	Repair	Add/Replace
House numbers			
Front porch			
Landscape			
Sprinkler system			
Trees			
Shrubs			
Lawn			
Hedging			
Fences			
Site drainage			
Hardscape			
Driveway			
Pathways			
Decks			
Patios			
Stone paving			
Brick paving			
Masonry			
Garage			
Garage doors			
Shelving			
Lifestyle Upgrades			
Security system			
Finishing basement			
Attic conversion			
Exterior gate			
Intercom system			
Wired for speakers			
Additional decking			
More outdoor access			

Item	Good	Repair	Add/Replace
Move walls to open kitchen			
Insulation for soundproofing			
Designed-to-Flip Techniques			
Interior Painting			
Walls			
Ceilings			
Interior doors			
Woodwork			
Exterior Painting			
Walls			
Masonry			
Siding			
Woodwork			
Window treatments			
Outdoor fountains			
Dressed-to-Sell Essentials			
Additional furniture for staging			
Accessories			
Flowers for sale day			

Your Fix-It Hit List Saves You Money

Every time you look at a potential flip house, you will want this Fix-It Hit List with you. Photocopy it ten times and keep the copies handy. Make notes on it every time you look at a flip candidate. It helps you quickly evaluate a property without missing any of the important items. A few fixes could make the difference between profit or not.

FLIP FLOP

He Didn't Keep Track—One novice flipper I knew was so excited about a house that he forgot to include the cost of a new heating and air system in his calculation. It wasn't until he had opened escrow and paid for the inspection that he made the $5,000 discovery. Had he gone through the checklist, he might have realized that the system was faulty, offered $5,000 less for the purchase price, and gotten it, instead of having to fight for the credit back after the inspection.

ESTIMATING AND GATHERING COSTS

You've identified the serious problems that you can solve, the System Upgrades you want to put in place, the Fix-It Essentials you *must* make, and the Lifestyle Upgrades you *can* make that will turn your Downright Ugly House into a beauty. "How much will this all cost?" is the question of the moment. Now you need to attach a dollar value to each and every one of those improvements. Feeling a wee bit overwhelmed? Stop thinking of it as "all" and start by breaking it down into manageable doses using your Fix-It Hit List as your basis for creating your Estimated Fix-It Budget.

GETTING PRICES

Getting prices is not brain surgery. All it requires is detective work, phone calls, and the willingness to make your way up the learning curve. On your first flip, getting estimates before you have made an offer can be tough. Here are the sources that made it easier for me:

Home-Improvement Centers

Big chain stores like the Home Depot and Lowe's are full of materials you will need, fixtures you will install, and ideas you can use. Expect to spend many hours at these places. After your first flip, they'll be giving you a parking place with your name on it. Whatever you're looking for is there in some form or another. You can comparison shop for everything from parquet flooring to ceiling fans, windows to washers. Many stores offer free design services, and all have informed staff that are there to answer your questions. Go. Ask. Write things down. Drive by the house. Go back. Ask more questions.

Weekend Home-Improvement Conventions and Home Shows

Found several times a year at convention centers in most major cities and advertised in the local papers, they are a great source of information in one place. With hundreds of vendors, the latest technologies, and helpful salespeople to answer questions, you can get ideas and learn about new services. You may also see me, since I often speak at seminars at these shows, and I will be happy to answer questions for you personally!

Contractors

The next chapter, "Starting the Work and Getting It Done," is going to review everything you need to know about contractors and tradesmen. But while you are still in the house-hunting stage, it can be tough to get individual attention from a contractor. These busy guys are reluctant to estimate a job if you don't even own the house yet. Try anyway. Let the contractor know you are planning to flip and you may luck out. But take heart: Once you have an accepted offer and are in escrow, and the prospect of work is real, contractors and tradesmen will suddenly appear! And by your second flip, your Dream Team will be in place and your contractor and tradesman will be eager to help you with estimates . . . even before you have made an offer on the house.

Pay a Contractor a Small Consultation Fee

Until you are experienced, once you have seriously identified a great flip candidate you may want to hire a contractor for an hour's consultation. Walk through a potential house and basically pick his brain about costs. Many contractors will be happy to do this, because not only are they getting paid, they are potentially locking in future business with you! Steve Wilder, who I have hired many times to consult, charges an hourly fee of

$200. It is always well worth it. Check him out at www.stevenwilderde-signs.com. Eventually, after you do one or two flips, you will be able to "guesstimate" your preliminary budget on your own with a few calls to your contractor and tradesman. "Hey Steve, how much to replace approx-imately ten rotten windows?" or "I've got an 1,800-square-foot house that needs new hardwood floors. How much?" Ask and you will receive.

Individual Subcontractors and Tradesmen

Unlike contractors, it is often possible to get these guys to the property before it's yours. When trying to put together your Fix-It Estimated Costs Budget, you can try to get some recommended subcontractors on the phone and ask them very specific questions: "Can you give me a ballpark price for replacing sliding-glass doors with three sets of French doors?" or, "I need to put a new roof on a seventy-five-year-old Tudor. What do you suggest and could you give me an estimate, please?" Sub-contractors, like roofers, plumbers, electricians, etc., can be very help-ful. Get multiple answers to each question and you'll begin to get a real picture of what your costs will be.

RENOVATION INDUSTRY COSTING GUIDES

Marshall & Swift is a division of McGraw-Hill. They publish their *Mar-shall & Swift Home Repair & Remodel 2005 Cost Guide,* a phenomenal re-source for a flipper at any level. It helps you estimate costs for fix-it projects, using a national average that is then adjusted based on your zip code for regional differences. I use this book all the time when I am try-ing to come up with my Fix-It Estimated Costs Budget. Of course, it's not quite as customized as a contractor's actual in-person bid, but it is still a fantastic reference point as you make your way through this new terri-tory, especially the first time. And as you become more experienced at flipping and fix-it projects, you will use it all the time to guesstimate cer-tain items on your own. It's also an accurate way to "cross-check" bids for your contactors and tradesmen—a real money saver. You can call the publisher toll-free at 800-526-2756, or go to www.MarshallSwift.com to get it.

MARSHALL & SWIFT COST ESTIMATES

The people at Marshall & Swift were kind enough to give me permission to include some sample charts of estimated fix-it project costs in this book. These projects include everything from bathrooms, electrical, and flooring to kitchens, windows, and more. They are figured by both room size—linear foot or square foot—and components. They break every job into three levels of finish—economy, standard, and custom, and then give every job a cost that is based on the national average.

These first two pages give you a breakdown of overall costs to completely replace either a half bath, full bath, or kitchen. These are amazing ballpark estimates that will really help you work out your Estimated Fix-It Budget.

The charts on pages 207–208 are samples of typical room layouts for both the kitchen and bath, along with a sample of pricing for individual components.

BATHROOMS

ROOM METHOD

Costs include replacing the bathroom completely. (New: fixtures, faucets, floor, ceiling and wall finishes.)

Note: If additional fixtures per room are required, add from the Unit Method.

HALF BATH
(1 toilet, 1 bathroom sink)

Room Size	Quality Levels		
(Square Foot Area)	Economy	Standard	Custom
25 Square Feet	$2,170.00	$3,800.00	$5,820.00
30 Square Feet	2,240.00	3,910.00	6,080.00
35 Square Feet	2,300.00	4,070.00	6,300.00
40 Square Feet	2,350.00	4,200.00	6,500.00
45 Square Feet	2,420.00	4,370.00	6,740.00
50 Square Feet	2,490.00	4,490.00	6,960.00
Over 50 Square Feet	2,540.00	4,650.00	7,230.00

FULL BATH
(1 toilet, 1 bathroom sink, 1 bathtub w/shower)

Room Size	Quality Levels		
(Square Foot Area)	Economy	Standard	Custom
50 Square Feet	$3,680.00	$6,180.00	$ 8,900.00
60 Square Feet	3,800.00	6,460.00	9,380.00
70 Square Feet	3,860.00	6,660.00	9,610.00
80 Square Feet	3,930.00	6,840.00	9,910.00
90 Square Feet	4,020.00	7,000.00	10,140.00
100 Square Feet	4,100.00	7,170.00	10,370.00
Over 100 Square Feet	4,160.00	7,350.00	10,650.00

3

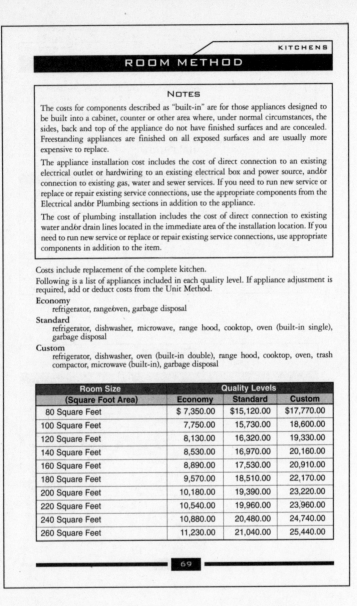

KITCHENS

ROOM METHOD

NOTES

The costs for components described as "built-in" are for those appliances designed to be built into a cabinet, counter or other area where, under normal circumstances, the sides, back and top of the appliance do not have finished surfaces and are concealed. Freestanding appliances are finished on all exposed surfaces and are usually more expensive to replace.

The appliance installation cost includes the cost of direct connection to an existing electrical outlet or hardwiring to an existing electrical box and power source, and/or connection to existing gas, water and sewer services. If you need to run new service or replace or repair existing service connections, use the appropriate components from the Electrical and/or Plumbing sections in addition to the appliance.

The cost of plumbing installation includes the cost of direct connection to existing water and/or drain lines located in the immediate area of the installation location. If you need to run new service or replace or repair existing service connections, use appropriate components in addition to the item.

Costs include replacement of the complete kitchen.
Following is a list of appliances included in each quality level. If appliance adjustment is required, add or deduct costs from the Unit Method.

Economy
    refrigerator, range/oven, garbage disposal

Standard
    refrigerator, dishwasher, microwave, range hood, cooktop, oven (built-in single), garbage disposal

Custom
    refrigerator, dishwasher, oven (built-in double), range hood, cooktop, oven, trash compactor, microwave (built-in), garbage disposal

| Room Size | Quality Levels | | |
(Square Foot Area)	Economy	Standard	Custom
80 Square Feet	$ 7,350.00	$15,120.00	$17,770.00
100 Square Feet	7,750.00	15,730.00	18,600.00
120 Square Feet	8,130.00	16,320.00	19,330.00
140 Square Feet	8,530.00	16,970.00	20,160.00
160 Square Feet	8,890.00	17,530.00	20,910.00
180 Square Feet	9,570.00	18,510.00	22,170.00
200 Square Feet	10,180.00	19,390.00	23,220.00
220 Square Feet	10,540.00	19,960.00	23,960.00
240 Square Feet	10,880.00	20,480.00	24,740.00
260 Square Feet	11,230.00	21,040.00	25,440.00

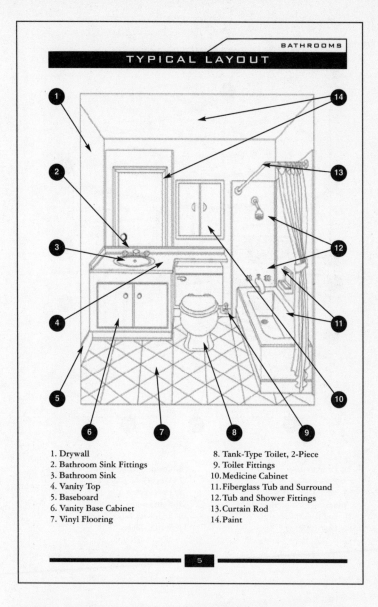

BATHROOMS

TYPICAL LAYOUT

1. Drywall
2. Bathroom Sink Fittings
3. Bathroom Sink
4. Vanity Top
5. Baseboard
6. Vanity Base Cabinet
7. Vinyl Flooring

8. Tank-Type Toilet, 2-Piece
9. Toilet Fittings
10. Medicine Cabinet
11. Fiberglass Tub and Surround
12. Tub and Shower Fittings
13. Curtain Rod
14. Paint

5

Source: Marshall & Swift Home Repair & Remodel 2005 Cost Guide. *Reprinted with permission of Marshall & Swift/Boeckh, LLC, Copyright 2005.*

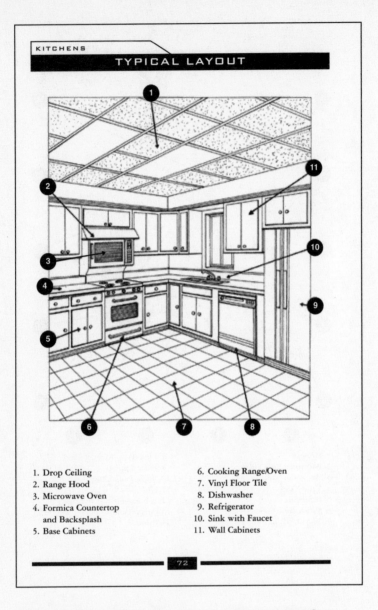

KITCHENS

TYPICAL LAYOUT

1. Drop Ceiling
2. Range Hood
3. Microwave Oven
4. Formica Countertop and Backsplash
5. Base Cabinets

6. Cooking Range/Oven
7. Vinyl Floor Tile
8. Dishwasher
9. Refrigerator
10. Sink with Faucet
11. Wall Cabinets

72

Source: Marshall & Swift Home Repair & Remodel 2005 Cost Guide. *Reprinted with permission of Marshall & Swift/Boeckh, LLC, Copyright 2005.*

BATHROOMS

UNIT METHOD

To replace individual items, use the costs below:

COMPONENT	QUALITY LEVELS		
(Price Each)	Economy	Standard	Custom
Accessories Set (paper and tooth-brush holders, soap dish, etc.)	$ 150.00	$ 205.00	$ 305.00
Bathtub	420.00	730.00	1,285.00
Bathtub Enclosure	305.00	370.00	450.00
Bathtub/Shower Combination	1,015.00	1,125.00	1,255.00
Bidet	540.00	705.00	965.00
Caulking—Bathtub	60.00	65.00	75.00
Faucet	145.00	200.00	295.00
Medicine Cabinet	125.00	170.00	240.00
Mirror	145.00	225.00	355.00
Shower Door	215.00	315.00	390.00
Showerhead	80.00	115.00	120.00
Shower (over the tub)	205.00	300.00	365.00
Shower Rod	28.00	34.00	39.00
Shower Stall	870.00	1,065.00	1,315.00
Sink—Built-in	305.00	370.00	465.00
Sink—Wall mounted	355.00	435.00	560.00
Toilet Seat	60.00	70.00	105.00
Toilet—Floor mounted	505.00	665.00	885.00
Toilet—Wall mounted	730.00	950.00	1,215.00
Vanity—Metal	315.00	370.00	445.00
Vanity—Wood	350.00	410.00	485.00

4

Source: Marshall & Swift Home Repair & Remodel 2005 Cost Guide. *Reprinted with permission of Marshall & Swift/Boeckh, LLC, Copyright 2005.*

Here is a list of some other selected cost items from Marshall & Swift, covering several different categories and Fix-It Levels of Improvements.

SAMPLE FIX-IT COSTS CHART

Electrical

The cost of electrical fixtures (light fixtures, outlets, switches, etc.) includes the cost of direct connection to an existing electrical outlet or hardwiring to an existing electrical box and power source. If you need to run new service or replace or repair existing service connections, use appropriate components in addition to the fixture.

Per individual items:

	Quality Level	
	Economy	**Standard**
Ceiling Fan—w/Light	$380.00	$510.00
Ceiling Fan	$235.00	$320.00
Door Chime	$100.00	$125.00

Heating/Air-Conditioning, Ventilation

To replace individual items, use the costs below:

Package Unit—	
Heating and Air System	$10,610.00
Exhaust Fan—Kitchen/Bathroom	$165.00
Chimney—Metal	$2,305.00
Thermostat—Programmable	$185.00

Windows

To replace individual items, use the per-square-foot costs below. Glazed windows (with insulating glass):

Double-hung—Wood	$34.00	$38.00
Fixed—Aluminum/Vinyl	$23.00	$26.00

Miscellaneous:

Hardware (each)	$47.55	$51.80
Paint, Trim (per linear foot)	$.45	$.50
Paint, Windows	$4.40	$4.55

Interior Doors

Wood Doors:

Closet, Mirror—Complete	$355.00	$410.00
French—Door and Hardware	$325.00	$375.00
Paint Door and Trim—per Side	$55.00	$60.00

Exterior Doors

Costs are for replacement of doors, unless otherwise noted. Complete doors include: door, frame, and hardware.

Garage:

Metal (sectional)—Complete	$675.00	$750.00
Entry Door Hardware—per Door	$80.00	$100.00
Paint, Garage Door—per Side	$80.00	$85.00

Wood Entry Doors:

Standard (stock)—Door and Hardware	$415.00	$550.00
French—Complete	$580.00	$710.00

Floor Finishes

Costs are for completely replacing and refinishing the floor, per room.

Medium Room Size: (81 to 144 square feet)

Carpet—Synthetic	$365.00	$390.00
Carpet—Wool	$770.00	$835.00
Carpet Pad	$80.00	$100.00
Ceramic Tile	$980.00	$1,085.00
Linoleum	$430.00	$555.00
Marble	$2,870.00	$3,625.00
Slate	$1,070.00	$1,390.00
Wood—Hardwood (unfinished)	$835.00	$800.00

Sand and Finish Damaged Floor	$225.00	$245.00
Regrout Tile Floor	$185.00	$205.00

Ceiling Finishes

Costs are for completely replacing and refinishing the ceiling, per room.

Medium Room Size: (81 to 144 square feet)

Paint	$100.00	$120.00
Repair Existing Plaster	$105.00	$145.00

Wall Finishes

Costs are for completely replacing and refinishing the walls, per room.

Medium Room Size: (81 to 144 square feet)

Paint	$300.00	$325.00
Molding—Ceiling	$130.00	$170.00
Paint, Molding	$55.00	$55.00

Exterior Wall Repairs

Costs are for replacement of exterior wall materials, unless otherwise noted. All square-foot costs are based on the area of the exterior wall.

Stone Veneer—Imitation	$9.15	$9.80
Stone Veneer—Natural	$22.40	$26.05
Stucco—On Framing	$4.20	$4.40

Sitework

To replace individual items, use the costs below, per square foot.

Paving/Steps:

Concrete Paving	$4.05	$4.50
Flagstone/Tile	$13.15	$14.90
Steps—Brick (per linear foot)	$36.45	$40.60
Wood Decks	$17.55	$21.95

Fences:

Redwood Fence	$16.00	$18.00
Split Rail (two rails)	$12.00	$13.35
Wrought Iron (per square foot)	$19.05	$23.95

Specialties/Equipment

Fireplace:

Chimney—Masonry (per linear foot)	$85.00	$120.00
Masonry Fireplace	$2,495.00	$3,295.00
Prefabricated Fireplace	$1,120.00	$1,565.00

Figures from *Marshall & Swift Home Repair & Remodel 2005 Cost Guide.*

CREATING THE ALL-IMPORTANT BUDGETS

Your true guide to the flip process is your budget. It will be your bible, the guideline you continually build, amend, develop, and flesh out. It will be your best friend and your worst enemy at the same time. There have been times when I've added and re-added or -subtracted by hand and then on a calculator, hoping the numbers would change. The numbers don't change. And they don't lie, either. But the budget will change, because you will actually create three phases of budgets, all of them based on your Fix-It Hit List.

- Budget One—The Fix-It Estimated Costs Budget

- Budget Two—The Fix-It Working Budget

- Budget Three—The Fix-It Final Budget

BUDGET ONE—THE FIX-IT ESTIMATED COSTS BUDGET

This is the initial Estimated Cost Budget that you will create. Plug the total into your Profit Calculation Chart to determine if a house is a possible flip contender. You need to create this budget to assess a candidate for its profit potential. It is usually 5 to 10 percent actual expenses and 90 percent best-guess estimates.

Using the Fix-It Hit List as your template, add in the estimated costs and you'll have a comprehensive basis for your Estimated Fix-It Costs Budget.

Fix-It Estimated Costs Budget (Budget One)	
Address _____	
Item	**Estimated Costs**
Additional Fix-It Costs	
Demolition	
Trash removal/Dumpster	
Permits/Fees	
Concrete removal	
Cleaning crew	
Systems	
Electrical System	
Panel	
Amperage	
Age of panel	
Plumbing	
Main line	
Sewage line	
Septic tank	
Main line clean-out	
Copper lines	
Hot-water heater	
Heating and Cooling	
Central air	
Forced air	
Heating and air	
Foundation	
Bolting	
Re-supporting	
Cement slab	

BUDGET TWO—THE FIX-IT WORKING BUDGET

Once your offer has been accepted and you are in escrow, you can take a break until you close and then start fixing, right? Wrong. The key to successful flipping is to have the house renovated on paper before you close! What do I mean by that? While you are in escrow, you will have thirty or sixty days to do all of your preplanning and preparations—so when your escrow closes, you can hit the ground running.

Review, Refine, and Add In

To develop Budget Two, you are going to review, refine, and beef up Budget One—The Estimated Fix-It Costs Budget. Take the Budget One worksheets and change your costs to your now more-educated guesstimates. Inspection day is critical to this budget. Not only will you be assessing the actual pros and cons of the property, but by following along with the inspector, you can ask him for ideas, gain insight into the actual scope of each fix-it project, and get some ballpark estimates. After a thorough inspection, you will be surprised at how much you missed from the walk-throughs you did prior to making your offer.

I also always ask my contractor to come on inspection day. If you're doing this without a contractor, then make sure that your subcontractors, such as a plumber or an electrician, can be there. The inspection allows you to add to and refine your Budget One, because you can:

- Get professional guidance from the inspector.

- Have the inspector identify all needed fixes from the first three of the six fix-it phases and maybe even offer some fresh ideas for the Profit Levels of Improvements.

- Get the inspector's unofficial ballpark estimates of costs.

- Have contractors, subcontractors, and tradesmen give you more accurate estimates and great ideas based on access to the property.

FLIP TIP

Budget for Lifestyle Upgrades—Review your proposed Lifestyle Upgrades with your contractor and tradesmen. Make sure they understand your vision and give you an itemized cost estimate for each item so you can add it to your budget.

Incorporating the Contractor's Estimate into Your Budget

You will need to ask your contractor to do a line-item estimate, which shows each individual fix-it project broken down by cost. Set your budget up the same way so you can simply plug his estimates right into your budget. Organize your budget by individual projects and assign each one a dollar value. By knowing what each project costs, you can pick and choose between them or scale down as needed. As the job progresses you will know exactly when you are over or under budget—and you'll stay in control.

FLIP TIP

Budget for the Final Fix-It Phases—Don't forget to add in costs for Designed-to-Flip Techniques and Dressed-to-Sell Essentials. Review those chapters and incorporate a few line items for those added techniques, including a budget line for staging or furnishings, window treatments, and sale-day items such as fresh flowers.

FLIP TIP

Trash It—Many novice flippers forget to add in trash and debris removal to their budgets. Every time a full truck or Dumpster is carried away, you'll pay from $200 to $400. It adds up.

BUDGET THREE—THE FIX-IT FINAL BUDGET

Budget Three is your final budget, the "hard" version of Budget Two. It is Budget Two with two additional columns: "Actual Cost" and "Overage/ Underage." It begins to come together by the time escrow is about to close and you have selected your contractor or tradesman for the job. As you start the actual work, make purchases, and begin to pay for each item, you enter the actual costs in the Actual Cost column. The Overage/ Underage gives you the actual dollar amount this item is over or under what you originally guessed. These two columns give you a running total of exactly how much over or under you are as the job progresses. This is invaluable because it helps you make decisions and stay in control of the project.

Fix-It Final Budget (Budget Three)			
Address _____			
Item	Estimated	Actual	Over/Under
Additional Fix-It Costs			
Demolition	1,700.00	1,900.00	+200.00
Trash removal/Dumpster	750.00	500.00	−250.00
Permits/Fees	150.00	225.00	+75.00
Concrete removal	450.00	300.00	−150.00
Cleaning crew	225.00	300.00	+75.00
Systems			
Electrical System			
Panel	1750.00	1,500.00	−250.00
Amperage			
Age of panel			
Plumbing			
Main line			
Sewage line			
Septic tank			

Systems			
Main line clean-out			
Copper lines			
Hot-water heater			
Heating and Cooling			
Central air			
Forced air			
Heating and air			
Foundation			
Bolting			
Re-supporting			
Cement slab			

FLIP TIP

Stay Current—Update this budget at least twice a week! I cannot emphasize how important this is. New costs come up, and you'll make slight last-minute changes. Take advantage of this budget, because you can stay profitable by eliminating nonessential items or tighten up the overall fix-it costs as the job progresses.

FLIP TIP

Repeat Your Business—As you begin your second flip, return to the suppliers you used for landscape, appliances, windows, doors, and flooring. Tell them that since you are working on another house and will be doing more soon as well, you would like to set up a tradesman or contractor discount. I sometimes even say I am looking at materials for "my client" for another "job" I am working on. "What is my trade price?" is often a good way to ask for a tradesman discount. It also allows you exclusive entry into wholesale nurseries and material suppliers. Just be polite and befriend the salespeople. They love repeat business and will be happy to work with you.

FLIP TIP

Free Money—Before you replace any appliances or other gas and electric components in your house, check with your utility companies for rebates. Many cities will give you big rebates and incentives to replace old or outdated appliances and components. You can receive money back from the electric company if you buy a new energy-efficient refrigerator. Certain brands will even give you a coupon for money off or a credit toward your electric bill. And they will offer to haul away your old one, saving you money there as well. Trust me; it is worth a few phone calls. On my Charl Place house, I received a $300 rebate on my pool pump, $100 on my new water heater, $50 each on the washer and dryer, and a $75 credit on my electric bill for the new refrigerator—a $575 savings on items I was going to replace anyway!

Twelve

STARTING THE WORK AND GETTING IT DONE

You've gotten prices and you've got a budget. You're ready to do the work on the property. But who is going to do it, how long will it take, and who is in charge? This chapter will cover it all, from starting the project, to managing it, and to finishing it. You'll learn how to:

- Assign the fix-it projects
- Hire the contractor or tradesman
- Get your contracts in order
- Schedule the work
- Manage the project
- Get the job done

PICK UP THE HAMMER OR PICK UP THE PHONE

First you have to decide whether you are going to do the work yourself or hire professionals, or some combination of the two. Here are some options:

- General contractor
- Subcontractors
- Individual tradesman or handyman
- Do it all yourself

GENERAL CONTRACTORS

General contractors are licensed, insured (liability and workers comp), and bonded professionals who manage every aspect of the work from start to finish. They are well qualified to review and refine your plans and ideas. They provide the crew, show you material samples, order building permits, supervise all work and its quality, and pay the subcontractors. In most cases, they bill their contractor fees via one of two methods: they build their fees into each item on your fix-it list, or they charge a percentage of the total cost of the job.

SUBCONTRACTORS

These are professionals in specialized fields. They are roofers, tile men, plumbers, electricians, landscapers, painters, carpenters, garage-door installers. Acting as a company or an individual, they are usually licensed, bonded, and insured, and they can often warranty their work. Subcontractors report to the general contractor and will bill him. If you are running the job, they work directly under your care and supervision. If so, use licensed, bonded, and insured companies. Make sure they provide you with all of the proper permits as well. Their bills will come to you for individual payment.

INDIVIDUAL TRADESMAN OR HANDYMAN

Yes, you can save a lot of money by hiring an individual tradesman or a handyman. But there are numerous disadvantages. Tradesmen may be highly skilled or specialized in a specific area, like tile, plumbing, floor refinishing, or electrical. They get most of their work by working under a contractor or a subcontractor. That way, they don't need to be licensed, bonded, or insured, because they work under the contractor's license and insurance. The same holds true for a handyman, who is similar to a tradesman but who has no specific area of expertise. Beware. With either individual, the bottom line is that *you* are responsible. And since they usually cannot warranty their work and are not licensed, you will have to file for your own homeowners permit to get work signed off by the city.

Do the Work Yourself

Forget it! Would you seriously hire YOU to do the work? Sure there are some fix-it projects you can do, but are you getting the feeling that in my humble opinion, you should let the pros do what they do best? You will pay dearly if you try to overstep your area of expertise. Besides, you are going to be too busy overseeing the entire project and becoming the project coordinator to be doing the big jobs yourself.

What the Pros Have That You Don't

I have found that people who gravitate to flipping are creative, like to be hands-on, and prefer to be their own boss. They know how to take initiative and love working under their own steam. There *are* projects that you can do yourself, but most require a level of expertise that you probably don't possess.

I actually enjoy doing the work and am fairly handy with a hammer. But I always use a contractor. First of all, I don't have the time, and secondly, I know my limitations. I learned early to rely on the proven expertise of successful professionals, and I strongly suggest you do the same. Here's what a contractor has that you don't:

- Expertise

- The right tools

- Experience in managing the process

- Knowledge of building codes

- Authority to pull permits

- Time

There are some jobs you will be tempted to do yourself. Here's how to decide. If you can answer all of these questions with a yes, then the job is one you can do yourself:

1. Is it a job that you *do not* need to have permitted?

2. Would your workmanship pass a building inspector's approval?

3. Do you know how to do the project according to building code?

4. Have you done it before?

5. Do you have the proper tools to finish the job?

6. Do you have the time to do it quickly and right?

7. Would YOU hire you to do it?

If you answered "no" to any of these questions, then you are not the man, or woman, for the job! Step away from the skill saw and call a professional immediately.

Quality of Workmanship Versus Saving Money

Of course, it would seem to make sense that if you do the work yourself, you will save money. Hey, I thought that in the beginning too, since I can actually do many fix-it projects with decent results. But when you are flipping a property for profit, you are creating a product for purchase in the marketplace. The buyer expects a certain quality level in workmanship and conformance to the legal standards and codes of the industry. As long as all the work you do has been approved by a licensed contractor or tradesman, you will be able to provide this.

A contractor will cost you 20 to 50 percent more than a handyman because they build overhead and project management into the cost. You pay more, but you don't have to deal with insurance or permits. If you choose to do some of the work yourself, you will save money in the short run. But if you ever have to refix your fix-it project to make it right, you are wasting both your cash and your time. So choose wisely.

Do You Have the Tools to Do the Job Right?

My dad built much of the house I grew up in. He always used to say, "You can do any job if you have the right tools." Well, I don't have a mitered tile-cutting skill saw or the latest coring drill bits all ready to go out in the garage—and I'll bet you don't either. By hiring a professional, not only do you get the labor and expertise, you get a pro with the tools to do the job right!

FLIP FLOP

Hardwood the Hard Way—There was a time when I believed that I could refinish the hardwood floors all by myself. Guess what? I was wrong. Imagine an episode right out of *I Love Lucy* . . . there I was trying to control a humongous and seemingly possessed industrial floor sander as it sanded wildly in every direction, dragging yours truly behind. I watched it carve out trenches in the sixty-year-old oak floorboards, my horror growing. I ruined the living-room floors, had to buy a big carpet to help minimize my new "distressed" look, and, of course, had to disclose the damage to potential buyers. That one day of "Oh, I can do it!" cost me dearly, but it also taught me a lesson.

Projects You Can Do

Go ahead and slap on the tool belt and do these projects:

- Demolition
- Cleanup
- Landscaping
- Spot painting
- Wallpaper removal
- Change out switch faceplates
- Replace door hardware

PROJECTS YOU SHOULD NOT DO

I always recommend a licensed contractor or subcontractor for the following:

- Plumbing
- Electrical
- Heating and air
- Asbestos removal
- Roofing
- Replacing new doors and windows
- Tile work
- Refinishing hardwood flooring
- Cabinet replacement or refinishing
- Countertop installation

A Contractor Has the Time—You Don't

Another thing to take into consideration is your timeline. Is it cost-effective for you to spend your time with a hammer in your hand?

If you have chosen the slow and steady path, which means you will be in possession of the property for two years, then yes, there should be more projects that you can take on yourself, except sanding floors . . . *Looocy!* I love having my weekend projects laid out for months and watching my "two-year" home project become a dream home over time. But even in that scenario, I still leave anything that needs a permit or professional craftsmanship to the experts. But if you are on the flipping fast track, just forget about doing it yourself. You are simply too slow for this steamroller process!

The Contractor Combo Team

Now that I have flipped so many houses, I find that I like to work with a combination of a contractor, some subcontractors, and a few tradesmen thrown in for good measure. The contractor handles multilayered fix-it jobs such as kitchens and baths. I hire the subcontractors myself for specific jobs such as roofing or heating and air, and call a tradesman to install a door or window, or handle small carpentry projects. But until you have gone through a few flips, please use a contractor. Yes, it will cost as much as 20 to 30 percent more than doing it yourself. But it will be well worth it to do it right and quickly. Plus, you'll get an invaluable education: You'll get to watch a pro in action and see how he hires, manages, and maintains quality.

FINDING THE PERFECT CONTRACTOR

Go straight to your Dream Team for referrals. In fact, if *your* Realtor has flipping experience, I would be surprised if he didn't suggest a great contractor or handyman. And of course, ask your friends who have rehabbed or flipped houses for references.

Pick Three and Choose One

Ultimately, you will want to interview at least three contractors and get three bids. But first, call the prospects. If you don't hear back within forty-eight hours, forget them. You want someone who is responsive. If they don't return a call promptly now, you can pretty much assume they'll behave the same way when you're in mid-demolition. Not a pretty picture. Set up interviews. If one doesn't show, again, forget him. Contractors and handymen are notoriously overbooked. If they can't make the interview, they are too busy to be on your Dream Team.

SIX QUESTIONS TO ASK EACH CONTRACTOR

1. **What are his specialties?** Residential rehab, commercial buildings, new construction?

2. **How big is his staff or his house crew?** How many men work for him full-time? Does he run an entire company or is he an individual contractor?

3. **Which jobs does he "sub out"?** Does he hire a subcontractor for the plumbing or electrical? Which jobs does he do with his "in-house" crew? It's good to know which are which. If he is subbing out for all the big jobs, you may want to negotiate to be able to hire some subcontractors yourself to save on his commission.

4. **How many jobs does he have going at the moment?** This is very important. Especially if his company is small, you want to make sure he is doing no more than four jobs at any given time.

5. **Ask for references.** This is harder than it seems. People are always a little funny about actually asking for references. I know I am. I always feel as if I am insulting the potential contractor. Well, I learned to get over that insecurity. And you can, too. If a contractor stalls with getting references, move on.

6. **Ask to look at examples of his work.** In this day and age, a contractor worth his salt will have before-and-after digital photos of his best jobs.

NINE FLIP TIPS FOR SELECTING THE RIGHT CONTRACTOR

1. While you can certainly hire a high-end pro, on your first flip, the mega-companies and most expensive firms are not for you. Look for someone who is creative and productive—and small enough to make a bigger deal of your project.

2. Look for contractors who are geographically desirable, i.e., close to your job site.

3. Look for pros who specialize in creative rehabs.

4. Interview only contractors who have been in business at least five years—under one name. (If Joe's Contracting Service had problems, Joe may surface a year later as "Joe's AAA Contracting Service.")

5. Go to a current job. A prospect should be proud to show off his work in progress.

6. Ask for both the general liability and workman's comp certificates from each prospective contractor. Then call the insurance company to make sure the coverage is current.

7. Ask for the names of suppliers he works with and check him out.

8. Go to the city building department and see if there are any complaints against him.

9. Pay attention to how timely, responsive, and businesslike he is in his dealings with you. How he is *now* is how he will be *later*.

GETTING THE BIDS

There is a science to getting your contractor bids. It starts with getting your ideas across clearly to a contractor or subcontractor and involves detailed communication about numerous topics. Be clear about what you want, or you won't want what you get. I often use pictures from magazines or books to illustrate what I want the finished product to look like. That way, we both have a "picture" (literally) of what I have in mind.

PREPARE A FIX-IT HIT LIST FOR YOUR CONTRACTOR

Before your meetings with each of the three contractors, prepare a complete and detailed Fix-It Hit List, make copies and bring them with you. Not only does this keep you organized and efficient, it also shows the contractor right from the beginning that you mean business, you're organized and effective, and that you expect the same from him. It also guarantees that each contractor is bidding on the same work to be done. As you walk through the house, you can both make notes. The contractor will spend more time analyzing and less time writing. And you'll have something to check his estimate against when you're reviewing his bid.

FLIP TIP

Listen for His Suggestions and Write Them Down—If he's a pro, he'll have cost-cutting approaches that achieve the look you want for less. It's important to work with a contractor who is creative and initiates ideas.

Getting Access to the House

To get the bids, you have to have access to the house. As we have discussed, inspection day is the perfect time. Have your Realtor contact the seller and ask permission to bring in your contractor. Explain that you want to get a jump-start on the renovation projects you will do after closing. Even though this is an imposition to the seller, they will be glad to hear you are investing your time and energy in the property—an indication that you are enthusiastic about seeing the sale completed.

FLIP TIP

Keep Your Plans to Yourself—*Never* ever discuss your proposed Fix-It Projects in front of the sellers. They probably love the lime-green shag carpet in the bedroom. After all, they put it there.

THE EIGHT MUST-HAVES IN A CONTRACTOR'S BID

1. **A Line-Item Bid of Costs**—Have all your contractors give you line-item bids. They list each fix-it project broken down item by item. This allows you more flexibility to negotiate certain items.

For example, if the new granite countertops and the kitchen installation seem reasonable, but the cost of the living room sliders seems high, you can ask, "Can you do better on that item?" It also allows you to manage your budget because you know item by item where you can spend more and where you need to spend less or eliminate.

2. **Material and Labor Breakdown**—Separate each item by cost of material and labor. For example, to install a Jacuzzi you want to see this kind of detail:

Master Bath Jacuzzi Materials:	$600 Jacuzzi tub
	$210 misc. (electrical box, pipes, fittings)
Labor:	$350
Total:	$1,160

3. **Materials Detail**—Have the contractor list all details related to materials, including quality, size, brand name, color, quantity, and need to special order.

4. **Any Exclusions**—You want to account for any and all items not included in the project price. For example, "New French doors for patio—complete installation *not* to include cost of materials and labor for handles and hardware."

5. **Statement of Insurance and Bonding**—Get written assurance that both the contractor and all subcontractors are licensed, bonded, and insured properly.

INSIDER SECRET

Get Named—Edward Bercow of Bercow Construction Company advises that you ask to be named as an additional insured party on his policy for the length of the job. It doesn't cost the contractor anything to do this, and you would thus be notified if his insurance lapses during the job.

---

6. **Debris Removal**—Get a guarantee that all debris will be removed from the job site and that the cost of such removal is included in the estimate.

7. **Completion Time Frame**—Have the contractor give you a projected completion date and timeline.

8. **Contractor Payment**—Get a payment schedule breakdown, including how much to start the job, when payments are due, etc. You also want to know how he bases his fee—in writing. Is it built into each individual item, or is he charging a commission on the cost of the entire project?

INSIDER SECRET

Don't Pay Twice—Edward Bercow explains that most contractors get paid via one of two methods. Either they build their fees into each item on your Fix-It Hit List, or they charge you a percentage of the total cost of the job. However, Ed warns that some contractors may try to do both. They may pad the cost of the item, and then *also* charge you a percentage of it. The way to prevent that is by getting three estimates and comparing items line by line.

FLIP TIP

Paying on Labor Only—Try negotiating to pay your contractor's percentage only on labor, not on materials. This will save you considerably. Why pay an extra 15 to 17 percent on expensive items such as appliances and carpeting?

FLIP TIP

Ask About the Day-to-Day Work Schedule—What time will workers begin in the morning? What time will they quit? What days of the week will they work? Which holidays do they expect to be off? Is he dedicated to this job or is the contractor fitting you into a list of other clients? If he seems overwhelmed, walk.

INSIDER SECRET

Ask the $65,000 Question—*After* the estimate has been presented, ask the single question that will save you thousands of dollars later: **"Does the price quoted for each of the projects listed include all materials and labor necessary to complete each project?"** Go line by line, then write in at the bottom of the contract: "The prices quoted for each of the items include the cost of all material and labor necessary to satisfactorily complete each item."

By addressing this right up front the contractor is aware that you are not going to accept any hidden costs, and he will be that much less likely to try to add them in.

FLIP FLOP

Learning from My Mistake—The contractor on my Bogart house had given me an estimate of $18,000 to supply and completely install 24" × 24" travertine stone floor tiles. This item had been a line item in the estimate and I had agreed to it. Once the job was finished, the contractor came back to me and asked if I wanted the tile sealed—for an additional $2,000! Now, in my book, sealing the tile floor is part of the job. But because it was not specifically listed in the estimate and I did not include the "total cost necessary to complete the project," he had me. And we both knew it. To keep the job moving forward, reluctantly, I acquiesced. I was not happy. But I was wiser.

CONTRACTOR CONTRACTS

You have hashed out the bid and discussed the contractor's prices and fees. Now you need to draft a contract with your contractor. Always do. It protects both you and him. Most established contractors have their own standard contract.

If there is something you don't understand, ask. You are at the bottom of a very steep learning curve. If you don't feel like you can ask this guy questions, he's the wrong guy for you. In addition to the Eight Must-Haves in a contractor's bid, this is a list of provisions you need in the contract to be protected:

- A description of the project, also called the scope of the work

- All permits, zoning, and regulations are the contractor's responsibility

- Change order procedures—There will be changes, and lots of them. This means that any project you add or take away has to be approved by both of you—in writing.

- Equipment warranties—This covers appliances and equipment he installs.

- Actual start and projected finish dates

COMPLETION DATES

You have to have a schedule and a consequence if it's not adhered to. Include a penalty for missing the completion date, say $75 a day. I also like to give a thirty-day grace period before any penalty starts.

You also have to know and accept that this is such a tricky area. Jobs are NEVER completed on time—for a variety of reasons. Sometimes it's the weather, delays in arrival of materials, additions and changes that you will ask to make, or slow subcontractors. Know that the job is going to take longer than expected and go easy with the completion date–penalty thing.

Payment Schedules

Always try to put down as little as possible. Upon signing a contract you will usually be asked to deposit 10 percent of the cost of the entire job, or $1,000.00—whichever is less. This just allows you to lock in a start date.

Once you get close to the beginning of the job, you have to really start forking over the cash. I always ask how much materials will cost to get started and then offer to pay 50 percent of that amount up front. That way the money is earmarked for materials. You will also have to make a payment toward labor. I like to pay that on the first day of work.

If there is no payment schedule in the contractor's standard contract, put it in yourself. Use the following payment suggestions as a guideline. And always ask for a targeted completion date with a penalty of 1 percent deduction of total price per week if the job is not satisfactorily completed on time.

Payment Schedule Breakdown

1. Fifty percent deposit on materials necessary to start the job upon signing of contract. These are materials the contractor will need to preorder or have ready to go when the job begins.

2. Ten percent of the *remaining* costs to be paid on the first day of actual work.

3. Three or four additional payments tied to performance—usually at the start of projects—such as:

   - Demolition

   - Framing

   - Electrical/Plumbing

   - Drywall

   - Cabinet installations

   - Flooring

   - Countertops

- Appliances/Electrical fixtures

- Painting

- Finish details

4. Hold back 10 percent until the final walk-through, completion of all details, and presentation of all the signed-off permits.

FLIP TIP

Keep the Cash—Pay with a check, never cash. That gives you a record in writing, literally, should there be a problem. If you must pay in cash, get a signed receipt with a full description of the work performed.

CHANGE ORDERS

Change is part of the process. You pick one kind of countertop, but it's back-ordered, so you choose another and it's more expensive. It's also a different depth, so you have to choose a less expensive tile. Change orders manage the inevitable and keep everyone on the same page. It is critical to stay current by adding them to the running budget as they occur.

FLIP TIP

Put Your Problems in Writing—If there is a problem that the contractor is not dealing with, get it in writing to him ASAP. Communicate your concerns; propose a reasonable timetable and either deliver the letter in person or via certified mail and request a return receipt. It gives them a chance to fix it and you a legal leg to stand on if they don't.

SUBCONTRACTORS

When working with specialized subcontractors—if you do not go the contractor route—you should have a detailed contract with each of them. Include the scope of the job and all the specifics. Include a timeline and the quality, color, and quantity of materials.

Hiring Tradesmen and Handymen

Hiring tradesmen can be tricky. Most of the specialized tradesmen that work independently and not for contractors are hard to nail down. They sometimes take on too many jobs at once. They have been known to take on new jobs to get those initial deposits and leave many of their other clients waiting for them to return.

Once again, a tradesman or handyman can save you money on small jobs. But if you are a flipping novice, ignorance can cost you money. Get referrals, get references, and check him out. Ask his hourly rate, but get bids on a per-job basis. Tradesmen and handymen generally don't have insurance, so make sure your insurance covers them. And draft a written agreement.

INFORMATION YOU NEED WHEN HIRING TRADESMEN

- Full contact information, including their job license if they have one

- References

- Complete written estimates—include all materials, their quality, color, and quantity

- Completion date in writing

TIPS FOR WORKING WITH TRADESMEN

- Pay up front only the cost of the initial materials needed to get the job started

- Pay 25 percent of the labor cost upon the actual start of the job

- Hold back at least 10 percent of the entire job until everything is totally completed

Now, in defense of tradesmen, they hate letting you hold back funds, because they are often cheated out of their money by homeowners who use any excuse or minor flaw in the job to get out of paying the final installment. Reassure them that a job well done will be paid in full.

This is exactly the way the tradesman left the fireplace. In fact, if you look closely you will even see the sledgehammer he left behind to the left of the semi-demolished fireplace. But after hiring a professional subcontractor to finish the job, I was very pleased with the final outcome.

FLIP FLOP

Here Today, Gone Tomorrow—In my Spaulding house, the fireplace in the living room needed the old brick facing knocked down and removed and a new, sleeker cement facade put on. I wanted a marble mantel and matching marble stoop. Not a huge job, but an integral part of my renovation that had to be done first.

I got the cell-phone number of a cement/brick tradesman. He came over, looked at the job and said, "No problem." He gave me a $2,500 written estimate and asked for $1,200 up front and immediately began the demo work. After an hour he left to get materials and promised to return in the morning. I was very impressed. No need to go though all the silly references, I thought, and gave him $1,200 in cash. The next morning, I waited for him, staring at the P.O. box address on his estimate, standing all alone next to a half-demolished fireplace, and repeatedly calling a cell phone that never answered. Lesson learned.

Don't Forget About Permits

To permit or not to permit, that is the question. Here is the answer: Spend the money, get the permits. Put it in the budget. It is important to have all your improvements be up to code and have a permit. You are going to be selling this house and you don't want to be liable for inferior workmanship that is not up to code. And you don't want to have to get a permit after the work is done, because then you may have to pay fines, too.

CONGRATULATIONS: YOU ARE NOW THE PROJECT MANAGER

Whether you hire a general contractor, individual tradesman, a handyman, or decide to do it yourself, YOU are now going to be the project manager! It really is the most important job of the project. Hand in hand with the contractor, you will be in charge of the two most crucial elements of this process: keeping the job *on time* and *on budget*.

I know you're saying, "But I just hired a contractor and I'm paying him to be in charge. Can't he just call me when the job is finished!?" The single biggest mistake a novice flipper or a homeowner doing renovations can make is to *not* take control of these duties. No matter who you have hired, you must take an active part and be in control of all of the details. This includes overseeing scheduling, budgets, and the quality of workmanship. Be prepared to be your own on-site project coordinator. To maximize productivity and profit, know from the beginning that you are going to be at that house all of your spare time, so clear your schedule! As the "big picture" person on the project, you're the one with the vision—which makes you the one to answer all those last-minute, job-halting questions. You need to be reachable to make changes on the spot when the unexpected arises. Otherwise, you'll pay for the cost of a day's work stoppage while the crew waits for you to approve the location change of a new light fixture.

Conducting Your Flip Orchestra

Project-managing the fix-it phase is like conducting an orchestra. From scheduling, to approving bids, to scrutinizing the workmanship, to juggling the budget, you must oversee this entire exercise in organized chaos in order to make it harmonious. One series of notes played out of order or at the wrong tempo will be somewhat less than music to your ears. But when you stay in control, and all your musicians play from the same score, it is a gorgeous thing indeed.

SCHEDULING IS IMPERATIVE!

During a renovation, numerous projects need to be performed in a certain sequence. Materials like tile, granite, new cabinets, and built-in appliances all need to be ordered early. Certain fix-it projects take longer than others, and some must be completed before others can proceed. You can't begin to retile the bathroom until the NEW plumbing is done. And never re-plumb until the plumbing fixtures have arrived and are sitting in your garage. Trust me; the new pipes will never be in exactly the right place unless you have physically lined them up with the fixtures. Learn to be a "schedule manager."

FLIP TIP

Don't Decide as You Go—A surefire road to fix-it disaster is to take the "I'll decide as I go" approach. This is no time to improvise. Yes, you'll have to be creative and adaptable as things come up, but first, you have to have a plan to stick to!

The Calendar Tool

Creating a timeline and calendar will be a joint effort between you, your contractor, and your subcontractors. Buy an eight-by-ten month-a-page calendar. Enter in all the jobs and how long each will take—no matter who is doing the work. Overlap them where you can and stagger them where you need to. It will keep the job on schedule and keep you sane! Oh yeah, write everything in pencil . . . it will change a lot!

February

Mon	Tues	Wed	Thurs	Fri	Sat / Sun
		1 CLOSE ESCROW!	2	3 MATERIALS ARRIVE ⟶ START ⟶ DEMO	4 / 5 ⟶
6 DEMO ⟶ TRASH REMOVAL DAY!	7 START ⟶ RE-PLUMBING	8 START ELECTRICAL ⟶ PANEL	9 ROOF ⟶	10	11 / 12 FINISH ⟶ RE-PLUMBING
13 FINISH ⟶ ELECTRICAL PANEL ⟵ ROOF ⟶	14 DOORS/ WINDOWS ARRIVE!	15 INSTALL DOORS/ WINDOWS	16	17 RE-TILING ⟶ BATH	18 / 19
20 FINISH ⟶ DOORS/ WINDOWS INSTALLATION	21	22 KITCHEN CABINETS ARRIVE/INSTALL FINISH ⟶ RE-TILING BATH	23	24	25 / 26
27 FINISH ⟶ KIT. CABINETS INSTALLATION	28 KITCHEN ⟶ TILING COUNTERTOPS START ⟶ OUTDOOR DECK				

This flip calendar shows projected start and end times of fix-it projects, as well as arrival dates of materials. It gives you a clear view of how overlapping projects can and will impact one another.

FIVE SCHEDULING TIPS THAT KEEP THE JOB MOVING SMOOTHLY

1. **Plan ahead.** Have your calendar set with all project start and completion target dates.

2. **Order materials ahead.** You know you are going to need five new French doors. It may take weeks to get them. Order them now.

3. **Confirm your delivery dates.** Don't wait until the day the materials are scheduled to arrive to check on them. You or your contractor must call three days ahead to check on delivery status. The sight of your workers sitting around waiting for materials that never come is a very expensive tableau.

4. **Keep in sequence**—Don't make the plumber wait for a tile man to finish his job. That plumber will drop you to the bottom of his priority list if he loses a day of work because the job is not ready for him.

5. **Only use in-stock materials**—Yeah, it's great to have custom or special-order items. But buying materials that are in stock won't leave your whole job hanging, unlike running out of a special-order tile and waiting for three weeks to get more.

FLIP TIP

Create the Buffer Zone—Here is a lesson I rarely remember, but maybe YOU will! Never schedule the contractor, material deliveries, and other tradesman to start on the day after escrow is set to close. That sounds like prudent scheduling, you say. Get everyone lined up and ready to go. The problem is that escrows NEVER close on time. And you will always be left with workers who are angry about losing several days of work, and a truckload of window, lumber, or appliances with nowhere to go. It is a costly nightmare and a bad way to start a job! For some reason I am always optimistic that the closing will happen on time, and I make this mistake over and over again! In this case, do as I say and not as I do! Give yourself a few days' buffer for the Big Fix to begin!

Part Three

FLIP IT!

Thirteen

DESIGNED TO FLIP

The Six Levels of Improvements
Fix-It Levels
    Serious but Fixable Problems
    System Upgrades
    Fix-It Essentials
Profit Levels
    Lifestyle Upgrades
    Designed-to-Flip Techniques
    Dressed-to-Sell Essentials

With weekly entrée to the multimillion-dollar homes of the incredibly famous and the fabulously wealthy, I have had a firsthand look at the work of today's masters of decorating and design. But it was through finding, fixing, and flipping homes that I learned how to make the choices that appeal to the broad universe of potential buyers. I've learned how to create a great look that is practical and, best of all, attainable.

From Malibu to Monte Carlo, with Dayna Devon, my cohost from
Extra's Mansions & Millionaires, I have traveled coast to coast
shooting the show at spectacular locations, all of which inspire me
with great new design ideas for my flip homes.

As host of *Extra* and *Extra's Mansions & Millionaires*, and through my work on other home shows, I have interviewed hundreds of wealthy and famous people. I have talked with them in the beautiful homes they are renovating, decorating, and putting up for sale. I have strolled through Jerry Seinfeld's Hollywood Hills home while it was on the market, spent the day with home style guru Kathy Ireland at her lovely Montecito estate, and spent an afternoon at Richard Gere's former Hollywood bachelor pad. I wandered around the home of Mary-Kate and Ashley Olsen. I interviewed the flipper who had just flipped Will Smith's country-style ranch and strolled the grounds of the golf green Will had built on the property. And recently, I was able to spend the day at Larry King's gorgeous Utah riverfront estate, where I got the full tour of all the fabulous new design additions he and his wife Shawna have made.

Kathy Ireland has incorporated so many of her home concepts and products into her beautiful Montecito home. She gave me a lot of design ideas that balance comfort, design, and practicality, all at the same time.

What was that clanking noise? Oh, that was just me name-dropping. Sorry about that, but it is my job, after all. And I was trying to make a point: Because of my good fortune to visit these homes and to interview great designers, I have been able to learn from the best and use these Designed-to-Flip techniques to great advantage in all my flips. Now you can, too.

Use these techniques to make your home stand out from the crowd, to create excitement, and to get a potential buyer's heart pounding. And once you have tackled the first four Fix-It Levels, it's time to fine tune. Put on your designer's hat, or at least try it on. These design tips and techniques add value, increase the aesthetic appeal, create an emotional response from your potential buyers, and win you the big profits.

Talk about curb appeal! Designer Brian Little created dramatic curb appeal from scratch on this Beverly Hills mansion. Even though he had a massive budget, the idea is the same at every level: create a dramatic and eye-catching look while staying consistent with the style of the house.

STEAL THIS LOOK

I am not a designer, nor do I want to be. So what's my greatest design secret? Find a design idea you like and steal it! I give you permission to blatantly steal and copy from TV shows, magazines, open houses, and your best friend's house. Yes, that's right, go around the neighborhood. Use what works in each and every home that catches your eye—from curb-appeal concepts to a fantastic sink in the powder room. Go to open houses in the neighborhood and look for good ideas you can use. There is nothing wrong with following a tried-and-true trend or a classic style. It's much faster and easier than trying to be different for the sake of being unique. Don't waste time trying to reinvent the wheel, just use the best of the best.

THREE DESIGNED-TO-FLIP KEY PRINCIPLES

- Don't personalize
- Stay consistent
- Keep it neutral

Don't Personalize Your Design Scheme—Keep It Simple

Celebrated designer Brian Little insists that when designing a house for a quick flip, you need to appeal to the broadest spectrum of tastes. Don't personalize. You want to walk that fine line of appealing to all tastes without alienating anyone.

You may adore purple, but most people don't want it on their walls. You may LOVE a cute gingerbread-style kitchen loaded with cookbooks and ceramic roosters, but not everyone can see past all that clucking clutter. So simplify. You want your flip house to have a beautiful, designed look, yet not be so style-specific that a potential buyer can't see himself and his own style in the house as well.

Buying a house is not an intellectual process for most buyers—it is an emotional one. Make choices that will help to elicit the "oohs" and "ahhhs" and emotional responses from buyers. Make ones that are aesthetically pleasing yet not so over the top or style-specific that they polarize or alienate potential buyers.

But My House Is Just the Way I Like It

But you say, "I've lived here for two years and I *love* the grapevine–and–harvest basket wall borders that I put all around the kitchen and breakfast room. It's so homey!" OK, you're in trouble! When all those buyers with no imagination come traipsing through your house on sale day and walk out with a subconscious desire to buy plums—but NOT your house—then maybe you'll take this advice. Unfortunately, by then your homey personal preference has just cost you a lot of tomatoes.

Consistency Counts

Think of your entire house as one whole project, one that works and flows together. Please don't think you can select a different design style for each room. I hate when people do that. It's just plain unsettling to the eye, not to mention completely impractical.

THREE REASONS TO STAY CONSISTENT THROUGHOUT THE HOUSE

1. **Create a Design Flow**—Give the house a sense of order, a well–thought out design and attention to detail that buyers will "feel" and love.

2. **It's Easier!**—Using the same materials throughout means fewer design decisions. You never have to worry about which colors and shades will work better in which rooms, because if you are consistent, they will all coordinate.

3. **It Saves Time and Money**—Not only will you be able to get a better price per unit when you buy larger quantities, but if you have leftovers you can use them in other rooms.

MAKE THE MATERIALS THAT MATTER MATCH THROUGHOUT THE HOUSE

1. **Cabinetry**—Keep all the cabinets the same. Use the same style or color in the kitchen, laundry room, and pantry as you do in the bathrooms.

2. **Countertops**—Whether you are choosing granite or Corian, marble or tile, use complementary color patterns in the kitchen and the baths.

3. **Carpet**—Stay with the same style and brand of carpet throughout. All bedrooms should be the same.

4. **Window Treatments**—Keep them consistent. Use the same style in all the bedrooms.

5. **Hardware**—I use a smaller version of the cabinet handles in the bathroom that I use in the kitchen. All doorknobs and door hinges should be the same throughout the house.

6. **Lighting**—Use the same type of recessed lighting throughout. You may use a smaller version in bedrooms or bathrooms than you do in the living room. But make sure they are all similar in style and trim color.

Keep It Neutral

Don't get nervous here. This is not about "the House of Beige"! But it is about getting a great, stylish look, quickly and simply—and making it easy to pull together. The way to have it all—style, color, and ease—is to select your floor coverings and wall colors in neutral tones and style. That way EVERYTHING else is easy to match and accessorize. Keep the big stuff neutral. Add in the color with the furnishings and accessories you will use when you dress your house for sale.

Keeping neutral and consistent is so very important, especially in high-traffic rooms like a master bath. Making sure all the elements and materials blend together creates the open and spacious feel that every buyer is drawn to. Remove any visual barriers, like the frames on shower doors, and replace them with frameless glass enclosures to expand the room even more.

PHOTOGRAPHY BY RAND LARSON.

My Charl house bathroom before and after demonstrates that without moving any walls I was able to create a space that visually looks more spacious. Keep it simple and keep your materials neutral and consistent. Less is more, and in this case, more elegant and sophisticated.

FLIP TIP

Go Classic—Think of your designed-to-flip house as a woman's classic little black dress. It looks look great on its own, but it can be accessorized with shoes, scarves, jewelry, or a jacket to create any number of terrific new looks.

LIGHT AND LIGHTING

It's all about the lighting. You hear that a lot in Hollywood, but it is just as true in flipping. And one surefire way to create huge value and Lifestyle Upgrades to your flip house is simply to upgrade your lighting. You can transform the drabbest of rooms with the flick of a switch. But before you turn on the electricity, always take full advantage of any available *natural* light.

Natural Light

There is nothing more nurturing and invigorating than walking into a sun-drenched room with patterns of light and shadows dancing slowly across the walls. It simply brings a smile to the face of any potential buyer. Any opportunities to open the house to more natural light should be maximized. Any time an exterior door can be replaced with a wood-framed glass door without sacrificing privacy or security, take advantage of it. And if privacy is an issue, consider white or rippled glass that still lets the light in but obscures the view. If you are replacing windows, try to enlarge them without making them out of proportion to the rest of the house. As discussed earlier, skylights work wonders.

Window Treatments—Bare It All

My dream has always been to live in a home or apartment with nothing but walls of glass on four sides—yet with total privacy. While that is impossible, there are lots of alternatives. And the first step toward letting it all in is to pull back those window treatments.

I personally don't like drapes and blinds. As a flip expense, they are very costly and considered part of the property when the house sells. I like to use a minimal amount of window treatment but still dress a room and make it look warm and inviting. But you never want to block any natural light. Lose the window treatments and expose the window itself. But don't forsake privacy. There are great products that you can use to create privacy while still letting the light shine and keeping your window-dressing bill down to nothing. This new technology uses crushed glass molded into paper thin sheets of plastic to give your glass a frosted look. They literally just cling to the window, come in great sophisticated patterns and are removable. I love this stuff. As a matter of fact, I was their spokesperson and sold it for them on Home Shopping Network. It's called "Wallpaper for Windows" and can be found at www.wallpaperforwindows.com.

Tears for Sheers

I made a discovery while getting my mom's house of forty years ready for sale. One day while she was out I pulled back every drape and shade and rediscovered a gorgeous home full of wonderful natural light. I installed inexpensive white sheers that let the light in but maintained privacy. When she came home, my mom actually started crying over the shocking transformation. The cost for the whole house? About $200. And the result? Tears of joy. I know this sounds corny, but it's true.

FLIP TIP

Make Windows Bigger—Create a sense of more space by hanging curtains slightly higher or wider than the windows they cover. You'll get the maximum amount of light and the windows will feel bigger.

Interior Lighting

You need to start thinking of light sources as ways to "paint" your room in light. I love recessed lights. They come in all designs and can be angled and "directionalized" to create pools of light in rooms. This visually sections off intimate groupings but still allows the feeling of open space in a room. And recessed lights allow you to get away from all those table lamps and floor lamps. Remember, we want to keep it simple.

THREE DESIGNED-TO-FLIP LIGHTING UPGRADES

1. **Dimmers**—Installing dimmers is so simple, but many people don't do it. For as little as five dollars each they can transform your room. After all, life is not about "on" or "off"—it's all about the in between. And so is good lighting.

2. **Halogen Bulbs**—Changing all the bulbs in your recessed lighting to halogen is an instant lighting makeover. Halogen lights create dramatic looks. All the new track-lighting systems use pin-spots in low-voltage halogen lights.

3. **Replace All Light Switches, Switch Plates, and Electrical Outlets**—This may sound like a small detail, but it is so important. Every time a buyer walks into a room, where do they have to look first? For the light switch. It is sometimes the first thing they will see in each room. New upgraded switches and plates also give the impression of new and state-of-the-art wiring and electrical systems—whether you have them or not.

PAINT AND COLOR

Paint transforms a flip house. After weeks or months of fix-it projects, patching and plastering, when the color starts to go on, the house comes alive. I have the painting done professionally, even on a low-end house. It may look easy, but what I can do compared to what a professional painting team can do is night and day. I see it—and buyers do, too.

FLIP TIP

The Right Finish—Please use the right paint finish for the right surface.

PAINTING FINISHES CHART

Interior

Walls	Flat
Ceiling	Flat
Kitchen Walls	Semigloss
Bath Walls	Semigloss
Woodwork	Semigloss
Cabinets	Semigloss

Exterior

Stucco	Flat
Cement	Flat or Semigloss
Wood Siding	Semigloss
Wood Trim	Semigloss
Gutters	Semigloss
Doors	Gloss

FLIP TIP

Hire a Full Crew—Hire a company that employs a painting crew—don't try to save money and hire one painter. I have had entire 3,000-square-foot houses painted in days when using a crew. How? Because they have the manpower and the equipment to do the job right. While some crew members are prepping, others are masking, and still others are starting on the trim. Even with all that manpower, it costs less because they are doing volume work.

FLIP FLOP
Pulling Out Your Hair—One time I decided to go without the big crew and went with the lowest bid of this nice fellow and his wife. They said they could paint the whole interior of the house for under $1,800—a good price—and I believed them, until I spent hours pulling paint-brush hairs off every surface on which they had slopped paint. Go with the pros—and use a crew.

FLIP TIP
Spraying Versus Hand Painting—Spraying gives a much smoother and more professional finish, especially when using semigloss paints in kitchens, bathrooms, and on wood surfaces. It's often cheaper too, and it takes half the time. But if you are doing the painting yourself, don't even try to wield one of those babies!

Color Your World . . . but Don't Get Crazy Here!

Color is a basic part of design. How you use it is crucial. Color creates energy and brings vibrancy into your home. Starting with the walls, the right color also creates depth and adds character to any existing architectural style. Painting is the quickest, simplest, and least expensive makeover for your home. It truly is the biggest bang for your buck. When done properly, you can add instant sophistication.

INTERIOR COLORS

The biggest mistake flippers make when trying to use color is to paint the walls wild and vibrant trendy colors. Wrong. For a perfect flip home, you want to keep your wall colors neutral. Limit your color pallet. Your walls are the backdrop upon which you will build your room. You don't want them to pull the focus off your room. You can make the room pop by adding more intense color later with your furniture, art, or select accessories. Think about it: Why bring attention to your walls? Our goal is to expand the space, not to remind the potential buyer of its boundaries.

I have developed a very practical and successful formula for taking the worry out of painting and choosing the right color scheme for the interior.

**DESIGNED-TO-FLIP THREE-COLOR TECHNIQUE
FOR INTERIORS**

Step 1: Choose the One Choose one great neutral color to be your overall base color—one found in nature, please! Choose from earth tones, desert tones, water tones, or forest shades.

Step 2: Three of a Kind Now select two *shades* of that color, a lighter shade of that color and a slightly darker one. You should now have three shades total—your original color plus a slightly lighter and a slightly darker version.

Step 3: Get Painting Most walls will be painted with your lightest shade. Paint accent walls and adjoining rooms with one of the two darker shades. For example, try the dining room in the darker shade, and the kitchen in the medium base.

The result is an instant picture-perfect look—with different shades in each room blending and complementing one another beautifully. It creates consistency and increases the feeling of space throughout the house, giving your property that sense of flow that makes even the smallest house feel expansive and inviting. Another hugely important payoff is that you have one base color to which you will match all of your furniture and accessories. That leaves you free to move them from room to room, giving you more flexibility when dressing your house for sale.

FLIPPING SUCCESS STORY

Richard Gere's House—Richard Gere's former Hollywood Hills home is a perfect example of my color technique. With a "driftwood tan" as his base color, each of the other two shades that Richard used complemented the other and highlighted the architectural details of his home. The technique made his home flow seamlessly and feel expansive. No wonder this 2,000-square-foot manse sold for more than $3 million.

FLIP TIP

Keep in Touch—Keep a set of sponge-topped shoe polish–applicator bottles filled with paint from each color, and label them by room. Give scuffs and marks a quick dab, and touch-ups will be a breeze. Your home will remain perfect through the sale process.

FLIP TIP

You'll Hit the Ceiling—Always paint your ceilings a shade of white. It neutralizes them. Visually it makes them disappear and thus gives a greater sense of height. And a white ceiling also reflects more light around the room. I never paint the ceiling a different color or one darker than the walls. My color of choice for ceilings is never a bright white, but a standard white shade known as Swiss Coffee or Ceiling White.

EXTERIOR COLORS

Your exterior color choices are extremely important. Not only do they create a lasting visual experience, but paint serves as a lasting protectant from the elements for your exterior surfaces.

Using paint to create a dramatic and inviting home is so simple, yet so often overlooked by beginning flippers and homeowners. Just as the old

Frank Sinatra song advises us to "accentuate the positive, eliminate the negative!" paint can emphasize any architectural detail and blend out any ugly elements.

Designed-to-Flip Exterior Three-Color Technique

Three is the magic number on the exterior paint scheme as well. Choose three colors to work with. Select a nice, neutral earth-tone base color for your large surfaces, such as the walls. Pick a second contrasting but complementary color for the trim and accent moldings. Go with a rich, strong third color for some very select accent items, such as the front door. The good news is that all major paint companies now have brochures and pamphlets that have already done the color combining for you. So head on down to your local home-improvement center and grab a handful of color combo ideas.

FLIP TIP

Mark Your Can—As you finish painting, clearly mark the paint cans. Use a piece of masking tape and identify the rooms and areas painted in each color. Not only will it be a time-and-money-saver for you for the inevitable touch-ups, but your buyers will appreciate the information and the effort when you leave the cans for them.

Adding "Brooches"

Contractor and design expert Steven Wilder has used this term for many years to describe the eye-catching accessories and special amenities that really dress up a house and make buyers take notice! Be creative. As you go to open houses, what individual items or upgrades catch your eye?

These Sample Brooches Will Add Untold Value to Your Home

- Add a lovely fountain as a focal point in the backyard or on a side deck.

- Replace the old thermostat with a new digital thermostat. Even if the heating and air system isn't new, it will appear as though it is.

- Install hotel-style, wall-mounted hair dryers in the bathrooms. At $29 each, they're a small expense, but buyers will talk about them when they go home that night!

- Put ceiling fans in the bedrooms if you're in a warmer climate. Please, use the kind *without* lights, and make sure to get a flush-mount style so that the fan is as unobtrusive as possible.

- If you are putting in an intercom, add a video intercom system. Spend a bit more for an eye-catching brooch.

- Customize the master closet in a medium to high-end house. Steal ideas from one of the closet stores and have your contractor install the elements.

OTHER DESIGNED-TO-FLIP TIPS

Mix and Match

Try mixing some expensive materials with inexpensive materials. You get the high-end look you want for a lot less money. The backsplash in the kitchen or above the stove is a great place to combine price levels. One nice piece of expensive tile surrounded by less expensive yet complimentary tiles will make the whole backsplash look more expensive.

Indestructible Carpet—I Love This Stuff

I have discovered the greatest maintenance-free home product since Teflon frying pans! A carpet company called Beaulieu has developed a product called PermaShield, which makes their carpets virtually indestructible. Carpeting treated with PermaShield is guaranteed not to stain from spills or pets, won't hold odors, does not fade, and can be steam cleaned as often as you like. It looks great, has a terrific designer-color selection, and will save you thousands by not forcing you to replace it whenever your terrier gets a little too territorial!

Put *You* on a Pedestal

Changing the vanity in a guest bath to a pedestal sink can make a small bathroom feel much more spacious and inviting. Just make sure there is plenty of in-wall cabinet space for toiletries.

A Mirror Science Lesson

Why do mirrors work so well to create space? It's because to the eye they appear to stretch space by reproducing it. If you hang a mirror on the longer wall of a narrow room, you will visually change its proportions by making the room seem wider.

Just Hang It Up

The easiest trick to adding space to a room is, of course, adding a hanging mirror on a wall opposite a window to maximize the light and view. But most people hang it too high or too low. Here's my tip: Put the nail on the wall seventy-two inches from the floor. And put the hook approximately three quarters of the way up the back of the mirror.

Reflections of the Past

Entire walls of mirror are a very dated look. And no smoked or etched-glass mirrors, please. To keep the mirror concept but update it, rip them down, paint the wall and replace them with a single, large, hanging mirror—framed, of course.

You Get Too High-Handed

Most people try to take up all the space on a wall and hang art way too high above their sofa. Tie the two together and make the art relate to the furnishings below. A good guideline is to keep the art only eleven inches above the sofa. Don't be afraid of a little blank wall space above.

Fourteen

TIME TO CASH OUT!: HOW AND WHEN

TAXES AND TIMING—YOUR PROFIT AND UNCLE SAM

If you have waited until this point in the process to decide when to sell your house, then oops . . . you have missed the prime decision time! The time to decide when to sell your flip is *the day you make the offer to buy it.*

There are numerous tax-law benefits afforded to flipping and selling houses. To take full advantage of them, you have to understand that how and when you sell your home will determine the amount of profit you get to keep. Miss a deadline by even a day, and you could pay up to 35 percent more of your profit to Uncle Sam. Let's examine in layman's terms the best ways to evaluate your situation and determine the most beneficial strategy for you.

DECIDE WHEN TO SELL *BEFORE* YOU BUY

When you flip, the difference between paying capital gains tax or a reduced percentage of capital gains tax can equal your profit. From the get-go, you need to decide on your sale date in order to make the most of the applicable tax laws. Is it going to be a fast-track fix-it flip that you flip in less than twelve months? Will you live in it? Will you sell immediately, or after one or two years?

Your Dream Team Accountant

Have I mentioned that I'm not a designer, contractor, lawyer, or professional landscaper? Let's add a tax accountant to that list! Tax rules are complicated. That's why an accountant who specializes in real estate tax accounting is a key member of your Dream Team. And it's up to you to ask, ask, ask in order to benefit from his expertise. Here is an overview of several ways to benefit from the tax laws.

FIVE SIGNIFICANT WAYS TO MAXIMIZE YOUR PROFIT AND MINIMIZE YOUR TAXES

1. Pocket up to $500,000 tax-free profit if you and your spouse/partner hold your property for two years or more and it has been your primary residence.

2. Keep up to $250,000 tax-free profit if you are single and hold your property for two years or more and it has been your primary residence.

3. Pay less, or even no capital gains, up to $250,000 to $500,000 prorated, if you move from your primary residence in less than two years and you qualify for the special circumstances I will discuss in this chapter.

4. Own the home for one year and a day, and pay significantly less capital gains tax than the day before!

5. Using the Federal 1033 tax-deferred exchange program, you can sell a property and roll your profit into the next one, no matter how short a time you have owned it—and pay NO tax on it! There are specific yet easy to understand guidelines.

TWO-YEAR PRIMARY-RESIDENCE TAX BREAK

Years ago, the only way to avoid paying tax on the sale of your home was to use the sale proceeds to buy another house. Today, the cornerstone of the tax-break tax laws for homeowners is the primary-residence capital gains rule. When the Taxpayer Relief Act of 1997 became law and went into effect on May 7, 1997, it completely changed the face of real estate flipping. It made it even more lucrative to flip houses, no matter which one of the four flipping paths you follow. In layman's terms, the rule is: If you have owned your primary residence for more than two years, when you sell you can keep up to $500,000 in profit if you are married, $250,000 if

you are single, and not owe any capital gains taxes. This tax law in particular makes it incredibly financially rewarding to find, fix, and then flip
your primary residence every two years. Not only are you able to make a
profit, but you are then *further rewarded* by being able to walk away with
all that profit tax free! It is a double bonus, like winning the lottery, except
better because when you win the lottery you pay tax on your winnings!

The Timing of This Tax Law Earned Me $60,000

I remember vividly when my first real estate agent told me about this
law. I had been flipping properties for about ten years, paying the capital
gains on the profit I had made on each flip—an average of 28 percent of
the profit. As there was no other option, I had to just factor this cost into
my Profit Calculator right from the beginning. I couldn't believe my ears
when I heard about this new tax break.

I was on *The Young and the Restless* at the time and had been completing a flip house that I was living in and planning to flip. It had been a little over a year since I had purchased this house for $375,000, and I was
about to list it for $695,000. With an $180,000 profit due to me, I was
facing a tax bill of approximately $50,000. But with the advent of this
new tax law, if I held onto the house for two years, I would be able to
keep all that profit! That was a crazy thought!

I called my accountant and mortgage broker. When they both con-
firmed this new tax law, I held off selling the house for ten months, then
put it on the market and asked for a sixty-day closing. I insisted that it
close exactly two years and one day from my purchase date. The market
was on the upswing and I sold it for $735,000, making a profit of ap-
proximately $250,000, tax-free!

By timing it correctly and waiting those additional months I increased
my profit from what would have been $180,000 − $50,000 in taxes =
$130,000, to $250,000, tax-free. That's a $120,000 increase!

This is such an important cornerstone of flipping properties that it
warrants further explaining:

- The property must be your primary residence. You have to live in
  it. You cannot claim this tax exemption on a house you are flipping as an investment property.

- You must have owned the property for a minimum of two years and have lived in it for any two of the five years before the sale.

- You can use the tax-free exemption every two years, each time you sell a home. There is no limit on how many times you can do this, as long as the flips are two years apart.

- When your gain doesn't exceed the limit, you don't have to file anything with the IRS. Ask your accountant to explain this to you.

- It's easy to calculate your profit or gain to be applied against your $500,000 or $250,000 break. Determine your cost basis for the home: what you paid for your flip house, plus all the fix-it improvements. Add in the closing costs, including the commissions to the Realtors, and then subtract those amounts from the sales price. That will give you the capital gains total on the sale of your flip. If it's less than $500,000 (if two of you own the property) or $250,000 if you are single . . . then you pay NO tax!

TWO-YEAR-EXEMPTION TAX BREAK

This one is HUGE! This tax law is one that very few people except the "insiders" know about. If you sell in less than two years but move more than fifty miles away because of a work relocation, health reasons, or unforeseen circumstances, you can prorate the taxes on your profit. That means you can keep 25, 50, or 75 percent of your profit tax-free, depending on how long you have owned your home. This is a tax advantage that EVERY qualifying homeowner should take advantage of to save thousands of dollars!

LONG-TERM VERSUS SHORT-TERM CAPITAL GAINS

There is a vast difference in the amount of tax you will have to pay on your flip profit by selling prior to one year of ownership (short-term capital gains) or by selling after one year (long-term capital gains). It's simple: Sell 364 days from the purchase date and you are one day short of a profit windfall. Sell it 366 days or more from the purchase date and benefit handsomely.

Just how much exactly *is* that long-term cap-gain tax? Well, this is where I point you toward your accountant. The laws have changed recently, and are due to change again. However, the rule of thumb is—if you are close to a year, hold out—long-term gains are always taxed at a much lower rate than short-term gains.

INSIDER TIP

Super Palm Springs Realtor Brian Hatch suggests that if you want to sell a flip and take advantage of the long-term capital gains, put the property on the market after ten months of ownership. Then insist on a sixty-day escrow so you close after one full year. Remember, it's a year from the date you take possession of the property to the date you sell it, not the date you list it for sale.

THE 1031 TAX-DEFERRED EXCHANGE

Here's another really valuable flipping tax law, the 1031 tax-deferred exchange. This little moneymaking tax law allows you to purchase a property, fix it, flip it, and then avoid paying any taxes by "rolling it" into a "like property." OK, what does that mean? Let me explain. You purchase the flip property for $250,000. You fix it and add in $50,000 worth of improvements and then market it for $415,000. Minus sales commissions and closing costs, that would give you a tidy profit of $84,000. Putting it up for sale after less than one year, you would have to pay the short-term capital-gains tax of approximately 28 percent, which would equal $23,500 going to Uncle Sam.

However, if you "roll" all the profit into another "like" property (meaning another investment-non-principle residence) of equal or greater value than your $415,000 sale price using the 1031 tax-deferred exchange, you avoid paying that tax bill. Since you are "deferring" your taxes, Uncle Sam allows you to keep rolling that money into more expensive properties each sale.

Keep in mind, there are some very specific guidelines associated with this IRS code: You must purchase a like property—investment property for investment property. You must identify one to three properties within forty-five days of your closing and purchase one within 180 days after that. Plus, your sale proceeds will have to stay in a special 1031 escrow account and then be entirely invested in the new property. So don't even think about touching that money!

I especially like this technique because it removes all possibility of spending any of your profit! Everything you make on your flip must go directly into the new property. It's like a forced savings plan and an automatic equity-builder that steps you up another rung on your financial ladder to success. Keep flipping and deferring, and eventually you'll buy your properties for all cash and never pay a mortgage again!

Get Your Accountant on the Phone Before You Buy!

There are many ways to enhance the profit you can make when you flip. By taking advantage of these tax laws, you can hold on to most *if not all* of your flipping profits, tax-free, as long as you work within the requirements and time frames of these tax laws. Get your accountant on the phone the minute you find a potential flip, and review all of your options. Don't wait until you're ready to sell to make your decisions. By then it's too late. You don't want to miss a single opportunity to keep all your hard-earned flip dollars!

Fifteen

FLIPPING THE HOUSE YOU LIVE IN

THE GOOD NEWS

You own a home. You realize that it's time to take advantage of all that equity and the tax advantages that are at your disposal. You can sell your home and reinvest, without having to scramble and scrimp for that first down payment and the initial capital, unlike a flipper starting from scratch. And if you've been in your home for a year or more, you have already built equity, which includes your original down payment, the amount you have contributed monthly toward principle, the amount the house has appreciated in an upward market, and any sweat equity you have earned if you applied any of my Find It and Fix It principles and techniques. Congratulations!

THE BAD NEWS

The bad news is that your home is completely personalized and full of the items that most people feel make a house a home. The closets are packed with stuff, the garage is stacked with boxes, and the backyard is full of projects that are half-finished but look "fine." Even worse, you have lost the ability to see your home objectively. You no longer notice that little stain in the ceiling in the upstairs hall. Everything that needs to be fixed, repaired, replaced, or upgraded is officially invisible to you. Your lovely home, no matter how perfect you think it may be, is not ready to be put on the market.

ANALYZE THE HOUSE YOU'VE GOT

You need to know what your house is worth right this minute—today, in its present condition. Easy enough to find out, right? Just bring in three Realtors for their expert opinion and market analysis.

Allow me to tell you in advance what they will say so there won't be any surprises. You'll hear "Your house is perfect, you'll get top dollar. Let's put it on the market right now!" Or, "You don't need to fix a thing, it won't make you any more money, and this is the time to sell." Or, "Something just sold for X up the street, but I am sure we should ask for more."

Why are you going to hear that? Because the Realtor wants the listing now! He won't make money until you sell. The time you take to get your house ready to flip, by making the improvements that maximize your equity and profit, will delay his receiving the listing. Plus, the additional $25,000 that you may make on the sale means only about $625 more to him. The $25,000 higher sales price × 6 percent commission = $1,500. Your Realtor's share after splitting it with the buyer's Realtor and his own agency leaves him with about $650. He is not inspired to wait for his share of your increased profit. He wants the listing now!

Calculate Your Current Profit and Capital Gains

Based on a Realtor's assessment of your home's worth, determine your profit and your capital gains. Here's the formula:

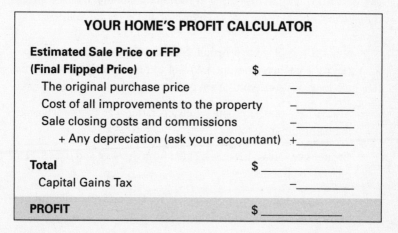

YOUR HOME'S PROFIT CALCULATOR	
Estimated Sale Price or FFP	
(Final Flipped Price)	$ _____
The original purchase price	–_____
Cost of all improvements to the property	–_____
Sale closing costs and commissions	–_____
+ Any depreciation (ask your accountant)	+_____
Total	$ _____
Capital Gains Tax	–_____
PROFIT	$ _____

HOW TO MAKE MORE PROFIT WHEN YOU SELL

So now that you know what you've got, let's see how you can get more! There is only one way to maximize your profit potential for the house you live in. You have to MOVE OUT! OK, not physically, but mentally and emotionally. You have "leave" in order to arrive at your house as though you were seeing it for the first time. You need to be a buyer before you can become the seller. With your Fix-It Hit List in hand, you are going to analyze your house using the Six Levels of Improvements.

FLIPPING THE HOUSE YOU OWN

Once you can see your house with the eyes of an objective buyer, you will follow a step-by-step process that squeezes the maximum amount of profit from your home. First, analyze it as you would any potential flip. Once you have calculated your FFP and identified all necessary fixes, get to work. Hire a contractor if the fixes are substantial. Hopefully, you were diligent and did many of the larger repairs when you purchased the home or over time. If so, you may only need to hire some specialized tradesmen.

LIVING THROUGH YOUR FIX-IT PHASES

Let me warn you up front—living in your home through the fix-it phase is no picnic. But there are ways to minimize the potential disasters.

- Stay on top of your scheduling and project coordinating, especially the kitchen renovation. Living without a working kitchen for too long gets costly, plus it's very draining to be kitchen drain–less.

- Always have one bathroom totally operational at all times. Stagger the bathroom fix-it jobs.

- Create "safe" areas that are shielded from the dust and debris. Seal off your bedrooms.

- Lock up or remove your valuables. Tradesmen will be in and out of the house for the whole process. Be smart.

- Remember the weather! Don't try to do a new roof in the middle of the rainy season, and don't replace windows in the dead of winter.

FLIP TIP

Save Your Receipts—Not only do you need to keep records of all your expenses, but you need to know which ones you will be able to count against your capital gains. It is obvious that when you flip a house, most everything you add to the house is counted as an improvement. However, if you are getting ready to flip the house you are living in, be prepared to argue with the IRS if they choose to audit after you sell. Protect yourself by showing your accountant or real estate agent the construction projects you are considering. They will know if the IRS will consider them home improvements, which are usable or general maintenance costs and therefore not applicable against capital gains.

YOU'RE NOT READY TO SELL YET

After completing the first five of the Six Levels of Improvements, you still have work to do. The house is probably packed to the rafters with your personal stuff. Before you even think about dressing your house for sale, you have to undress it first!

SAVE IT, STORE IT, SELL IT, OR CHUCK IT!

As I mentioned, you need you to move out in your head and emotionally prior to doing any Fix-It Improvements. Well, now I'm telling you to move out physically! The only way to even begin to get the house ready is to start packing up to move or, as I say, save it, store it, sell it, or chuck it!

I guarantee that there is far too much "of you" in the house. Get rid of what you're not using, then edit and organize the rest. Start in one room and systematically go through every drawer, every closet, and every shelf. Throw or give away what you haven't used in over a year.

Continue through the house room by room, and then make sense of what you have left. Your first reaction is going to be, "Oh, dear God, I don't have the time to do that." Believe me you don't have the time not to.

Create Space

Downsizing and clearing out personal belongings goes against our pack-rat natures. But it is a technique you can learn. The benefit is a feeling of space and a house that's ready to be Dressed to Sell.

Next time you enter a room packed with furnishings, accessories, and knick-knacks, take a moment and notice how you feel. No matter how expensive or well arranged they are, I'll bet you'll feel a little closed in, tight, and constricted. Then, next time you find yourself in an open, bright, airy, minimally furnished space like a museum or a well-done shop, stop and check yourself out. Chances are you'll feel more relaxed, open, and lighter. This is how you want your BUYERS to feel when they enter your home. To get that feeling, you have to create space.

THREE STEPS TO CREATING SPACE

Step 1. Give Yourself a Two-Day Space Break .

This may sound odd, but it really works. Select a particularly cluttered corner of the room, or a wall that has too many hanging photos or objects. Remove them! Put them in another room or, better yet, in the garage. You are going to hate it. "Arghhh . . . it looks so bare!" Don't worry—this is only for forty-eight hours. By the next day, it will start to look more normal. And by day two, when you try to put the all the items back, you won't be happy. It will feel too crowded. Congratulations! You have just learned how to edit. You are on your way.

All the things that comfortably fit back in the room, you *save*. With everything else you need to decide what you are going to put into *storage*, what you are going to *sell*, and what you are just simply going to *chuck* or give away.

Step 2. Take on the Whole Room

Use this same technique with that whole room now. Remove the accessories on the coffee and end tables, any bric-a-brac, and photos. Next, pull out anything broken or in need of repair, especially any furniture that you have been promising yourself you would re-cover or clean. This is the time. Strip the room to the bare minimum of furniture.

"Oh my God, I can't live like this for two days!" I can hear you mumbling that now. You may even feel a bit naked. But hang in there—like before, that feeling will pass.

In forty-eight hours you are allowed to put things back—but only half of the items you took out. In fact, I'd prefer you only put back one quarter of the furnishings, but I am not going to push you . . . well, maybe later.

Step 3. Take on the Whole House

Go room by room and do this same process. This includes the baths and, of course, the kitchen. Promise me you will get rid of at least half of those plaster roosters and bottles of decorative fruits and vegetables sealed in oil. Clean it out.

This is the time for your house to take center stage, not your 387 family photos or the Murano glass collection you brought back from Italy.

The Garage Is Not the Dumping Ground

Get that garage cleared out, too. Don't make the mistake of permanently storing everything there as you clear out each room. You are eventually going to have to store the garage contents as well. If something is meant to be chucked, throw it out. If it is meant to be given away, mark the boxes and set up a Goodwill pick-up date a week or two in advance.

Remove Anything That Is "Polarizing"

When clearing out the house, remove any polarizing elements—anything religious or political. Everyone has strong emotional reactions to religious artifacts and political mementos or statements. Don't give your buyer a chance to prejudge your home because of your political or religious beliefs.

FLIP TIP

Use Off-site Storage—My favorite trick is to use a company here in California called U-Store-It. They bring a giant, eighteen-foot-high storage "room" to your door, which you can neatly fill with all your newly marked boxes and extra clothing and furniture. You lock it up and they come and take it away. Remember, your next house will be a fixer, and it will take a good deal of work before you can fully move in, so you're going to have to clear things out and store them anyway. This way, they're held indefinitely for you, and once you've moved, they deliver the box to the door of your NEW home! (Call 888-U-Store-It, or go to www.U-Store-It.com to find one in your area.) It's incredibly easy. And the cost of the storage will be offset by the profit you make at sale time.

ORGANIZE WHAT'S LEFT

Remember, to the buyer, a perfectly organized house implies that by living here, their home life will be organized as well.

ORGANIZE KITCHEN AND BATHROOM CABINETS

This may seem silly, but I promise that you will be shocked at what a remarkable change it makes. Organize your food cabinets by like items. Put all the cereal boxes together, all the cans together; all the coffees together, etc., then "directionalize" them. Huh? What does that mean? Go to a grocery store and see how things are arranged on the shelves. All the labels face forward, making everything look neat and organized. That's directionalizing. Do the same for medicine cabinets. It's a Dressed-to-Sell must-do!

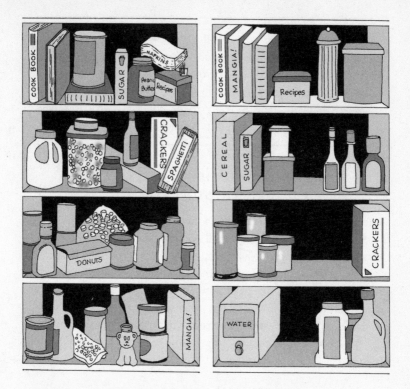

*Not only do you want to organize and directionalize your
cupboards and pantry, you want to make sure there is lots of
empty shelf space, which implies spaciousness and plenty of
storage.*

Edit Plates and Glasses

Go through all your cabinets and throw out all those mismatched single
glasses, coffee cups, and plates. You should have only your nicest matching tableware in view from now on. This does not mean your good
china. It means your everyday wear. Lose the Scooby-Doo promotional
plastic cups that have been on the second shelf since 1989. Stack all
your cups with the handles facing the same direction. And if you have
cookbooks, make sure they look like they're on a bookstore shelf!

FLIP TIP

Clean the Kitchen Junk Drawer—Everyone has one. I certainly do. It's the one drawer where you throw everything without an obvious place to call home. Well, I can guarantee that 75 percent of everything in there is ready to be chucked. Give it a new home—the trash. And organize what's left.

MAKE YOUR CLOTHES CLOSETS LOOK
DEPARTMENT-STORE PERFECT

Go to Bed, Bath & Beyond and buy four dozen hangers of the same type. It will cost you $49. Throw out all your mismatched hangers. I know this sounds a little like *Mommie Dearest*, but it will transform your closets. First, group your clothes together by category: Shirts, pants, short dresses, long dresses, etc. Then group each category by color. You will never want to have your closets any other way again. I do this now in all my closets all the time, and not because I'm obsessive about my belongings, but because it saves me so much time each morning deciding and finding what I want to wear.

FLIP TIP

Sheets and Towels in Line—Empty your linen closet. Group sheets and towels by color, throw out all the mismatched ones, then fold neatly and stack the rest.

Clean Up Outdoors

Don't think you can get away with clearing out the house and organizing it meticulously, but then ignoring the outside. Oh, no. The same technique applies to the front, back, and side yards. Throw out those old hoses, that rusty rake, those piles of old wood scraps, your tool area, and all those terra-cotta pots that someday you mean to reuse.

CREATING SPACE IN YOUR HOME
CREATES SPACE IN YOUR LIFE

There is a wonderful added benefit to this clearing-out process. I am referring here to my personal philosophy: *Create a Lifestyle That Leaves You Time for Your Life!*

Not only are you getting your house ready for sale, *but when you create space in your home you also create space in your life!* Remember, your home is a mirror of you and how your life works, so *as you simplify your home, you simplify your life.* By investing the time needed to clean out, edit your possessions, and organize your entire house, you will give yourself more time for your life. Plus, you are on the road to creating a home and home lifestyle that not only functions better, but looks more appealing and valuable to your potential buyers. You are increasing the value of your home and simplifying your life. Talk about a win/win!

Sixteen

DRESSED TO SELL

The Six Levels of Improvements
Fix-It Levels
  Serious but Fixable Problems
  System Upgrades
  Fix-It Essentials
Profit Levels
  Lifestyle Upgrades
  Designed-to-Flip Techniques
• **Dressed-to-Sell Essentials**

Here it is, the sixth and final of the Profit Level Improvements: Dressed-to-Sell Essentials. And as they say, we are saving the best for last. But why is it the best? Because this is the one phase that only the professional flippers and real estate insiders know is the deal closer. Dressed-to-Sell techniques are equally invaluable for any homeowner about to sell his property. This important level transforms a house into an inviting, emotionally engaging home that is irresistible because it personifies a lifestyle. This is where you maximize the profit your house can generate by creating the emotional appeal that quickens the pulse of even the coolest customer!

Dressed-to-Sell techniques create "perceived value." Perceived value is not a quantifiable improvement like copper piping or a new hot-water heater. It is purely qualitative because it is the price a buyer is willing to pay based entirely on the emotional appeal of the house. The more emotionally invested the buyer becomes in the house, the higher the perceived value . . . and your profit. Dressed-to-Sell techniques have one goal: to inspire your potential buyers to say the words that are instant cash to any flipper, "I LOVE this house. It feels like HOME! I HAVE to have it!"

Dressed-to-Sell Components

- Staging

- Create emotional appeal

- Room vignettes

- Seduce the senses

  - Lighting

  - Sounds and music

  - Scents

  - Touch

- Camera-ready

- Squeaky-clean

- Sale prep setup

Your House Becomes a Broadway Show

Think of the sale of your home as a big theatrical production. Just like a Broadway show, you're setting the stage, and creating a mood through lighting, music, or even adding just the right scents to attract an "emotional buyer," the buyer who walks through your front door and has an emotional or visceral reaction, not a rational one. What happens when you put this theatrical magic to work? You have a hit—and a top-dollar sale.

How I Learned That Showmanship Sells

My background in TV, stage, and film has given me a real appreciation and understanding for dressing a house to sell. I know from experience that when a buyer's first impression of a house is both emotional *and* visual, it is more powerful and long-lasting than just a visual impression alone.

I learned this through my years in TV, especially commercials, where you have thirty seconds to convince the audience to purchase your product. You need to stimulate all of the senses pull the viewer's heartstrings at the same time. Well, you want to do the exact same thing with your flip house. During that first walk-through, you want the buyer to *experience* all the beautiful, inviting, and practical elements he sees in your home and to connect them to his positive, visceral response! If the buyers can sense warmth, vitality, tranquillity, and security—all sensations of cherished family moments—they're sold!

I have often heard buyers say things like, "The house was smaller than I had wanted" or "There weren't as many bathrooms as we needed," then finish their thought by saying, "but I just had such a good feeling about the house that we bought it!" Your job is to create that *feeling*!

I have New Yorker friends who, after weeks of frustrated househunting in the San Fernando Valley, fell in love with a house that had fabulous flow and East Coast touches such as crown molding and parquet floors. They joked that it probably snowed there in the winter. They didn't realize it was short a bedroom until they moved in. *That* is the power of emotion!

STAGING—THE HOT NEW SELLING TOOL

On *Extra* and *Extra's Mansions & Millionaires* I interview Realtors, big designers, and renovators all the time. One of the hottest trends in real estate is "staging," the practice of dressing a house with carefully chosen furnishings and little touches that say "home." Why? It's transformational.

How Staging Works

Simply put, you treat the house like a stage set, adding furniture, accessories, plants, artwork, and a host of details, right down to placing a few carefully chosen clothes in the closets. Does this sound crazy? Well, it's crazy smart! This technique has become so valuable to making a profit when selling that there is new breed of professionals in metropolitan areas who specialize in staging. Known as house fluffers, stagers, or property enhancers, they are well paid for their services. What do they know that the novice flipper doesn't know? A *staged* house sells faster, and for more money!

Why Stage Your Flip

One of the best of these transformation specialists in Los Angeles is Meredith Baer. She knows all the ways to get buyers to respond emotionally to a house, and all the elements that need to come together to guarantee top dollar. She is paid handsomely for her expertise, and rightfully so.

One of Meredith's many success stories concerns a home in Beverly Hills. The owner had interviewed her and decided not to use her. He didn't want to pay her fee, which includes not only her expertise but her warehouse full of great furniture and accessories that she uses. Well, the house sat empty and unsold for six months. When he finally changed his mind and hired her, Meredith added in all her buyer-snagging, grab-their-heartstrings techniques, and it sold in two weeks for $50,000 over asking price with multiple offers! Obviously, he was more than repaid for the cost of her services.

But why does staging work? No matter what size the house is, from cottage to mansion, your flip home will benefit from staging for the following reasons:

FIVE MAJOR STAGING BENEFITS

1. Gives buyers a visual blueprint of what life will be like in the home

2. Makes an empty home feel warm and more inviting

3. Creates proportion in a big room through furniture groupings

4. Makes a tiny room feel larger with customized furnishings

5. Showcases positive features and downplays negative features

---

Buying a home is a very emotional experience, so you need to get the buyers to respond emotionally. Meredith explains that everyone wants a home that represents an idyllic lifestyle, but they need to be shown how to create it. Walking into an empty house is just that . . . empty. You have to show buyers how to live in your space.

Open Floor Plans Are a Challenge

Everyone wants open floor plan today. If not staged in some way, they can be very scary to buyers because they don't know how to make them work. Just by laying down a few rugs that delineate the areas and adding a grouping of club chairs and a love seat, you give the buyer both an idea and a *feeling* of how an open floor plan can work.

PHOTOGRAPHY BY RAND LARSON.

This is my Bogert house, before and after. It has a big open floor plan, but without staging it looks empty and cold. Once I added in some furniture groupings, it was instantly transformed into a home.

Staging Accentuates the Positives and De-emphasizes the Negatives

If a home is very small, staging it properly can show a buyer how a smart decor can take advantage of every available area to make the home seem more spacious. If it is larger, staging will make a home feel cozy.

People need help visualizing. That's why furniture stores have mini-rooms on showroom floors instead of a room stacked full of chairs or beds or tables. They're selling a lifestyle—what *happens* on the chairs, etc. Staging helps your potential buyer to see the life they could have in your house. You have the power to make it a very desirable one.

FLIPPING SUCCESS STORY

Staging Makes a Room Larger—A few days prior to staging my Orlando Avenue house, a potential buyer came to the door and asked to come in. While I usually never let buyers see the house until it is totally finished and prepped, she said the front of the house was so adorable that she just HAD to get in right now. Against better judgment, I acquiesced. Upon entering the empty bedroom she said, "Hmm, this room feels so small, I don't think my bed will fit in here along with the dresser." When she came back a week later and saw the room staged, with the bed and the dresser, two nightstands, a reading chair and ottoman, and room to spare, she had to have it. Unfortunately for her, it had already sold the first week.

Staging Defines the Spaces

Professional designers and stagers have a variety of techniques that showcase the best features of a house's layout. What might be just an extra room off the living room becomes a cozy den when dressed with a leather sofa and a club chair. That funny alcove under the stairs becomes a home office area when staged with a small writing desk and some shelving. With a small glass-topped table and four café chairs, the odd leftover space off the kitchen becomes a breakfast room. And that slab of cement off the slider from the guest room becomes a private sun patio for house guests when furnished with an outdoor lounge chair and side table.

FLIP TIP

Model Homes Are Not Always Model—I learned many staging techniques by going to developers' open model homes, and you will, too. For me, they are so OVER-decorated that I find it hard to breathe! But go see for yourself, learn what you can—and then simplify!

FLIP TIP

K.I.S.S.—As Meredith Baer suggests when it comes to staging your flip house, don't go crazy, don't overdo it. She said she lives by the "K.I.S.S." rule of decorating: Keep It Simple, Stupid!

Spell It Out. Show It Off.

Always put a few articles of clothing in the closets, strategically placed, color-coordinated, and perfectly hung or neatly folded. You are creating a feeling of order and space. The same goes for kitchen cabinets and bathroom medicine cabinets. You are setting a stage and creating a "feeling" of ample storage and a well-organized life. "Yes, Mr. and Mrs. Buyer, if you buy this house your closets will look just like this! You will never again lose those gray dress pants in an overstuffed closet. You will never miss a meeting because you couldn't find the right tie." Get it?

Stage It . . . but with What?

So now you are ready to stage your flip, but just in case you don't have an extra house full of furniture sitting around, where does the furniture come from? When you are first starting out, get it anywhere you can.

I have often borrowed from Peter to pay Paul when staging. In the beginning, I just moved the furniture out of my own home. To stage my Orlando Avenue house, I cleared out all my furniture and slept on a mattress on the floor for a month. But when it sold the first week at about $8,000 over asking price, camping out in my own home was worth it!

I often get calls from other flipper friends asking, "Hey, can I borrow that big six-foot mirror and your tan club chair?" I always help out, and I know they will do the same for me!

Eventually, as you begin to flip more houses, you will accumulate some basic pieces that you will be able to use and reuse in your flip homes. I now have a garage full of extra furniture and accessories that I can pull out at any time. But for your first flip, furnish your flip house from three sources:

- Your own home or apartment

- Borrowed pieces from friends

- Consignment or secondhand stores

Remember, you are only going to need the furniture for thirty to sixty days. Once the house is on the market and you have an accepted offer with the contingencies removed, you can begin to remove your furnishings.

Best of all, you don't have to furnish the entire house. You just have to give a suggestion of a furnished home. Of course, the more you do the better, but go easy on yourself. Do the best you can. For example, if you can only furnish one bedroom, then do the one. But make it look terrific!

INSIDER SECRET

Don't Just Throw Anything in There—Meredith Baer says that to get a buyer's heart pounding, use furnishings one quality level above the quality level of the actual house. (It's better to leave some rooms empty than to throw Uncle Frank's overstuffed chair in the corner.) The buyers will not realize that they are responding positively to the upgraded furnishings, not just the house itself.

FLIP TIP

Keep the Furniture Classic and Simple—Always buy new furniture with flipping in mind. Buy pieces that will work with one another in any room or configuration. Remember, your furniture is also a staging designing tool!

FLIP TIP

Create Focal Points in Every Room—Draw the buyer's eye to the farthest point in the room and create a sense of space. See for yourself. Put an orchid on the bedside table farthest from the door, and voilà! It instantly feels both livable and larger.

FLIP TIP

Face It! Don't Turn Your Back on It—To create a visual focal point that extends well beyond your interior walls and creates a feeling of space, orient some of the furniture in your room to face a window or a sliding-glass door. Chances are you already have a configuration oriented toward the fireplace or TV center. Add in two comfy chairs and a side table that face an outside space as well.

FLIP TIP

Color Your World—An inexpensive and dramatic way to add color to your space is to use accent pillows and simple accessories. They make the room pop.

FLIP TIP

Mirror, Mirror on the Floor—Lean a tall oversized mirror against the wall opposite a window or sliding-glass doors. This reflects the outdoors as you walk into a room. It also creates the illusion of an additional wall of windows. Not only does it do its job of giving you more outdoors indoors and visually expands your interior space . . . it now becomes a piece of accent furniture.

INSIDER SECRET

I Have Found the Perfect Houseplant—With leaves so beautiful and colorful you would swear they are fake, Chinese evergreens (Aglaonemas) are the perfect houseplant. Why? They are easy to find. They thrive in low to medium light. And they are almost impossible to kill. You only need to soak them with water twice a month and then let them dry out in between and their full and striking appearance really brings the outside in. To add drama to any room, put one in a big colorful ceramic pot on the floor.

FLIP TIP

Bring in Fresh Plants—No dead plants! Buy new ones or throw them out!

FLIP TIP

Clear Countertops in the Kitchen and Bathroom—Go minimal. Remember that counter space is a valuable commodity. When it comes to stuff, less is more.

FLIP TIP

Stay Perfect—Keep the house looking perfect all through your buyer's inspection and contingency period. Until your buyer is LOCKED in the deal, every time he or she comes to the house you want it looking exactly as it did when they fell in love with it.

STAGING THE HOUSE YOU LIVE IN

Dressing your house for sale techniques also apply to any homeowner who is about to sell the home they live in. You need to create a positive emotional response from your buyer to maximize your profits.

If you are living in the house you are flipping, in some ways it is easier than staging an empty house. You do not have to scramble for furniture and accessories. They're already there. But as we discussed in chapter fifteen, "Flipping the House You Live In," you probably have too much to choose from. However, if you followed all the steps from that chapter, you're ready to fine tune what you have.

Get the Kids to Help

If you have children, you have a lot of stuff. And of course, your kids need to be able to play and continue on with their everyday lives. So how do you get the house looking perfect for every showing? *Involve your kids.* Make the process a game and get them to participate.

Children love to feel like they are part of the setup. Let them understand that it's time to put the house on display and that you all need to set the stage together. Have them pick their favorite toy and stuffed animal to showcase in a perfect spot each time for the show, and put the other toys away. You will be surprised how cooperative the kids are and how much fun they have when you yell "Showtime!"

THE EMOTIONAL EDGE—HOW TO GET IT AND MAKE IT PAY

Most home buyers make a yea or nay decision on your house in the first five minutes. That's how long it takes to formulate an "impression" of your home. And because this is not a logical thought process, you must immediately grab them emotionally.

With the clock ticking, you've got five to ten minutes from the moment they approach the house to grab their heartstrings. You want them to feel "at home." Each room should elicit a specific emotional response. Living rooms must be inviting and gracious. Bedrooms should exude a sense of relaxation and comfort. Kitchens should be so clean, spacious, and organized that the buyer can practically hear their friends offering to chop carrots while they clean the lettuce.

What Home Feels Like

As Meredith Baer says, "Some call it staging, but we feel we put the heart in a home." Here are some key words that represent the feelings that trigger positive—and profitable—emotional responses:

- Tranquil
- Warm and cozy
- Exciting
- Secure
- Welcoming
- Private
- Relaxing
- Empowering
- Inclusive
- Homey
- Entertaining

- Organized
- Spotless
- Spacious
- Serene
- Inviting
- Productive
- Comfortable
- Romantic
- Fresh
- Together

ROOM-BY-ROOM VIGNETTES

Go through the house and identify places where you can elicit positive emotional responses. Create "living still lifes," three-dimensional snapshots of a heart-filled home. Set up vignettes or small lifestyle areas that fit your target buyer. You want your buyer to feel like spending a little time in your home. You want your buyer to feel welcome and comfortable. If you can create at least a dozen vignettes throughout the house, you are certain to grab your buyer where he lives (pardon the pun)!

The Front of the House or Condo Hallway

Play on their emotions the minute they step out of their car or walk down the hallway to your front door. In a condo, have a handsome wreath hanging on the front door. Spend five dollars for a top-of-the-door

Christmas-wreath hook. Run over to Pottery Barn or Crate & Barrel and get an all-season wreath for around $40. It will make a huge difference.

If you have used all of my curb-appeal techniques from chapter ten, "The Big Fix: The Profit Improvement Levels," then your front door should be ready to receive and seduce your buyer. Emotional keyword: "Welcoming."

Entryway

The entryway must be inviting yet simple. Place a side or parson's table along the wall inside the front door. Dress it with an attractive tray, a set of keys, and a lovely orchid. Hang a good-sized mirror above it, and you have the perfect first and last impression for your buyer! Emotional keyword: "Welcoming."

Kitchen

Put an open cookbook on a book stand next to the stove. Add in props such as a nice butcher-block knife set. Have a bowl of fresh fruit. I like apples, lemons, and grapes for a good color combination and a great stacking/draping effect. It sends a subtle and clean citrus fragrance wafting though the kitchen. Emotional keywords: "Entertaining," "Inviting," "Fresh."

Breakfast Room or Eat-In Kitchen

Create an inviting table setting at the breakfast table with white plates, polished silverware, and colorful napkins. A house flipped with a target buyer of a couple with a child might like a cheerful breakfast table with cereal bowls at each setting, a bowl of oranges in the center, and a morning newspaper ready to read at the head of the table. Emotional keyword: "Togetherness."

PHOTOGRAPHY BY RAND LARSON.

This is the breakfast room in my Bogert house—simply dressed, yet very inviting.

Master Bedroom

A bed with fluffy white pillows and a white duvet cover is a classic look that inspires tranquillity and security. Flowers or an orchid by the bed is a nice touch. If the bedroom has a window seat or a reading chair, place an opened hardcover book and a pair of reading glasses there. No magazines, please. The hardcover book implies value. Emotional keywords: "Secure," "Tranquil," "Serene."

FLIP TIP

Go with White—Hotels use all-white sheets and towels for a reason. White always looks fresh and crisp and reflects more light. They also can be used and reused over and over again no matter what the decor or house style is. And cleaning is a breeze; throw them all in the wash with hot water and bleach. No need to do loads for different colors.

RAIKO HARTMAN PHOTOGRAPHY.

This is one of Meredith's bedside stagings. It creates such a three-dimensional snapshot of a well-lived lifestyle that it will emotionally engage your buyers.

Master Bathroom

You want your bathroom to look like a sophisticated hotel bathroom or spa. Fold a set of fluffy white towels. Add a white terry-cloth robe on a hook or a small basket of rolled-up hand towels. Keep it simple. Emotional keywords: "Relaxing," "Private."

Powder Room or Guest Bath

Make sure you always keep your powder room or guest bath stocked with toilet paper and some nice fresh hand towels. Some of your prospective buyers will need to use the facilities, and you want them to feel right at home. Emotional keywords: "Comfortable," "Thoughtful," "Gracious."

Living Room

It is always wonderful and welcoming to light your fireplaces for showings if the weather permits. In colder climates, a staged lit fireplace is a must. Use either gas logs, or real logs and stack fresh logs for an inviting and cozy outdoor scent. The reading chair with the open book is a classic look. And I love to keep a short stack of *Architectural Digest* magazines on a coffee table to add panache. Emotional keywords: "Homey," "Inviting."

Dining Room

Never set up a vignette in the dining room. It is OK to do a table setup in a breakfast room or outdoor patio, but the dining room will be overkill. Yes, there should be a table with a flower arrangement or a set of matching candlesticks, but no table setting. Emotional keywords: "Entertaining," "Organized."

Laundry Room

Dressing the laundry room is really important. A stack of neatly folded towels on top of the washer does the trick. Emotional keywords: "Spotless," "Organized."

Small Patio Area or Balcony

Two comfortable outdoor chairs with two wineglasses and fresh fruit on a side table will attract a young couple. Emotional keywords: "Romantic," "Relaxing."

Backyard

If weather permits and there is an outdoor dining area, stage an outdoor table setting. If you have a separate barbecue, stage a nice set of barbecue mitts and barbecue tools next to the barbecue. Be creative. I have seen a backyard staged with a croquet set, as though there were a game in progress. Or if there is a pool or spa, include rolled white towels and a terry-cloth bathrobe draped by a Jacuzzi. Emotional keywords: "Tranquil," "Serene."

PHOTOGRAPHY BY RAND LARSON.

Dressing this outdoor setting creates an emotionally engaging moment. The buyers can visualize themselves having a relaxed Sunday brunch by the pool. This will be a "feeling" that they take with them as they go home to discuss their buying decision.

PHOTO COURTESY OF MEREDITH BAER.

This is one of Meredith Baer's staged patios. By merely adding a wicker chair, a coffee table, and some flowering potted plants, she created an outdoor living room out of an otherwise underutilized empty space. The buyers went crazy over this!

SEDUCE THE SENSES

In addition to designing, staging, and creating vignettes, there is one more "trick." You've got to subconsciously seduce four out of the five senses! Sight, sound, touch, and smell. The only taste you have to worry about here is your own taste in design! Remember, when they say, "I just love the way this house feels!" Cha-ching! You've seduced them.

Unlike any other celebrity I have visited, the amazing country superstar Naomi Judd has created a home that embraces and soothes you the moment you walk in the door. Her home is her sanctuary, and when you cross the threshold, you know you are in sacred space. How does she do it? Naomi adds the sensory elements of sound, scent, and touch throughout the house.

Sounds

Indoor or outdoor fountains, melodious wind chimes swinging in a light breeze, or soft music drifting throughout. Basically, any source of pleasing sound will stimulate the senses. Keep it soft, soothing, and barely audible. It also subconsciously creates a fullness and tranquillity to your home. This also helps to shut out traffic noise or sounds from the neighborhood.

Touch

A chenille throw across the back of a chair, the arm of a sofa, or draped on a bed feels wonderful to the touch, is very inexpensive, and says "cuddle up."

Scents

Studies have shown that citrus scents in the home can be the most appealing when they are from natural sources—real citrus! So don't go spraying or use those horrible plug-in things or stacked-up scented soaps. Simply squeeze a fresh lemon carefully in the sink, wipe it out with a paper towel—perfect. Be careful about scented soaps. They are often overused. Personally I am allergic to perfumes and colognes. And there is that old standby of baked bread (use Pillsbury crescent rolls— bake just one or two before a showing) or cinnamon sticks simmering on the stove. But only try these "cooking" scents when the weather is cold. A hot oven in the middle of the summer is not appealing.

Sight

You are pretty well covered with designing and staging for the visual stimulations. However, during the day, make sure all the window coverings are pulled back to show as much natural light as possible. At night, put lights on dimmers to create a warm, inviting mood.

Life Is a Breeze

I love the feeling of a warm, breezy day. But indoors? Why not? Ceiling fans are a fantastic addition to bedrooms and dens. They make you feel like you are being gently caressed. (And who doesn't like that?) But ceiling fans are meant to be *felt*, not *seen*, so flush-mount the fans to keep them tight to the ceiling, and keep them the same color as the ceiling so they disappear as much as possible.

INSIDER SECRET

Take a Flip Tip from Nick Lachey—You would never expect that rock star Nick Lachey, the husband of Jessica Simpson, would have a great design sense, but he does. His penthouse condo in Los Angeles employs a wonderful and inexpensive design trick that really feeds your senses. Nick added very thin white sheers on a high-tension wire that he can stretch across the arch separating his open-plan living room and dining room. When he opens the windows even a little, the sheers practically dance in the breeze, creating the most visually beautiful light and shadow patterns. You can almost hear the tropical breezes blow.

PHOTO COURTESY OF STEVEN WILDER.

Lovely sheers gently blowing in the breeze are . . . a breeze. They are so inexpensive and yet create such a dramatic look. Designer Steven Wilder often uses them in his flip homes. He used them here on an outside deck to great advantage.

IS YOUR FLIP "CAMERA-READY"?

When you have finished staging, give your house a screen test. After all, if it's going to star, it's got to look great. And the camera does not lie. Start outside from the street where your potential buyers will park. Go ahead, be corny—hold up your hands like you are a director checking a camera shot—but take a picture with a digital camera. How does the "shot" of your house look? Is everything perfect? This is the first impression your buyer will have of your flip. Do you need more flowers? Are the new numbers perfectly straight? Open the front door and take photos in every room. Look at them. And then make the necessary changes.

SQUEAKY CLEAN

Of course, your house not only has to look good, it needs to be spotless. No one likes to get on their hands and knees and scrub. You'll say, "I don't even do this in the house I live in!" or "My mother never cleaned this hard or this much." Well, if you can make $5,000 to $10,000 at sale time, I'd say it's worth it! You should be able to eat off the floors. The windows, glass, and mirrors must sparkle. The sinks and toilets should look five star–hotel perfect.

FLIP TIP

Wipe the Walls—After a remodel, you will also notice that everything seems be covered in a fine dust. It's from sanding and patching drywall. You won't see it, but trust me, it's there. If your buyers run their hands on the walls, they'll notice it. Use a clean, lightly damp towel to wipe everything down, including the walls.

SALE DAY—GET READY FOR THIS WILD RIDE!

I want to mentally prepare you for the work that sale day brings. Whether you are living in the house or not, be mentally and physically prepared to "show prep" your house for each showing. Even though my Realtors are fantastic, they are busy and often arrive at the same time as the buyers. They may not have the opportunity or time to "show prep." But I do, and so should you.

When the buyers arrive, you must have this house ON! Every light set perfectly, the music softly playing, the fireplace going, the doors and windows open if weather permits, and the temperature exactly right. Remember, you are selling a lifestyle where everything about this house—and the life a buyer would experience in it—is perfect!

SHOW-PREP CHECKLIST

I have a really busy schedule, and there have been times when I've had to rely on the Realtors or on friends to do the show prep. If I'm flipping the house I'm living in at the moment, I take extra care to keep it dressed for sale every day. So when I leave the house in the morning, the beds are always made and the bathrooms are totally pulled together, which saves time for those last-minute showings. Before every showing, just accept that you'll be nuts for about a half hour running through the house like a white tornado! I use a Show-Prep Checklist. Make copies, mark off items as you complete them, and you'll always be ready at the ring of a cell phone.

Show-Prep Checklist	
Item	*Completed*
Air out the house for half an hour Open doors and windows, weather permitting Vacuum and dust	
Kitchen Make sure stove, oven, and sinks are spotless All surfaces are freshly wiped down Clear all countertops Grind a fresh lemon in the garbage disposal All cabinet contents are "faced" Floors mopped	
Bathrooms Put out fresh hand towels All cabinet contents are "faced"	
Bedrooms Beds made perfectly Nothing lying around Kids' toys are staged, not flung	
Powder Room Hand towels Toilet paper	
Sensory Preps Turn on all lights—even the one above the stove Turn on all fountains Adjust the temperature Turn on fireplace (or start fire)	

Item	Completed
Check on your orchids or flowers Set the music	
Front Yard No leaves Hoses put away No cars in the driveway	
Backyard No leaves Trash cans put away All toys cleared	
Garage Neat and tidy	

Get It Ready and Get Out

Once you have gone through the Show-Prep Checklist and the house is ready for its close up, get out! You want the buyer to feel that this is *their* beautiful house. After you have worked so hard to control every aspect of their experience, don't muck it up by lurking around. You'll spoil the fantasy—and the sale.

I Can't Live Like This—Dressing the House You Live In

One interesting note: When you flip the house you have been living in, living in your home will feel different. You'll wonder "How can I keep the house this perfect or this clean forever . . . and where are my things?" Well don't worry. If you truly dress your house for sale, it's going to sell right away and you will be moving soon. Since your things are packed, well-organized, and edited down to what is essential because you purged your closets and cleaned out the garage, moving will be a snap. You will be shocked at how little you actually need for the three months you are in the "sale process." And I guarantee it will change your relationship to "stuff" forever, because *when you simplify your home, you simplify your life*.

FLIP TIP

Maintain Your Privacy and Safety—Believe it or not, people will look through your drawers at open houses or showings. I guess it's just human nature. Make sure they are accompanied by a Realtor. And don't keep anything in the house that you don't want anyone else to see. That includes personal documents and valuables.

FLIP TIP

Share Your Show-Prep Checklist—Review the "Show-Prep Checklist" and make sure your Realtor has a copy. If there is a showing that you can't prep yourself, he'll know the drill.

FLIPPING SUCCESS STORY

By my third house in L.A., my Dream Team was in place and word was out. When Realtors who had seen my previous two flips heard I was readying my fourth, they set up five showings, sight unseen, with prequalified buyers to whom they uttered that magic phrase, "Bring your checkbook!"

This happens because the houses I flip always have a sense of excitement and elicit an emotional response from the buyers. My flips have all the bells and whistles—they're all dressed to sell! By consistently applying these techniques I have built a reputation. Your flip houses will do the same for you.

Seventeen

LET THE SELLING BEGIN

OK, the house is dressed and ready for sale day. Now it's time to get down to the business of selling. In order to get the maximum dollar, you need to be on top of all aspects of a successful sale, including:

- For Sale by Owner—think again
- Setting the selling price—your "final" Final Flipped Price
- The listing agreement
- Getting your Realtor ready for sale
- Marketing—your Realtor's game plan
- The buyers and the offers
- Surviving the closing escrow
- The two selling escrow arenas

FOR SALE BY OWNER—THINK AGAIN

Going the For Sale by Owner route is like performing your own surgery or being your own defense lawyer at a murder trial. As we have discussed in chapter three, "Your Flipping Dream Team," when buying your home, you really want to leave it to the professionals. The same goes for selling.

You don't have the time, the expertise, or the market access to show and close the deal. The money you *think* you will save on commission might be equal to the higher price a Realtor could get. But most likely, it will be less. Leave the selling of your house to a pro and you'll benefit.

They have the resources to get top dollar for you, and it's in their best interest to do so.

In addition to all the things a Realtor can do for you when you're buying, here's what they can do when you're selling, which you simply can't:

- Deal with buyers objectively

- Deal with the buyers' agents directly and professionally

- Shield you from personal interaction with the buyers

- Create excitement with other agents in their home office

- Use proper selling procedure

- Keep the closing on track

- Negotiate any concession requests from the buyer

- Keep the buyer on their closing timeline

SETTING THE SELLING PRICE—YOUR "FINAL" FINAL FLIPPED PRICE

Even before you made an offer on this flip property, you determined your future Final Flipped Price (FFP). You had to make that calculation to determine if this property was a good flip candidate and would make you a worthwhile profit. As you worked on the three phases of your budget, you kept one eye on expenses and renovations and the other on the competition and the temperature of the market. You have been adjusting that FFP in your head all along. "Oh, that house down the block just sold for more, so I can raise my price . . . Hmmm, a couple of comparable houses just came on the market at my price, maybe I need to drop it to stay competitive."

Well, now comes the day of reckoning—final pricing day! All of the work is done, and the house is dressed and staged and ready for market. *Only now* will you know how much your house is really worth!

No Realtor Until It's Ready!

Never let your Realtor see the house before it is dressed for sale! Especially if this is your first flip. Realtors will always say, "Oh I have a good eye." I am sure they do. But when your Realtor sees the house for the first time, you want him to have the same experience that your buyers will have. That way, when you price the house together, your Realtor will feel—and factor in—the emotional edge and lifestyle you worked so hard to create.

After all, unless your Realtor knows you have read this book, he will probably assume you did a "nice" renovation and updated the kitchen and baths. He does not know that you have created a buyer's *Dream Home*!

Intellectually, and over the phone, a Realtor bases price on the comps, the neighborhood, what he or she "envisioned" you would do, etc. But only after you use these dress-for-sale techniques, and then invite them over so they personally experience the emotional appeal you created for the buyer, can your Realtors really set the sales price.

FLIPPING SUCCESS STORY

You Have to Let Them Experience It—After seeing my Martel house in Dressed-to-Sell mode, my Realtors upped my original Final Flipped Price estimate from $675,000 to $749,000. Not only did it sell the first day, but at $5,000 over the asking price. Through my Dressed-to-Sell approach, I increased the house's value an additional $80,000! The Realtors had an emotional reaction to the house and they knew the buyers would, too!

After fixing this house on all Six Levels of Improvements and dressing it for sale we upped my original Final Flipped Price estimate by $80,000 . . . and got it!

THE LISTING AGREEMENT

Commissions

I agree that a 6 percent commission, which is the standard for the industry, does seem high. It certainly seems higher than it used to be. That's because ten years ago, buying a house for $100,000 was commonplace. And $6,000 to be split between the Realtors and their respective real estate companies didn't sound like a lot. After all the splits, your Realtor may have gone home with $2,000 to $2,500, which seemed more than fair. But with homes routinely selling for $500,000 to $1.5 million, a 6 percent commission is from $30,000 to $90,000 per transaction, which means a Realtor gets $12,000 to $45,000 for the same exact work. Yikes.

Here's the reality: Until there is a national overhaul of real estate commissions, whether the market is hot or cold, we all need to bite the bullet and pay it. Why? Well if you tell your Realtor you only will pay a 4 percent commission for the sale, you have now handicapped your house—*if* he accepts the listing. Here's why:

Your house is selling for $600,000. With a 4 percent commission, that's $24,000 to the Realtors. However, there is a house down the street for sale for the same price. It may not be as nice as yours, but with a full commission of 6 percent, the Realtors are going to split $36,000 at the time of sale. Do you think a buyer's real estate agent is going to encourage his client to buy yours? He'll push for the other one, because he gets extra commission for the same amount of work.

To help your sale now, you'd have to drop your price. So by trying to save $12,000 you may have just lost $25,000 or more. And I promise you, a reduced commission does not get as much Realtor and buyer traffic, either, which means it will sit on the market longer. Saving that 2 percent defeats everything you have done to make the house stand out.

DOUBLE-ENDING THE SALE

There are two situations in which I recommend negotiating on the commission:

1. **When your Realtor brings in the buyer himself and there is no other agent involved.** In this case, include a clause in the listing agreement that if your Realtor "double-ends" the deal, the commission is reduced to between 4 and 4.5 percent. This is a significant savings to you.

2. **When the buyer comes from a Realtor in your Realtor's home office.** Since the home office will receive a split on both commissions, they can offer you a break without taking any money from the Realtors' split. In this case I ask for a 0.5 to 1 percent reduction—as part of the listing agreement.

No Realty Agency Fee

Some realty offices include an extra $250 agency fee in the listing agreement. Look for it in the listing contract and have it crossed out.

Limit the Term of the Listing

You should ask to limit the listing agreement to a maximum of ninety days.

Cancellation Fee

Make sure there is no cancellation fee in the contract. If there is, have it crossed out. Should you decide not to extend the agreement beyond the ninety days because the house hasn't sold, then you shouldn't have to pay a fee.

Your Realtor Should Be Present for All Showings

Specify in the listing agreement that the Realtor will meet every prospective buyer and their agent and show the house himself. The alternative is that he leaves a computerized lockbox with a key to the house so that prospective buyers and their Realtors can see it on their own. By doing this, you lose on several fronts. You want the Realtor present for these reasons:

- Your Realtor knows the house and will steer the buyer to its strong points.

- He can answer any questions or address any concerns on the spot.

- He can show-prep the house if you can't. Remember, the lights, the music, and the other little touches make a huge difference in the "feel."

- Especially if you are living in the house, a lockbox is an invitation to security issues. You want your buyers attended by your Realtor at all times.

- You want your Realtor to be the only one who has the code to your alarm system, and he or she should avoid giving it out to other agents and their buyers.

GETTING YOUR REALTOR READY FOR SALE

You may say, "Oh, the Realtor is a professional and it's his job to have everything ready." Yes, that's true. But I have heard horror stories from sellers whose Realtors let some of the final details slip through the cracks. Make sure all of the marketing elements are ready so that when you're ready to put it on the market, your Realtor has the full arsenal of selling tools at the ready.

THE MARKETING GAME PLAN

Are you and your Realtor are on the same page in the "Marketing Book"? You will be if you are clear about what you expect. Start by revisiting who your perfect buyer is. Everything your Realtor does should be targeted toward that individual.

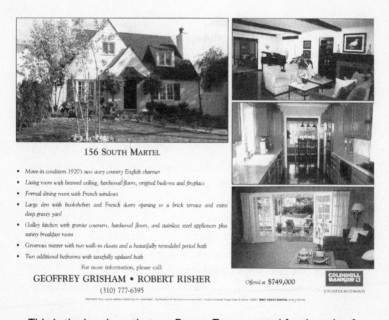

156 SOUTH MARTEL

- Move-in condition 1920's two story country English charmer
- Living room with beamed ceiling, hardwood floors, original built-ins and fireplace
- Formal dining room with French windows
- Large den with bookshelves and French doors opening to a brick terrace and extra deep grassy yard
- Galley kitchen with granite counters, hardwood floors, and stainless steel appliances plus sunny breakfast room
- Generous master with two walk-in closets and a beautifully remodeled period bath
- Two additional bedrooms with tastefully updated bath

For more information, please call:

GEOFFREY GRISHAM • ROBERT RISHER
(310) 777-6395

Offered at $749,000

This is the brochure that my Dream Team created for the sale of my Martel house. It has lots of great color photos and wonderful descriptions of the house's features.

- Marketing plan—Who is the buyer and what is the best way to reach them in terms of photography, language, and style of materials? What will the Realtor do beyond the expected to attract buyers?

- Photos—Are they beautiful? Do they telegraph what's great about the home?

- Brochures—Are they attractive and well-written? Is all the information correct?

- Open houses—What is his strategy and schedule?

- Presentation One-Sheets—Are they gorgeous and compelling?

- Newspaper ads—What do they say and how often will they appear?

- MLS Listing—Does it use the language of the ads/brochures/one-sheets?

- Internet—Is the house on the Realtors' Web site and other realty Web sites with full-color photos and glowing detail?

INSIDER SECRET

Get It Online!—The Internet is critical. According to Curt Truman of Coldwell Banker Realty Beverly Hills North, "Seventy percent of all buyers will look for a house at some point on the Internet. They may not have access to the online MLS, but they will have access to realtor.com and any other local real estate listing site. Make sure your Realtor has your home listed with multiple photos and well-written descriptions." It takes several days for these Internet submissions to process and go live. Make sure your listing is submitted a few days before sale day.

SALES STRATEGY

There are many strategies for selling. Here are a few that my Realtors have used with great success for me:

Hold Back

My Realtors build excitement by refusing to show the house prior to the first caravan, the day that all the Realtors in Los Angeles drive around in a caravan to view all the properties that have come on the market that week. Because no one gets a sneak preview, all the interested buyers will rush over during the first few days and hopefully submit offers all at once. It works. In many other cities, however, Realtors merely list the new properties on the MLS and then show them to interested parties.

Hold No-Offer Pre-showings

This one is a teaser. The Realtor offers sneak previews but accepts no offers until the caravan or first day of sale. Once again this stockpiles offers and often creates the seller's dream come true: the ever-popular bidding war.

FLIP TIP

Avoid Open Houses Prior to Officially Listing the House— Never allow your broker to "presell" your house before it lists in the MLS. Show it, yes. Sell it, no. If your broker is trying to presell your house, what he is really doing is trying to grab commissions from both you, the seller, and from the buyer that he is hoping to bring in ahead of the pack. You want maximum exposure in anticipation of going into a multiple-offer situation, forcing buyers to bid against each other and thus driving up the price. The most powerful words your broker can say to a potential buyer are, "I believe there is another offer coming in!" Everyone wants something more when they think can't have it.

Hold Out a Carrot

If there is significant interest from a qualified buyer, let them see the house a few days before opening day. A smart and hungry buyer will know they have an advantage and use it by making an offer at full price or more to beat the competition. You can then decide to respond and accept, or wait until opening day.

A Little Help from Above

I am not particularly superstitious. But I do believe that anything you put your attention to you create. So here is an old house-selling custom for you to enjoy. I am not sure where it originated, but if you bury a small statue of Saint Joseph in the front yard upside down and facing your house, it will supposedly speed your sale! I never understood this one, especially the upside down part. I would think that Saint Joseph would be very, very angry about being upside down. But people swear that this speeds the sale.

INSIDER SECRET

Put the Sign Up but Keep the Door Shut—Curt Truman of Coldwell Banker Beverly Hills North says, "Put the for-sale sign up in the last month that you are finishing up work on the house. But never let anyone in until the house is done. Buyers will call your Realtor for information. Your Realtor will take their name and number and tell them as soon as the house is ready, he will call them for a first look. Hopefully you will have built up a long list of targeted potential buyers in that month prior to the big sale day."

THE BUYERS AND THE OFFERS

OK, you're ready to put the house on the market. Now it's time to meet the potential buyers—and let the games begin!

Here Come the Offers—and the Shoe Is on the Other Foot!

Just as when you bought your home and had to offer, negotiate, and then suffer through escrow, it's time to do it all over again—only in reverse! And now all those negotiating tricks that you learned as a buyer will be used against you. So let's hope that your buyer has not read this book. If he has, you are going to have to be a tough negotiator. But not to worry—there are many ways to negotiate on price and terms that will make both of you happy.

HERE COME THE BUYERS—FIVE TYPES OF BUYERS TO AVOID

1. **Sale-Contingent Buyers**—If they are offering to buy your home contingent on the sale of their home, say "No, thank you." Ask them to come back when they are ready to buy. If your home is still on the market then, you will be happy to strike a deal.

2. **Buyers Without Prequalifying Letters**—In a hot market, if a buyer hasn't already been prequalified, they're a bit suspect. In a cold or downward market, ask for a prequalifying letter in a counteroffer, especially in a multiple-offer situation.

3. **The 0- to 10-Percent-Down Buyer**—Chances are your flipped house will be setting a selling-price high mark for comparable homes. A mortgage company will find it very difficult to appraise your house for buyers with little or no money down, and you will have to put your house back on the market again when such a buyer's mortgage falls through. I have seen it happen far too often.

4. **The Bully Buyer**—This buyer starts by listing all the things that he thinks are wrong with the house, even as he presents an offer. Thus, he will be even more difficult to work with in an inspection process. Trust me. This bully approach is a prelude to tying up your house in escrow and then trying to get concessions by nit-picking the disclosure and the inspection.

> 5. **The Sight-Unseen Buyer**—In a hot market, it is not unusual to have an offer from a buyer who has only seen photos of your house. This buyer is trying to tie up your house and get if off the market until they have a chance to really look at the house. Don't deal with them.

HOW TO ANALYZE YOUR OFFERS

Think of the offer from the buyer as the offer you originally placed on the house. The *highest* price may not be the *best* price. Now, as the seller, you want the OPPOSITE terms. You want:

- Fewest possible inspection contingencies
- Shortest possible mortgage contingency
- Strongest deposit
- Largest down payment
- Flexibility on the mortgage terms
- Ability to rent back

Your goal in pushing for shorter contingency terms and maximum flexibility in their mortgage terms is to lock them into the deal as soon as possible. This is the opposite strategy from when you brought the property. Then you wanted the terms to give you the ability to walk away from the deal until the last possible moment.

FLIP TIP

Give Them a Warranty—In many states, it's customary to provide a homeowners warranty for your buyer, an insurance policy against any first-year repairs. This is also a terrific hedge against liability. If their heating and air system goes out in the first year, they won't come running back to you. The $350 to $600 cost is an incredible value. Speak to your Realtor about American Home

Shield or one of the other home-warranty companies out there. For a $35 to $45 service-call fee, they will repair any malfunctions in almost any system in the house.

BACKUP OFFERS

Having a backup offer is the next best thing to seller's insurance. It means that just like in the Miss America pageant, if Miss America is unable to fulfill her duties for any reason, the first runner-up will wear the crown! The same is true for real estate sales.

If you get multiple offers on your flip (and we hope you do), then pick the best one. But have you Realtor advise the second-best offer that if they are willing, they can have a backup position. The backup is in no way obligated to buy the house if it becomes available, but they do get right of first refusal. Even if you do not have multiple offers at the time of the first offer, I always expect the Realtor to let it be known that we are looking for a backup offer.

WHY SECURE A BACKUP OFFER?

- It puts your buyer on notice that if they ask for too many concessions, you can very easily walk away from the deal and go with the backup.

- It allows you to hold a bit firmer if the buyer asked for credits or repairs after an inspection.

- If the buyer fails to meet his or her obligations in a timely manner, you can cancel the escrow—sometimes being able to keep their deposit—and move right away to open escrow with the backup offer.

- If the buyer decides to pull out of the deal, you have someone else in place and can avoid the cost of remarketing the property.

SURVIVING THE CLOSING ESCROW

This escrow process is going to be slightly easier than the purchase escrow. And yes, I did say slightly. When you bought this flip house there were three distinct arenas progressing all at once. Now it's a merely a *two*-ring circus. But you are still the ringmaster juggling all the balls in the air, running from ring to ring making sure they finish at the same time. And whether you are "in escrow" or "under contact" the show that goes on is basically the same.

THE TWO SELLING ESCROW ARENAS

KEEPING THE BUYER ON TRACK

Make Sure the Buyer Does His Inspections Quickly

You want to get this contingency covered and signed off on immediately. Have your Realtor encourage the buyer to schedule his inspection as soon as escrow is opened. Also, the more money and time a buyer has invested in a purchase via appraisals and inspections, the less likely they are to walk away over minor differences or negotiations.

Once the buyer has his inspection, he will want to negotiate *something*. He will want you to repair *something*. Be prepared and don't take it personally. Chances are you have completely fixed, replaced, and upgraded everything in the house, and your flip is flawless. But personally, I am suspicious of a buyer who *doesn't* ask for something to be addressed, even if it's minor.

However, if the buyer presents a litany of expensive and costly requests, then you need to examine your bargaining position. Is this a good buyer with a prequalified loan and a good deposit? Do you have a backup offer in line? I usually find that most buyers are willing to split the cost of any requests. Weigh the cost of any concessions against the carrying costs of putting the house back on the market. Remember, when flipping you want to get in and get out with the most efficiency, as well as the most profit.

KEEPING THE BUYER ON SCHEDULE

Keeping your buyer on track and on time is your real estate agent's responsibility. However, one of the greatest pieces of advice I can give you in the selling escrow process is to make it your business to stay on top of the timeline as well. Find out from your Realtor, your escrow officer, or your lawyer exactly what the buyer's deadlines are for submitting his deposit monies, signing off his inspection contingencies, and obtaining his mortgage. Mark them in your calendar.

June

Mon	Tues	Wed	Thurs	Fri	Sat / Sun
1 ACCEPTED OFFER SALE AGREEMENTS SIGNED	2 ESCROW OPENS! BUYER TO SCHEDULE INSPECTION	3 BUYER TO SCHEDULE APPRAISAL	4 SUBMIT DISCLOSURES, PLOT MAP, PERMITS	5 REQUEST ESTIMATED CLOSING COSTS	6 / 7
8 BUYER'S INSPECTION	9 BUYER'S APPRAISAL	10	11 INSPECTION CONTINGENCY EXPIRES	12	13 / 14
15	16 BUYER'S MORTGAGE CONTINGENCY EXPIRES	17	18	19	20 / 21
22 REQUEST ESTIMATED CLOSING COSTS	23	24 COMPLETE TERMITE OR OTHER BUYER-REQUESTED REPAIRS	25 CALL TO TRANSFER UTILITIES	26 REVIEW ESTIMATED CLOSING COSTS	27 / 28
29 FINAL WALK-THROUGH OF PROPERTY	30 ESCROW CLOSES! CONGRATULATIONS	$ $ PROFIT			

This is an example of a thirty-day closing escrow timeline. Create this kind of calendar and keep your escrow on track.

Even though the buyer and his loan officer are responsible for scheduling the appraisal, it will benefit you to have your Realtor help move that along. You will want to know as soon as possible if your house is appraising at your sale price. Chances are, you are selling this house at the top of the comps, and it can sometimes be a push to justify the price.

You will also want to make sure your Realtor, escrow officer, or lawyer constantly checks the status of the title policy, termite inspection report, and buyer's insurance.

YOUR SELLER ESCROW PAPERWORK

Right about now you should be having déjà vu. Wasn't I just IN escrow? Well, yes you were, when you bought the house. And even though that was months or even a year or more ago, time flies when you are in the middle of a fix-it project. But here you are, hopefully with a nice selling price for your house, and a cash profit only thirty to sixty days away. But the task at hand is to manage this escrow and be the ringmaster again and complete all of your escrow responsibilities:

- Review the escrow instructions

- Turn in your disclosure statement

- Deliver all permits

- Get the termite certification

- Request and review the estimated closing cost statements

Review the Escrow Instruction

As you were when you purchased, you will be asked to sign the escrow instructions. These should reflect all the items that you have agreed to via your buyer's offer and subsequent counteroffers. Review them with your real estate agent before you sign.

Supplying Your Disclosure Statement

Let me see, how shall I put this to get my point across? Disclose, disclose, *disclose*! Legally, in almost two-thirds of the country now you are required to disclose material facts about the property and its condition to potential buyers. This is called your disclosure statement. In California it is a preprinted, itemized form that you must fill out to the best of your knowledge.

However, I like to go one step further and list all of the work that has been done to the property. I list anything that has been done without a permit, as well as all the systems that have been replaced or upgraded. If there has been a roof leak, I disclose it. If there is still slight moisture in the basement, I disclose it. Why? Well for two reasons. One, it's the honest thing to do! And two, it protects you. If a buyer discovers a problem after the purchase, even one the inspector misses, and he can show that you were aware of the problem and didn't disclose it, he can come after you. So I need to say this again: Disclose, disclose, disclose.

FLIP TIP

The More Inspections, the Better—Encourage a buyer to get all the inspections he or she needs to feel comfortable: home, geological, chimney, sewer, foundation, termite—whatever. Ultimately, it benefits you, since once a problem has been identified and thus disclosed, you can never be accused of hiding problems after the sale.

Deliver All Permits

As you are progressing through your fix-it phases, make sure you get copies of all the signed-off permits from your contractor or tradesman. Have them ready to present to your buyer.

Request and Review the Estimated Closing Cost Statement

It is imperative that you request and carefully review your Estimated Closing Cost Statement. It is also imperative to ask for an updated copy at the beginning of escrow, during escrow, and right before closing. This gives you a chance to review all the charges and credits and have time to negotiate them.

If you really want to save money on all those closing costs and fees, you need to review the statement long before the closing date, and ask as many questions as you need to. Just as when you purchased, there can be numerous "junk" or "garbage" fees thrown into the closing statement. Review the list of junk fees from chapter eight, "How to Survive Escrow and Come Out a Winner," and eliminate or negotiate them from your closing-costs statement.

Also, you will need to remind your escrow officer, or lawyer, if you had purchased a title binder when you purchased the house. If you did, good for you. That means you have saved yourself a big chunk of money now that you are selling.

FLIP TIP

Check for Prepayment Penalties—The good news is that you will not have to worry about loan fees, but you may need to make sure you haven't been mistakenly charged a prepayment penalty. This can be a costly mistake if you don't catch it.

FLIP TIP

Don't Leave Money Behind—When you sell your flip house, make sure you contact your insurance company and see if you have any prorated money due you from the insurance you have already paid in advance. This could be substantial. The same holds true for a home warranty policy that was paid up for a full year in advance.

DELIVERING THE PROPERTY

Delivering the property is an important issue. Just because you have sold the property doesn't mean you should hand over the keys and shout

"Good luck!" as you drive away. I am a big believer that you need to deliver what you promise. And when creating a home and lifestyle, you want to deliver just that!

THE BUYERS' WELCOME PACKAGE

I always like to prepare an information booklet for the buyers, which should include:

- The address

- The alarm codes

- The location and current schedules for any sprinklers, light timers, pool equipment.

- The contact info for:

  - Gardener

  - Utility companies

  - Cable or digital-satellite info

  - Garage-door company

- The trash pickup day

- The paint-color chart: This is the chart that lists, room by room, all of the names and brands of the paints used throughout the house. Fortunately, if you follow my three-color indoor and outdoor paint technique, you won't have dozens of different paints to list.

Also provide an envelope with:

- All the warranties and instructions for all appliances, alarm systems, built-ins, etc.

- The keys

- The garage-door clickers

The Final Touches

The very last thing you want to do before the sale day or the day before the owner takes possession is to make the house look as terrific as possible for their move-in day. Not only is this a wonderful thing to do for your buyer, it is also a very smart way to hedge against the buyer finding last-minute things wrong after they've moved in. Leave the buyers thinking, "Oh, the seller took such care when he moved out. Let's not bother him with this or that."

- Touch up any paint scratches or scuffs
- Make sure the front and backyards are trimmed and beautiful
- Remove any trash or garbage from the property
- Clean the house from top to bottom

And for the final touch, put a lovely orchid on the kitchen counter with a note that says simply, "Enjoy!"

Eighteen

CONGRATULATIONS—SOLD! NOW STEP AWAY FROM THE CASH!

OK, so you've sold your flip and now have a big pile of money! You get your down payment back, along with all the money you invested in renovations, plus all your profit! Congratulations! NOW . . . step away from the cash! Calm down and remember your goal: a lifetime of financial security. Believe me, you are going to be tempted to spend it, to buy a new car or take that vacation. Don't.

If you're having trouble keeping your hand out of the cookie jar, please feel free to e-mail me at my Web sites MichaelCorbett.com or FindItFixIt FlipIt.com, and I will be happy to talk you out of it. I will be the first to remind you that this profit is your seed money and is off-limits! It's what you will use to nurture and grow your financial independence. That's how I turned my initial $10,000 investment into millions in real estate!

You will now use that money to find, fix, and then flip your *next* house. When you are ready, you are going to start all over again, this time with more money to apply to a larger down payment. If you choose, you can afford a slightly more expensive house in a slightly better neighborhood, or you can stay at the lifestyle level you are at now and simply amass more equity with each house, bringing you one step closer to buying your dream house—mortgage-free. Whether you want to take the fast track, the slow and steady path, or any path in between, you are now ready to build your financial independence.

We all work very hard to pay the bills while striving to bring in additional money and to build financial security. If we only had the ability to do both. . . . Well, now you do! You can work smarter using your flip profit to continue to create a second revenue stream through flipping. And while that won't "buy" time, it can certainly create a lifestyle that allows you to make time for your life, to make millions in real estate and never pay a mortgage again—one house at a time. All you have to do is Find It, Fix It, Flip It!

My *Find It, Fix It, Flip It!* Experts

Meredith Baer

Meredith Baer was a screenwriter who pursued design as a hobby until, through word of mouth, she found herself at the heart of a new Hollywood industry. With her writing background, she focuses on the story behind the furniture. Meredith has done hundreds of homes, owns millions of dollars worth of staging furniture, and has been featured on *Home and Garden* television, ABC, NBC, The Discovery Channel, *Los Angeles Times Magazine, Brentwood Magazine,* and *Wallpaper Magazine.*

Edward Bercow

As president of Bercow Construction, Ed personally manages high-end projects from large kitchen renovations to complete house remodels. He stresses that every home is a sanctuary for the people who live there, and that it's his responsibility to construct it with the care and attention that he would for his own family. He enjoys working with designers with whom he has developed long-term relationships, as well as with new designers.

Rex A. Berkebile

Rex A. Berkebile, an escrow-industry expert, is a senior escrow officer with Escrow Exchange West, Inc., an independent escrow company in Beverly Hills, where he handles escrows for the sale of business, commercial, and residential properties. He also has experience working within a title company as a settlement processor, and is well-versed in the nuances of both West Coast and East Coast escrows.

Jeff Beuth

Jeff Beuth, a resident of Los Angeles, has been a successful real estate investor and has flipped more than 200 homes over the past ten years. Starting with homes in the $60,000 price range, Jeff has successfully flipped his way up to the multimillion-dollar price range. His company, City Corp Ventures, specializes in high-end luxury homes. Visit www.citycorpventures.com.

Natalie Dalton

Natalie Dalton is the manager of Design-at-Home Services for the Home Depot EXPO Design Center. She oversees their design professionals and is well-versed in design and renovation trends.

Jim Gillespie

Jim Gillespie is the president and CEO of the Coldwell Banker Real Estate Corporation, and is responsible for the company's more than 3,500 independently owned and operated residential and commercial real estate offices and 112,000 sales associates globally.

Brian Hatch

Brian Hatch is a successful Realtor specializing in residential real estate. He's the top-producing Realtor with Sotheby's International in Palm Springs, California. His background in design and construction makes him a triple-threat Realtor for anyone looking to invest in real estate in the Palm Springs area. His Web site is www.brianhatchrealtor.com.

Brian Little

Brian Little, a native of Minnesota, established his design/construction firm in Los Angeles nearly twenty years ago and has become one of L.A.'s foremost designer/contractors in the restoration and ground-up construction of many premiere trophy homes. His endless attention to detail and respect of classic architecture and landscape has established

him as a renaissance designer for many homes in the vintage neighborhoods of Hancock Park and Beverly Hills.

Suze Orman

Suze Orman is an internationally acclaimed personal finance expert,
whom *USA Today* has called a "one-woman financial advice power-
house" and "a force in the world of personal finance." From her earliest
childhood years and the stress of her father losing his business, to her
post-college job working as a waitress, to climbing the ranks in the investment world, to becoming a best-selling author, Suze has lived and
learned many hard financial lessons. She has translated these experi-
ences into frank, savvy financial advice that has transformed the lives of
millions around the world.

Anthony Robbins

For more than a quarter of a century, Anthony Robbins has served as an
advisor to leaders around the world. A recognized authority on the psy-
chology of leadership, negotiations, organizational turnaround, and
peak performance, Robbins has directly impacted the lives of nearly fifty
million people from eighty countries with his best-selling books and au-
diotape products, public-speaking engagements, and live appearances.
Since fathering the life-coaching industry, Robbins has produced the
number-one audio coaching system of all time.

Curt Truman

Curt Truman is a Previews International Estates Director at Coldwell
Banker Beverly Hills North and a member of the prestigious International President's Elite. He is ranked in the top 4 percent of all sales associates internationally, and was named by *Los Angeles* magazine as one
of L.A.'s Real Estate Super Agents. He specializes in luxury home sales in
the Sunset Strip, Beverly Hills, and West Los Angeles areas.

Steven Wilder

Steven Wilder Designs is a registered building contractor and architectural interior design service. Established in Los Angeles in 1986 by Australian-born and -educated designer Steven Wilder, the company primarily specializes in the creative remodeling of homes, and also has experience remodeling bars, restaurants, and night clubs.

Internet Resource Guide

www.americanhomeshield.com	Home warranty site
www.ashi.org	American Society of Home Inspectors
www.buywithnocredit.com	Site dedicated to buying real estate with no credit
www.citycorpventures.com	Super flipper Jeff Beuth's real estate site
www.brianhatchrealtor.com	Top Realtor Brian Hatch's site
www.crimecheck.com	Crime-rate statistics by neighborhood
www.eloan.com	Online loan resource
www.equifax.com	Personal credit site
www.experian.com	Personal credit site
www.forfeitedproperty.com	Foreclosures
www.homefair.com	Home-listing site of realtor.com
www.homes.com	Homes for sale, rentals, foreclosures, and more
www.homesales.gov	Homes for sale by the U.S. government
www.homeseekers.com	Homes for sale, agents, foreclosures, and more
www.househunt.com	Homes for sale and more
www.marshallswift.com	Renovation charts
www.michaelcorbett.com	My home site
www.mortgage.com	Online mortgage resource
www.myfico.com	Fair Isaac & Co. (FICO), featuring Suze Orman's FICO-improving kits and more

www.home-listings.org/ 　MLS-Multiple-Listings-Service.asp	Real estate resources and links
www.real-estate.com	Homes for sale, real estate agents, mortgage rates, and more
www.reals.com	Real estate "directory" with links to national listings and real estate resources
www.realtor.com	Official site of the National Association of Realtors; home listings, and everything about Realtors
www.registeredoffenderslist.org	Megan's Law listing
www.rentnet.com	National online rental listings
www.stevenwilderdesigns.com	Site of top Los Angeles designer
www.suzeorman.com	Financial guru's home page
www.transunion.com	Personal credit site
www.thehomeshow.com	National Home Show locations, dates, and more
www.ustoreit.com	Portable-storage company site
www.wallpaperforwindows.com	Home-improvement product site